Praise for *A Way to God*

"This wise and marvelous book will profoundly inspire all those who love Merton and want to know him more deeply."

— ANDREW HARVEY, author of
The Hope: A Guide to Sacred Activism

"*A Way to God* inscribes a profound intersection of lives — Merton, Fox, and more — in the history of Christianity, Catholicism, and the emerging Creation Spirituality so relevant to our globe's current cultural evolution. Perhaps Merton's lament on the 'lost art of listening' can be assuaged significantly by the profound potential impacts of this new book."

— KURT JOHNSON, PhD, coauthor of
The Coming Interspiritual Age

"The changes to the Earth community that will take place during the twenty-first century will surpass in magnitude anything that has happened in all of human history. It is impossible to be optimistic about the extent of the destruction that will be brought down upon humanity and life as a whole. The future of Christianity itself will depend upon its ability to reinvent its forms and practices so that it might become a mutually enhancing presence within the dynamics of life. Among current spiritual theologians, no one has a more comprehensive vision of the necessary changes that must take place than Matthew Fox. In *A Way to God* he shows how Thomas Merton's work can be understood as a powerful current within the Creation Spirituality tradition that is so essential for this reimagining of Western religion."

— BRIAN THOMAS SWIMME, professor of cosmology,
California Institute of Integral Studies

A WAY
TO GOD

Books by Matthew Fox

Stations of the Cosmic Christ (with Bishop Marc Andrus)

Meister Eckhart: A Mystic Warrior for Our Times

Letters to Pope Francis: Rebuilding a Church with Justice and Compassion

Occupy Spirituality: A Radical Vision for a New Generation (with Adam Bucko)

Hildegard of Bingen: A Saint for Our Times: Unleashing Her Power in the 21st Century

The Pope's War: Why Ratzinger's Secret Crusade Has Imperiled the Church and What Can Be Saved

Christian Mystics: 365 Readings and Meditations

The Hidden Spirituality of Men: Ten Metaphors to Awaken the Sacred Masculine

The A.W.E. Project: Reinventing Education, Reinventing the Human

A New Reformation: Creation Spirituality & the Transformation of Christianity

Creativity: Where the Divine and the Human Meet

Prayer: A Radical Response to Life (formerly *On Becoming a Musical, Mystical Bear*)

One River, Many Wells: Wisdom Springing from Global Faiths

Sins of the Spirit, Blessings of the Flesh: Lessons for Transforming Evil in Soul and Society

The Physics of Angels (with biologist Rupert Sheldrake)

Natural Grace (with biologist Rupert Sheldrake)

Wrestling with the Prophets: Essays on Creation Spirituality and Everyday Life

The Reinvention of Work: A New Vision of Livelihood for Our Time

Sheer Joy: Conversations with Thomas Aquinas on Creation Spirituality

Creation Spirituality: Liberating Gifts for the Peoples of the Earth

The Coming of the Cosmic Christ: The Healing of Mother Earth and the Birth of a Global Renaissance

Illuminations of Hildegard of Bingen

Original Blessing: A Primer in Creation Spirituality

Meditations with Meister Eckhart

A Spirituality Named Compassion

Confessions: The Making of a Post-denominational Priest (revised and updated)

Hildegard of Bingen's Book of Divine Works, Songs & Letters

Whee! We, Wee All the Way Home: A Guide to Sensual, Prophetic Spirituality

Religion USA: Religion and Culture by Way of "Time" Magazine

Manifesto for a Global Civilization (with Brian Swimme)

Passion for Creation: Meister Eckhart's Creation Spirituality (formerly *Breakthrough: Meister Eckhart's Creation Spirituality in New Translation*)

In the Beginning There Was Joy (children's book)

Western Spirituality: Historical Roots, Ecumenical Routes (editor)

A WAY TO GOD

Thomas Merton's Creation Spirituality Journey

MATTHEW FOX

New World Library
Novato, California

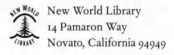 New World Library
14 Pamaron Way
Novato, California 94949

Text design by Tona Pearce Myers

Library of Congress Cataloging-in-Publication Data
Names: Fox, Matthew, date.
Title: A way to God : Thomas Merton's creation spirituality journey / Matthew Fox.
Description: Novato, CA : New World Library, 2016. | Includes bibliographical references.
Identifiers: LCCN 2016006215 (print) | LCCN 2016008302 (ebook) | ISBN 9781608684205 (alk. paper) | ISBN 9781608684212 (ebook)
Subjects: LCSH: Merton, Thomas, 1915–1968. | Fox, Matthew, 1940– | Eckhart, Meister, –1327. | Spiritual life—Catholic Church.
Classification: LCC BX4705.M542 F69 2016 (print) | LCC BX4705.M542 (ebook) | DDC 271/.12502—dc23
LC record available at http://lccn.loc.gov/2016006215

First printing, May 2016
ISBN 978-1-60868-420-5
Ebook ISBN 978-1-60868-421-2
Printed in Canada on 100% postconsumer-waste recycled paper

 New World Library is proud to be a Gold Certified Environmentally Responsible Publisher. Publisher certification awarded by Green Press Initiative. www.greenpressinitiative.org

10   9   8   7   6   5   4   3   2   1

I dedicate this book to my brother Thomas Merton and to all the people he has touched and will touch — people young and old, believers and unbelievers, who "seek a deeper dimension of consciousness than that of a horizontal movement across the surface of life." A special memory to three Mertonphiles in my life, Michael Toms and Dan Turner and Thomas Berry. And I thank Tom for the *honor* of interacting with him in the way I have in this book, even as I praise him for his deep and generous gifting, his mystical and prophetic gifts that keep on giving after all these years.

I am glad you are going to work on spiritual theology.... I do think we are lying down on the job when we leave others to investigate mysticism while we concentrate on more "practical" things. What people want of us, after all, is the way to God.

— THOMAS MERTON,
letter to Matthew Fox, January 23, 1967

Contents

Introduction

In 2015, I was invited to speak at Bellarmine University in Louisville, Kentucky, on the occasion of the centennial anniversary of Thomas Merton's birth. In a very auspicious decision just one year before his untimely death at fifty-three years of age, Merton chose to leave his papers and documents at Bellarmine. Merton's death on December 10, 1968, occurred in an annus horribilis: it was the same year that Dr. Martin Luther King Jr. and Robert Kennedy were gunned down. December 10 was also the date of Merton's entrance, in the winter of 1941, into the Abbey of Our Lady of Gethsemani, located just a few miles from Louisville.

The title assigned to me for my talk was "Vocation, Merton and Myself." I added Meister Eckhart to the title, since he was so pivotal to Merton and still is to myself. I thank the organizer, Mark Steiner, along with the Thomas Merton Center, for their invitation, since it encouraged me to think more deeply about my journey with Thomas Merton — and because of Merton. Out of my Bellarmine talk, and the workshop the following day, I have developed this modest book about the connections between Merton's journey and my own (as well as both of us with Meister Eckhart). The closer I looked at Merton's journey, the more interesting "connections" (one of his favorite words) emerged, and I have been quite surprised (and pleasantly so) at the number of intersections where our paths have crossed. I have come to learn how deeply Merton and I shared a common break away from dualistic spiritualities to a creation-centered way of living our shared religious heritage, and so some of my own ideas and autobiography also appear in this book.

This book is in part a thank-you to Thomas Merton and an acknowledgment of my debt to him, a debt that is quite unique in some ways. I offer it also as an outreach to others, monastic or not, who may not be familiar with the Creation Spirituality tradition, which has not only marked my life and work but, I am now certain, did the same for Merton in the last decade of his life. Many times since 1968 — in the face of culture's rapid leaps and profound evolutions — I have lamented Merton's untimely death, asking myself the question many others have no doubt asked as well: "What would Merton say?" and "What would Merton do?"

Risking gross understatement, I dare to say that Merton's thoughtful and deep commentary on spirituality and on cultural and historical events has been sorely missed these five decades since his death. Nor am I alone in this stance. For example, the late Michael Toms — the "Socrates of radio," who for decades gifted the world with brilliant interviews with some of our culture's greatest thinkers on his radio program *New Dimensions* — told me on more than one occasion: "I am a Thomas Merton Catholic." By this he surely meant a thinking, critically minded, and justice-oriented Catholic. Pope Francis, in his talk to the US Congress in September 2015, invoked Thomas Merton, saying, "Merton was above all a man of prayer, a thinker who challenged the certainties of his time and opened new horizons for souls and for the Church. He was also a man of dialogue, a promoter of peace between peoples and religions." I would maintain that much of Merton's spiritual journey parallels the articulation of the Creation Spirituality tradition and its Four Paths, which have proven foundational in my own journey. How could this be otherwise, since Meister Eckhart was so pivotal to Merton's journey from 1958 up to his death in 1968? Eckhart, so fully a creation-centered mystic and prophet, has been a guide to me as well — and indeed a "lifeboat," to use Merton's phrase.

I will confess that for decades I resisted over-associating myself with what seemed to me to be a veritable "Merton industry," or what Merton himself called "Mertonism." As I forged my theological and spiritual way — not only in my writings and research but in designing educational programs that would make an engaged mysticism more accessible — I shied away from institutional power trips wherever I sensed them, whether they came from religious institutions or academia. Of course, this reaction related in part to my own wounds at the hands of both. This does not mean that I neglected Merton's genius. I hosted courses on his work, I assigned his books for reading by my students, and I included him in my writing. It's just that I felt the need to keep my distance a bit from the "Merton machine," which sometimes seemed to suck all the air out of the room.

With this project, however, I feel a certain reconciliation — with Thomas himself, and with Merton scholars and the institutions Merton was closely related to, including both Bellarmine University, where Merton left many of his papers, and the Trappist Order within which he lived his adult life. I praise Thomas for his fidelity to his vocation, and I praise his monastery for keeping his work alive and providing ever more resources from his rich legacy. I especially salute with a loud kudo the wisdom of the Trappist Order for taking Thomas in, first of all, and then for eventually encouraging him to write what was in his mind and heart, for giving him logistic and personnel support, and for assisting in the dissemination of his work both before and following his death. They deserve praise for being so integral a part of the deep journey of Thomas Merton, sharing their lineage with him but also being humble enough to learn from him along the way.

I have been moved in my writing of this book to rediscover my roots and intersections with Thomas Merton. Merton was born in 1915; I was born twenty-five years later, in 1940. We were obviously of different generations, but Merton and I connected at many levels and on many occasions. Merton was born in southern France, while I was "reborn" in southern France, as I was busy writing my doctoral thesis while living on a simple Basque farm. It was there one day, while sitting at my typewriter, that I said out loud to myself: "I am a writer. Because I am so happy writing and putting ideas together and in a form I can communicate with others. And I learn so much doing this."

Merton was a very prolific writer, having written over fifty books in a period of about twenty-seven years. Writing brought Merton joy, though it could be a burden at the same time. I have experienced this same thing, and I, too, have been called prolific. However, where Merton took a vow of poverty to an institution and was spared the demands of having to make a living, much of my life and writing time has been tempered by years of administration. I designed and guided programs at Barat College, and then at the Institute of Culture and Creation Spirituality (both in Chicago and Oakland). I also launched and ran my University of Creation Spirituality with a master's program that operated in conjunction with the Naropa Institute of Boulder, Colorado, which was founded by a friend of Merton's, Chögyam Trungpa Rinpoche. Yet despite our differing positions in the world, the spiritual journeys Merton and I underwent and shared with others — our vocations, therefore — ran very parallel, as this book shows.

I end the book by citing Merton's own words about a "perfect circle." I argue that his life was that way for him personally, but also he carried the rest of us to that new beginning by completing a full circle back to his (and our) Creation Spirituality roots. The very writing of this book has proved to be a great circle for me. I first encountered Merton when I read his autobiography as a teenager, and I have been deeply moved in writing this book at how deeply he and I have journeyed together, with Eckhart as a guide to each of us, ever since. This was happening all along without my being deeply aware of it. Deep down, though we were twenty-five years apart in age, and though I have lived longer than he by another twenty-two years, we have been traveling together on a "way to God" that I have come to call Creation Spirituality.

While Merton, as in the citation that opens this book, talks about "*the* way to God," I am happy to talk about his and my journey via Creation Spirituality as being *a* way to God.

Regarding the translations of Meister Eckhart in this book: When I cite from Merton when he employs Meister Eckhart, I have left the translations Merton used as he presented them. I have done the same with Suzuki's translations of Eckhart. Most often, these are the translations by Blakney, which while lively are not always accurate, since Blakney wrote before the critical German works were published. When I cite Eckhart, I draw from the critical German editions that have appeared since Merton's death and from my translations of them.

It brings joy to my heart to know that Merton's encouragement to me nearly fifty years ago to go to Paris to study has not been fruitless, and I hope that, in my small way, I have contributed to carrying on the honest search that he was also on. Or as he put it in 1965 in the prologue to *Raids on the Unspeakable*: "Shall this be the substance of your message? Be human in this most inhuman of ages; guard the image of man for it is the image of God." Humans are not the only image of God, but we are the most dangerous and the most endangered species as a result. The wisdom Merton offers and Eckhart offers and Creation Spirituality offers can be medicine for our souls and societies, I am sure.

— MATTHEW FOX,
December 10, 2015 (the centennial of Merton's birth,
the 47th anniversary of Merton's death, and the
74th anniversary of his entrance into the Trappist community)

Merton at his hermitage. Merton and I were both living at our respective hermitages the same year (1965), though he on a part-time basis.

CHAPTER ONE

"The sign of Paris is on me, indelibly!"

My Intersection with Thomas Merton

*It is important to have seen the jagged outline of the towers of Car-cassonne against the evening sky. To have smelled the sun and the dust in the streets of Toulouse or Narbonne. There are times when I am mortally homesick for the South of France, where I was born....
The high roofs of Strasbourg, Tauler's city. Streets known to Eckhart.*

— THOMAS MERTON

Like many young Catholic men growing up in the fifties and looking at a possible vocation in the religious arena, I was moved to read Merton's autobiography, *The Seven Storey Mountain*. I was then a teenager attending my local public high school, West High School, in Madison, Wisconsin. I remember sitting down with the vocational director of the Dominican Order in the Midwest, Father Gilbert Graham, who told me that "portions" of Merton's autobiography were "quite immature" but "it was a good book to read anyway." I did find it uplifting and expansive, exciting and full of derring-do and adventure, which appealed to

1

my budding religious manhood. The book was heralded as a classic, and no doubt it brought many people into the Trappist Order, which is a very ancient and strict order. It held special appeal to the postwar generation, many of whom had seen so much suffering and death in World War II (and often developed what we now call post-traumatic stress disorder) that they sought a more contemplative and peaceful life such as the Trappists offered.

While Merton's autobiography did not entice me to join the Trappists, his vocational treatise set my goals for the contemplative side of religious life quite high when I joined the Dominican Order. During my youthful days, the vocation that I sensed growing in me was to embody both contemplation and action together, and I took the Dominican Order at its word that these need not be antagonists.

In many ways, Tolstoy most influenced my vocation. Reading *War and Peace* during the summer between my junior and senior years of high school, I had what can only be called a mystical experience (I had no vocabulary for that at the time). I told a friend that "it blew my soul wide open," and I wanted to pursue what happened to me. Later, I was struck by Charles du Bos's comment on *War and Peace*: "Life would speak thus if life could speak." That mystical experience was at the heart of my joining the Dominican Order, and no doubt it has been core to my entire vocation or calling since. It could readily be said that all of my books are about that experience in one way or another — that and how to relate it to social justice action. This combined perspective grew during the sixties with the civil rights movement and the anti-Vietnam movement, and in the seventies with the ecology movement, the women's movement, and the gay movement as well.

Another early intersection with Father Thomas Merton and myself emerged during my training as a Dominican. That training included two years at Loras College in Dubuque, Iowa, where aspiring Dominicans lived together in a dorm called Smith Hall under the supervision of two Dominican priests; then a year of novitiate training in Winona, Minnesota; and then three intense years in philosophy school in River Forest, Illinois. This was followed by solemn vows and a move to the Aquinas Institute of Theology in Dubuque, Iowa (today both schools are located in St. Louis, Missouri). The spiritual experiences I underwent along the way were powerful and meaningful, and during my last year in River Forest, when I took them to my confessor, he said to me: "You should consider becoming a hermit."

This was not at all on my radar. I considered myself quite an extrovert, whether I was relating to my other Dominican brothers or playing sports or in my aspirations to teach and to preach. But the advice kept eating away at me, and by the time I landed in theology school in Dubuque, I was entertaining at least the possibility of checking out a hermetical life. After some research, I found a colony of hermits on Vancouver Island overseen by a former Belgian abbot and biblical scholar named Dom Winandy. I went to my superiors and asked for permission to visit the place in the summer. They were not particularly supportive — indeed, Father Gilbert Graham, who was by now provincial of my province, told me, "That is a crazy thing to do. The only ones from the province who have done such a thing in the past went off the deep end. If you do this, I cannot guarantee you will be ordained a priest." I responded that that was okay with me, but I had to pursue this option. After all, it had not been my idea but that of my priestly confessor.

So Father Graham relented and allowed me to journey from Dubuque to Vancouver Island for the summer of 1965, though he told me I was to tell no one on my return (a promise I kept). In a similar way, Father Thomas Merton also had to fight with his superiors to be allowed to have his own hermitage on monastery grounds. It was not an easy battle, lasting for about six years, but he did eventually win out. As it turned out, both Merton and I were both living in our respective hermitages the same year (1965). Merton remained in his hermitage from 1965 until his final journey to Asia in 1968. In January 1967, Merton wrote to me, saying he had "found what he was looking for" in his hermitage, and he told me that he knew Father Winandy. This was yet another intersection. In January 1960, Merton wrote in his journal about how an article written by Winandy on the canonical situation of hermits "reopened everything" for him. "The big wound bleeds. I think certainly I have been unjustly treated. But what can I do?" This fed Merton's efforts to create his own hermitage. Later, in 1967, Merton spoke at some length about Winandy's hermit community to a group of contemplative nuns. In this way, Merton and I were also both indebted to the vision of Dom Winandy.

I found the summer I spent in the Vancouver Island hermitage to be a profound and energizing experience — indeed, I told a friend later that I ran on that energy for twenty-five years. It was utterly "simple living"; my room consisted of a mattress on the bare wood floor, a candle, and a small table. No electricity, no shower, and so on. I remember on the last day there I took a bar of soap into the nearby river and bathed that way. About half a dozen hermits lived there, and they were not allowed to speak to one another, though they could speak to me, an outsider. I appreciated learning their interesting stories. A couple were ex-Trappists; one worked during the year atop a tower in the Canadian woods as a forest ranger, so he was hermit-like both in the hermitage and in his work. I kept a journal, and the abbot asked me to read it toward the end of my stay. He then advised me to return to the more "active" life of the Dominicans but to remain true to my contemplative vocation at the same time. He said to me, "One day you will be a hermit while living in a great city." So he was advising me to turn my back on a rural vocation as much as the hermetical vocation. More than once since, whether living in Paris or in Oakland, those words have echoed back to me.

I returned to Dubuque very much energized. Among other things, I was given the responsibility to "bury" our philosophical magazine with the modest title *Reality* and start up a new magazine, which I called *Listening*. This became a very successful publication during the sixties, when so much was happening in Catholic and ecumenical theology due to the Second Vatican Council then in progress in Rome. When we launched *Listening* magazine, I chose the name deliberately as a reference to Martin Heidegger, who says: "Being-with develops in listening to one another." Merton read Heidegger with appreciation also, and he once tartly criticized the lost art of listening: "Since language has become a medium in which we are totally immersed, there is no longer any need to say anything. The saying says itself all around us. No one need attend. Listening is obsolete. So is silence."

With the help of able-bodied Dominican brothers living and studying with me, we put out a publication that soon became the pride of the province. We published Hans Küng, Yves Congar, M. D. Chenu, Edward Schillebeeckx, and many others who were key thinkers and movers and shakers at the council. Perhaps the most impactful piece for me was Chenu's article "The End of the Constantinian Era," which we published in the autumn 1967 issue. Little did I imagine that I would be studying with him one year later. His article put the Vatican Council in historic perspective, tracing the detour that Christianity had been making for centuries, and it traced the walls of lies (the spurious "Donation of Constantine") and obfuscation that had been erected to defend an empire. I was not the only one affected by Chenu's historical criticism on the history of empire and religion. Merton, too, was very approving of Chenu's teachings, and on reading one of his books, he was struck to comment in his journals:

> How much we have done to lead ourselves astray with theories about ages of the world, and extrapolations from prophecies of Daniel about the Roman Empire — to Charlemagne — to Barbarism and what not. This was the contribution of a Cistercian, Otto of Freising. We have never given up thinking in such terms. No one, however, has yet formulated anything about the "Western" realm of America being the heir of the Holy Roman Empire — or perhaps some Spaniard did. Yet that is how we think, still, and it is built in to our Christianity as a permanent delusion.
>
> So also the delusion of Holy Russia.
>
> There are too damn many holy empires with archimandrites to shower them in holy water.

But there *is*, I learned while doing my thesis in Paris, a quasi teaching of America being the heir to the Holy Roman Empire — and it was promulgated by none other than the media genius Henry Luce and the Luce media empire (which has been followed by other media empires). Luce called America the nation "most chosen by God" since the Israelites to lead the world, and he called for a "Pax Americana." Merton was alert to Luce and alluded often in unflattering ways to *Time* and *Life* magazines on several occasions.

Two days later in his journal, Merton continued his reflection on empire and religion that was inspired by Chenu.

> Otto of Friesing was so convinced that Constantine had finally inaugurated the Kingdom of God, that he spoke at last only of *one city* in his history of the "Two Cities." When the Emperor became Catholic, the Christendom = the Kingdom of God, i.e. the Christian politico-religious world is the kingdom of God.

Hence there is no more to be done, but to preserve the status quo of the kingdom, if necessary by violent repression, coercion rather than apostolate. The apostolate of united coercion!!

Here we see the profound impact on Merton of Pere Chenu's understanding of history and the "End of the Constantinian Era." The lesson Merton drew from Chenu's insights was this: "The true responsibility — to receive the Holy Spirit and cooperate with His transforming work in time now."

In the third issue of *Listening* (autumn 1966), I devoted much of the editorial to Thomas Merton's decision to live as a hermit, calling it "noteworthy" that "one of the men who spearheaded American Catholicism's coming of age has chosen to live as a hermit. Because we know Thomas Merton from his words and outspoken stands on war, civil rights, the role of the Orient, his decision strikes a jarring note into the melee of political, educational and ecumenical revolutions which so occupy our attention today." I pointed out how we need to respect "those who will experiment in the Church — experimentation not only with new forms but perhaps with some of the oldest as well."

One Dominican priest teaching in our theology school who followed the birth of our new magazine told me one day, "*Listening* magazine is the biggest political coup in the history of the province." All I know in retrospect is that I enjoyed doing it, and we found good work for lots of my fellow brothers in training, and I think it benefited many who were following the radical changes in the church in the wake of Vatican II. The circulation reached about thirty-six thousand readers, and they were avid, judging from the correspondence that came our way. I honed skills of many kinds, and it was a project that others could take pride in. And my energy to do that task as well as my studies in theology and the priesthood came from my visit to the Vancouver

Island hermitage. The fact that I risked losing the priesthood before I even entered into it enabled me to get my priorities straight, and it served me well long after I was ordained.

Years later I learned that my provincial, Father Gilbert Graham, had sent Abbot Winandy a letter when I set out to join him that more or less threatened him. It said something like, "This is one of my best prospects and you must not steal him from me or you will pay." Did this influence Abbot Winandy to direct me to return to the Dominicans? I guess I will never know. Then again, under Father Graham, I was first sent to Paris to study spiritual theology and study with Pere Chenu and get my doctorate at the Institut Catholique de Paris. Father Graham told at least one brother that he "sent me out of the country to get rid of me," since he felt I might emerge as a political force in the province (a second "political coup"?). Here, too, Thomas Merton enters the picture in a big and direct way.

In the midsixties I pestered my Dominican superiors about the need to hire a person with a degree in spirituality to teach on the faculty. We had no courses on spirituality as such, and though we underwent lots of spiritual practices on a daily basis — from fasting to vegetarianism and meditation and rosaries (mantras) and celibacy and voluntary poverty — there was little or no discussion of the meaning behind it all. When I would go to priests about the spiritual experiences I was undergoing, I got little or no help. Finally, a younger priest in the house said to me, "What you are experiencing I don't think any priest around here knows anything about. You have to get used to the idea that you are on your own." This sort of observation confirmed what I was thinking and inspired me to pester the order to get someone trained in spirituality. I said, "My generation is going to be less interested in religion and more interested in spirituality, so you really should get someone on the faculty with that kind of training." And I added, "I am happy to volunteer."

My pushing was not in vain. In late 1966, my superiors came to me and said: "Good news! You can go to Europe to get a doctorate in spirituality." I said, "Great! Where do I go?" They said: "Why not go to Spain?" I said, "No, thanks. We don't need more sixteenth-century Spanish Carmelite spirituality." "Well," they said, "then go to Rome." I said, "Rome? For spirituality? You must be kidding." They said, "Well, wise guy, where do you think you should go?" I said, "I don't know. But let me write Thomas Merton and ask him where to go." With that, they shook their heads and gave me the distinct impression that they felt I was crazy.

So in January 1967, I wrote Thomas Merton and asked him where I should go. I do not have a copy of my letter to him. I know that I mentioned my time with Abbot Winandy in the hermitage, and I emphasized the need for an ecumenical perspective and my work with *Listening* magazine, among other things. To my surprise (and to the surprise of my superiors), Thomas answered me with a full-page letter, which I reproduce and exegete in the following chapter.

The gist of his reply was: Go to the Institut Catholique de Paris. With that letter I went back to my superiors and said, "I need to go to Paris." They said, "No way! We have never sent anyone to Paris who came home again!" I replied, "But Merton says, and he knows what he is talking about." They said no, and so it went back and forth for several months, with me taking that letter and beating it over the head of my religious superiors until they reluctantly gave in, perhaps exhausted, and granted permission to study in France.

Thus I can say without correction that I owe to Thomas Merton all the trouble I have gotten into since my sojourn in Paris. But the research I have conducted, the books I have written, the classes I have taught, the programs I have designed and administered over the years upon returning from Paris — this, too, I owe to Merton. For it was in Paris that I received much training and learning and, above all, where I met my mentor, Pere Marie-Dominique Chenu. It is he who named the Creation Spirituality tradition for me. And that has been my vocation ever since — to research and teach and preach and make known that much-forgotten and often-maligned tradition. Without Merton's counsel, I never would have gone to Paris and never would have met Pere Chenu. Merton read and respected Chenu very much, as is clear from his journal entry on December 9, 1962: "M. D. Chenu's article on Theology and History in the 12th century is, like everything else of his, instructive and important."

Thomas Merton's parents met as art students in Paris. His father was from New Zealand, and his mother was from America, and Thomas was born and raised in southern France. In 1966, Merton wrote movingly of what France meant to him:

It is important to have seen the jagged outline of the towers of Carcassonne against the evening sky. To have smelled the sun and the dust in the streets of Toulouse or Narbonne. There are times when I am mortally homesick for the South of France, where I was born.... The high roofs of Strasbourg, Tauler's city. Streets known to Eckhart.

Merton talked of Paris as the cultural capital of Western Christianity and exclaimed, "The sign of Paris is on me, indelibly!"

I can say the same. I remain in debt to Paris and the French for more than just my theological awakening. I was influenced by a doctoral theological system that encouraged thinking over rote memorizing and anal-retentive footnoting; by a culture that was old and sophisticated but also very critical and artistically focused; by the history of the streets and places of Paris, where my earlier Dominican comrades, including Aquinas and Eckhart, walked and lived and learned and taught; by the wonders of Chartres

Cathedral and Notre Dame and other architectural Gothic marvels, all dedicated to the goddess, Mary; and by a cosmopolitan gathering of students from all around the world, especially from Latin American countries.

Numerous faculty besides Pere Chenu also impacted me. Among these excellent thinkers were l'abbe Yves Marchasson, who fed me his methodology of critically analyzing old French newspapers to find the philosophy of culture embedded in them and who became director of my doctoral thesis on *Time* magazine and American cultural and religious values. Abbe Louis Cognet taught a three-year lecture course on the history of Christian Spirituality and wrote many books on the same, which I devoured. Others in Paris included Paul Ricoeur, from the University of Chicago; the Jesuit Michel de Certeau; Henri de Lubac, and many more. Paris was, in Ernest Hemingway's memorable wording, a *feast*. Said Hemingway: "If you are lucky enough to have lived in Paris as a young man, then wherever you go for the rest of your life, it stays with you, for Paris is a moveable feast." For me, it was not just a culinary feast, but an intellectual, artistic, historical, architectural, and theological feast.

I also managed trips to other countries, including Russia, which was still under the Soviet Empire at the time. I was blessed to spend a long summer writing my doctoral thesis in southern France, during which I made pilgrimages to Carcassonne and the other cities Merton mentioned. During that exciting time just after the close of the Second Vatican Council, I made friends with other students who were studying in Paris, especially some smart and alive Catholic sisters from America. I also connected with young Dominicans who were keen on reforming the order. Many were studying theology in Germany and elsewhere and gathered at Trier, Germany, for a convocation at which I played a somewhat prominent part.

All this I have Thomas Merton to thank for. I was changed forever by my French experience. I owe Thomas Merton big-time. In 1994, I had a dream that spoke movingly of my vocation, which was formed in the streets of Paris, and I repeat it here from my autobiography, *Confessions: The Making of a Post-Denominational Priest*.

> Ash Wednesday, February 16, 1994
>
> Dream last night (I cried in the dream) — I'm at an old gate, outdoors, made of iron. It is like a cemetery gate and I hear the statement (have I been teaching it?): "Everyone is here for a purpose. God has a role for everyone."
>
> And then I hear a question: "Has my role been to make creation spirituality known?" With that I cry because of the simplicity of it and the clarity of it and (I think) because it says something about my life and its many choices, including the recent one to become Episcopalian and the Vatican's choice to dump me. And also because it suggests that maybe my life and life work have had some meaning after all.

The gated place, particularly with a gate that is rusty and dying, might mean several things: my expulsion from the order and even from a Garden of Eden existence, but it might also mean the rusty and dying ecclesial institutions as we have known them and the end of the modern era and the industrial age. Clearly, the dream is about vocation and moving from a modern to a postmodern time. "I am no longer protected by the cloister and the garden it represented, as in my novitiate days," I wrote. "But the vocation continues." The tears were of grief — but also of joy. I wrote, "Joy is deeper than sorrow. In spite of the expulsion, my vocation continues. Inside or outside, my vocation goes on. Everyone's does."

In Bangkok on the final journey of his life, in his final talk delivered two hours before he died, Merton himself spoke about how we can no longer trust institutions but must instead develop a deeper spirituality. Merton died on December 10, 1968 (for more on this, see chapter 7). That was my second winter in Paris. Merton's death occurred only some seven months after the riots in spring 1968 that brought down Charles de Gaulle's government and after my classes with Pere Chenu, where I first learned the term "creation spirituality."

Merton meets the Dalai Lama. The Dalai Lama reports that Merton was the very first Christian he had ever met!

CHAPTER TWO

"The first place that comes to my mind"

Merton's 1967 Correspondence with Me

I am glad you are going to work on spiritual theology. The prejudice in some Catholic quarters against mysticism is a bit strange, when outside the church there is such an intense and ill regulated hunger for and curiosity about spiritual experience (what with LSD and all that).

— THOMAS MERTON

I reproduce here the original correspondence Thomas Merton sent to me in January 1967. This was followed several months later with a package that contained articles, most of which he had not yet published, and also many bound copies of notes he had used in his teaching of the history of monastic spirituality to the novices at Gethsemani Abbey. A note said, "Some day these may be of interest to you." This was a very generous and thoughtful thing to do, to bother to collect all these papers and mail them to a young fellow like me (for a complete list, see the select bibliography). Merton died about fifteen months after I received that package.

Jan 23, 1967

Dear Matthew

I'll do my best to answer your questions. Unfortunately I
am not too well informed as to what is available academi-
cally in this country. The first place that comes to my mind
is the Institut Catholique in Paris. However I know that you
ought to be able to get good comparative religion courses
at places like Columbia and Harvard. My line is Buddhism
more than Hinduism and I know there have been good Buddhist teachers at both these places.

For information I suggest you also write Dom Aelred
Graham at Portsmouth Priory, Rhode Island, who is pretty
well up on all this. If you get a chance, by all means go to
India. You could spend some time at the Ashram of Dom
Bede Griffiths in Kerala (Kurisumala Ashram, Baghamon
P.O., Peermade, S. India). He too will provide information
I am sure. There are plenty of Yoga schools in India, like
the Yoga Vedanta Academy at Rishikesh, somewhere in the
north. I don't know exact address.

Nearer home, in Montreal, there is the R. M. Bucke Me-
morial Society, at McGill University, specializing in comparative spirituality. They might be the most helpful at this
point.

Your general direction seems good: but where is Mystical and Ascetical Theology on your program? I don't think
History of Spirituality covers it well enough. Maybe you
include it in moral. If I can dig up a set of notes for the
course I gave in Mystical and Ascetical Theology, I'll send
it along. Admittedly, one has to start all that from scratch.
The Tanquerey approach just won't do. My own stuff is out
of date after five or six years.

You can do a great deal by reading the right books. The
Bucke Society can keep you in touch with the new literature.

I am glad you are going to work on spiritual theology. The prejudice in some Catholic quarters against mysticism is a bit strange, when outside the church there is such an intense and ill regulated hunger for and curiosity about spiritual experience (what with LSD and all that). I do think we are lying down on the job when we leave others to investigate mysticism while we concentrate on more "practical" things. What people want of us, after all, is the way to God.

I wish you luck in your search. Pray for me here in the woods. I feel very fortunate to have found what I was looking for. I keep you in my prayers. God be with you in everything.

Cordially yours in Christ,

As I've said, this letter spurred my decision to go to Paris and played a decisive role in getting the order to support my study there. Among other things, Thomas Merton's advice that I seek out Bede Griffiths has been fulfilled several times over.

I met Bede Griffiths in person for the first time in the eighties when Bede made several visits to the Bay Area. Later, we met on numerous occasions, including a public dialogue at Holy Names College in America not long before his death in India. In that dialogue he declared that "the future of spirituality is creation spirituality and the future of theology is the Cosmic Christ theology." He said the same thing to me in our personal correspondence. In addition Father Bede assisted me in my book on Thomas Aquinas, *Sheer Joy: Conversations with Thomas Aquinas on Creation Spirituality*. He wrote the book's afterword, and over several revisions, he upgraded my translations from the Latin into something more akin to the queen's English.

Aquinas was very important to Bede. After he graduated from Oxford as an atheist, Bede converted to Christianity upon reading Aquinas. C. S. Lewis became his sponsor or mentor as he probed the Christian tradition, a journey that took him eventually to the Benedictine Order and then to India. In their ashram refectory, Bede had his monks read several of my books publicly during meals as they ate in silence, including *Original Blessing* and *The Coming of the Cosmic Christ*. So we met first by way of our books.

Father Bede Griffiths was also close friends with British biologist Rupert Sheldrake, with whom I teamed up on a number of public dialogues, and with whom I have published two books, *The Physics of Angels* and *Natural Grace*. This is another way in which Father Bede and I have met. Rupert moved to India after his graduation from Cambridge. Though an atheist at the time, he became taken with the rich spiritual tradition of India, and on the advice of others, he sought out his countryman, Father Bede Griffiths, in the south of India. Rupert and Bede became fast friends. Bede was rejuvenated by Rupert's descriptions of the new science, and Rupert converted to Christianity; he and his wife, Jill Purce, are serious practitioners to this day.

Father Bede and I also met over the subject of my somewhat controversial relationship with the Vatican. As it turned out, after Bede's death, the truth came out about how much flak he had endured over the years both from the fundamentalists in the Vatican and from Hindu fundamentalists in India. But he endured it quite stoically and responded to it quite gently in his time. Father Bede told me, in what would turn out to be our final conversation before he died, that I should not put a lot of energy in trying to please my Vatican critics. He said, "Don't worry about the Vatican. Don't even think about them. Continue to do what you are doing, planting new shoots for a new Christianity. The Vatican will all come tumbling down some night, just like the Berlin Wall." Father Bede, like Merton, did not suffer fools easily and neither spent a lot of time arguing with fundamentalists and anti-intellectuals.

As Merton recommended, I eventually tackled the ideas of

Adolphe Tanquerey in several of my early books. Tanquerey was a deep dualist who promulgated an anti-body, anti-earth spirituality, yet he was widely taught. His book *The Spiritual Life: A Treatise on Ascetical and Mystical Theology* was used for training priests and sisters in Europe, America, and beyond. You will look in vain in his work for any reference to compassion as justice-making, committed as he was to an ascetic spirituality rooted in the three paths of purgation, illumination, and union (which I critique later). Merton was critical of Tanquerey for all these reasons, yet as regards ascetic theology, I do not think Merton understood its deep limitations. This is and was an area where perhaps Merton and I disagreed — though later in his writings Merton seemed to acquire a deeper critique of the same. I sensed early in my writings that the prophets were not ascetic. As Rabbi Abraham Joshua Heschel taught in his classic work *The Prophets*: "Asceticism was not the ideal of the biblical man. The source of evil is not in passion, in the throbbing heart, but rather in hardness of heart, in callousness and insensitivity.... We are stirred by their passion and enlivened imagination.... It is to the imagination and the passions that the prophets speak, rather than aiming at the cold approbation of the mind." Research has taught me that the very term "ascetic theology" was born in the seventeenth century (1655 to be exact), which I do not consider a high point in the tradition of Western spiritual consciousness by any means. Indeed, it was the time that religion separated from science, and psyche and cosmos were split. Of course, much depends on what one means by "asceticism," but I do think that much damage has been done by the promulgation of dualistic teachings that too glibly preach a battle between spirit and matter, body and spirit, earth body and human flesh. Merton himself wrestled with the term continuously.

Wisely, Merton added to me that "one has to start all that from scratch." In many ways, his words were very liberating and very radical. And since then, that is what I have done — start over from scratch. Consistently in all of my writings I address the fear of matter and I celebrate the sacred flesh of the universe, the earth, and our own bodies. Early on, I laid out an important distinction in my second book, *Whee! We, Wee All the Way Home: A Guide to a Sensual, Prophetic Spirituality.* I distinguished *natural ecstasies* — such as experiences in nature, art, literature, music, lovemaking, and friendship, which are experiences of the Creator as well — from *tactical ecstasies*, which are devices or methods that religions have developed over the years — including fasting, vegetarianism, introvert meditation, chanting, mantras, and more — to bring about ecstasies.

To his credit, in his 2015 encyclical on the environment, Pope Francis takes up the dualistic spiritual tradition that is so often linked to asceticism and points out that it was not the way of Jesus. He criticizes the "unhealthy dualisms" that "left a mark on certain Christian thinkers in the course of history and disfigured the Gospel." In contrast, Jesus himself "is far removed from philosophies which despised the body, matter and the things of this world." For he lived "in full harmony with creation" and "his appearance was not that of an ascetic set apart from the world, or of an enemy to the pleasant things of life."

As Merton advised, "You can do a great deal by reading the right books." In fact, this was Merton's way of continually staying abreast of things. He read a wide array of books, from the ancient fathers to contemporary novelists and poets and theologians. It was his intellectual and spiritual nourishment, and as he commented more than once, the monastic tradition encouraged extensive reading. The *lectio divina* was a spiritual practice after all. Merton did not have that much formal training as a theologian — in many ways he was self-taught. He did not consider himself a theologian as such, calling himself in one diary entry "a frustrated intellectual, pseudo-contemplative pseudo-hermit." In a letter to Rosemary Ruether, he said, "I am not enough of a theologian to be really bothered by theological problems." But he was a profound commentator on culture and values and the experiential side of religion. Spirituality was his specialty. But he was postacademic in his learning, and I suspect that is one reason he communicated so well and so deeply to so broad an audience. As a monk he took time to ponder the scriptures and pray them and to contemplate nature and current events — something academia is slow to indulge in.

Merton's observation that his work was "out of date" after five or six years is strikingly humble. He was most likely referring to his classes on mystical and ascetic theology that he was then teaching his novices. Nevertheless, I found it liberating then, as I do today — and also challenging. The implication is that one's task is not just to regurgitate a tradition but to shake it up and dig deeper. With the blessing of Thomas Merton, this is a vocation I have tried to persist in for all these years.

Merton did indeed "dig up a set of notes for the course" he gave in mystical and ascetical theology, and he sent them to me several months after our initial correspondence. As I mention above, I remain grateful for his doing this; I list these items in the bibliography, and I periodically quote from them in this book.

Merton's last paragraph in his letter very much struck home with me: our task is to "lead people to God" and a God experience. At that time, more secular movements, including those involving LSD experiments, were exploring mystical experience, but religious orders and seminaries were not even raising the right questions. It was for this very reason that I was so interested in pursuing a spirituality education more vigorously. Then and now, I agreed with his observation that "the prejudice in some Catholic circles against mysticism is a bit strange." In many respects, much if not all of my work has been to redeem the word *mysticism* and the practice of it. I have linked mysticism with our prophetic traditions and with the Wisdom tradition of Israel, which scholars today agree was the lineage of the historical Jesus. All this sets the table for an ecologically based spiritual consciousness and action. In my first book, published in 1972 with the unlikely title *On Becoming a Musical, Mystical Bear: Spirituality American Style* (now called simply *Prayer: A Radical Response to Life*), I wrestled with the meaning of "mysticism" and its dialectical relationship with "prophecy" or social justice. That book is foundational to my thought to this day. In it, I avoided the terms *contemplation* and *action* because I felt they were too often used in an either/or, dualistic relationship. I felt a new language was necessary.

Yet the term *mysticism* was problematic in Christian circles. One reason was that for some time it had been used to refer to a flight from social justice and commitment. Also, it was overidentified with a sin-oriented religious philosophy that was anti-matter and anti-body, that is to say, one that was founded on asceticism. The number one question I brought with me to my studies in Paris was this: How do you reconcile mystical experience with prophetic action? Is that task possible at all? This was the breakthrough I received from Pere Chenu when he named the creation tradition for me — he who was the grandfather of Liberation Theology and a former worker priest himself. My work on creation-centered mystics through the ages — such as Hildegard of Bingen and Meister Eckhart, St. Francis and Thomas Aquinas, Nicholas of Cusa and Julian of Norwich, and others — has, I think, answered that question of the radical compatibility of mysticism and prophetic warriorhood. All the mystics of that tradition right up to Sister Dorothy Stang today have taken on forces of power while not abandoning their love affair with life and being. Such a marriage is found obviously in the work and life of Thomas Merton himself.

Merton's reference to his having found "what I was looking

for" in the woods and in his hermitage was quite moving —
but in retrospect it is not totally convincing, as he never ceased
searching. Less than two years after he wrote my letter, he made
a pilgrimage to the East, where he had, among other things, a
breakthrough and breakout mystical experience at a famous Buddhist shrine in Ceylon. He also met the Dalai Lama and other
notable Eastern spiritual adepts, all of whom made a profound impression on him. In 1966, Thich Nhat Hanh had visited him at his
monastery and both were moved by their encounter. Thich Nhat
Hanh later described it this way: "It is hard to describe his face in
words, to write down exactly what he was like. He was so filled
with human warmth. Conversation with him was so easy. When
we talked, I told him a few things, and he immediately understood
the things I didn't tell him as well. He was open to everything,
constantly asking questions and listening deeply." Thich Nhat
Hanh later nominated Merton for the Nobel Peace Prize. Merton
devoted the final pages of his book *Mystics & Zen Masters* to the
teachings of Thich Nhat Hanh and credits him with an "ontology of non-violence." The Dalai Lama reported that Merton was
the very first Christian he had ever met! While his hermitage was
important to Merton, clearly his Asian sojourn was something he
needed as well. In addition, before he left for Asia, he made trips
to Northern California, Alaska, and New Mexico in search of a
more rigorous eremitical place where he could get away from the
distractions of his hermitage at the Abbey of Gethsemani.

One thing to admire in Thomas Merton is his readiness to
be continually learning and growing — and to be self-critical in
an amazingly objective way. As he wrote in May 1968 in *Woods,
Shore, Desert*:

> In our monasticism, we have been content to find our way
> to a kind of peace, a simple undisturbed thoughtful life. And
> this is certainly good, but is it good enough?

I, for one, realize that now I need more. Not simply to be quiet, somewhat productive, to pray, to read, to cultivate leisure — *otium sanctum!* There is a need of effort, deepening, change and transformation....

But I do have a past to break with, an accumulation of inertia, waste, wrong, foolishness, rot, junk, a great need of clarification of mindfulness, or rather of no mind — a return to genuine practice, right effort, need to push on to the great doubt. Need for the Spirit.

Hang on to the clear light!

It is interesting that here, in the last journal he ever approved for publication, Merton offered self-criticism along with institutional criticism. He critiqued monasticism as well as his own role in it. A very postmodern thing to do! Right up to his death, Merton was seriously contemplating moving to the West, to spend a few years as a hermit in communion with the wilderness there. "I dream every night of the West," he tells us in his journal. He still wanted to die a member of the Gethsemani community, but he was feeling the call to live beyond it for a while.

Merton's fame as a writer and spiritual guide was a two-edged sword for him. While he was pleased to be contributing to the spiritual growth of others, and while he delighted in entertaining guests from Joan Baez and Daniel Berrigan to Jacques Maritain and John Howard Griffin, he was also beset by many people who showed up at the doorstep of his hermitage unannounced. He tells one story of actually hiding behind a tree to wait for some visiting priests to leave the hermitage; they had arrived without notice and were hoping to meet him. His introvert side needed attention. This is why he separated himself partially from the larger monastic community in the first place by moving into a hermitage on the monastery's grounds. But it proved to be just a half-gap measure.

CHAPTER THREE

"Eckhart is my lifeboat"

Merton Encounters Meister Eckhart

Eckhart trusted men to recognize that what he saw was worth seeing because it brought obvious fruits of life and joy. For him, that was what mattered.

— THOMAS MERTON

Thomas Merton's intellectual and spiritual debt to Meister Eckhart was profound and long lasting — as a student at Columbia University in 1938, Merton wrote about Eckhart in his master's thesis, and during his final journey to the East in 1968, Merton was invoking him. In 1966 Merton wrote: "Meister Eckhart may have limitations, but I am entranced with him nevertheless. I like the brevity, the incisiveness of his sermons, his way of piercing straight to the heart of the inner life, the awakened spark, the creative and redeeming Word, God born in us." Many of Eckhart's ideas — such as "ground of being," letting be and letting go, the Apophatic Divinity, the Godhead, the "unborn self," the "spark" of God — pop up regularly in Merton's work.

But the greatest impact on Merton regarding Eckhart came about through Buddhist scholar Dr. D. T. Suzuki, with whom Merton had been in dialogue since about 1958, about the time of Pope Pius XII's death and the election of Pope John XXIII. In their dialogues Suzuki highlighted the importance of Eckhart. This dialogue became a life-changing experience for Merton, one that set him on a path of ecumenism between East and West and of prophetic action and consciousness that changed his spirituality forever. From that time until his final journey East, Merton was indebted to Eckhart. Eckhart changed him from being the dualistic and sentimental Augustinian-tainted monk of the forties (as reflected in his autobiography) to being a prophetic Christian who, as it turned out, was the first religious figure in America to come out against the Vietnam War. This decision may have cost Merton his life (see chapter 7).

Just before that Asian journey, in May 1968, Merton sojourned to Northern California, where he visited a group of Cistercian nuns and discussed Eckhart with them. In his journal, he compared one of the sisters to a fictitious woman whom Eckhart wrote about and who shares a similar name: "Sister Katryn to be an obscure descendant of Eckhart's Sister Katrei. Sister Katryn and Sister Christofora were the ones who seemed to respond the most knowingly whenever Eckhart was mentioned." Merton began his final journey East by flying out of San Francisco International Airport, and his body was returned by way of Oakland, California, my home for the past thirty-two years.

Why was Eckhart of such importance to Merton? As we shall see, Eckhart is the spokesperson par excellence for the wisdom-based and nature-based mystical and prophetic tradition called Creation Spirituality. His love of life and being, of animals and earth — as well as his appreciation for silence and the Apophatic Divinity and his teachings on art and creativity and on justice and compassion — deeply nourished the soul and teachings of Merton as, in the last decade of his life, he put on his wings of both contemplation and prophetic criticism. Eckhart's teaching that "compassion means justice" and "the person who understands what I say about justice understands everything I have to say" supported Merton at this time of cultural and moral upheavals in the sixties.

Eckhart was also an uncanny and unparalleled deep ecumenist — indeed, Dr. Suzuki put Eckhart at the front of the pack of Western thinkers who are representative of a spirituality where East and West meet. In his classic work *Mysticism: Christian and Buddhist*, Suzuki's entire first chapter, "Meister Eckhart and Buddhism," is devoted to how Eckhart's thought parallels Buddhist teaching in so many deep ways. In the preface, Suzuki writes, "Eckhart's thoughts come most closely to those of Zen and Shin....Eckhart, Zen, and Shin thus can be grouped together as belonging to the great school of mysticism."

My most recent book, *Meister Eckhart: A Mystic Warrior for Our Times*, is devoted to exploring Eckhart's ecumenism. The book's entire methodology is to put Eckhart in conversation with thinkers from various world spiritual traditions: Thich Nhat Hanh, Ananda Coomaraswamy, Rabbi Abraham Joshua Heschel, Black Elk, Carl Jung, Rumi, and so on. Perhaps no thinker in the West went as deeply and broadly as Meister Eckhart, who reached a place of universal truth where all the contemplative traditions gather. Surely this was part of what endeared Merton to Eckhart and fed him right to the end of his life.

In 1329, a week after Eckhart died during his trial in Avignon, France, he was condemned by church authorities, but Merton himself dismissed this. He wrote in *Conjectures of a Guilty Bystander*:

> He was a great man who was pulled down by a lot of little men who thought they could destroy him: who thought

they could drag him to Avignon and have him utterly discredited.

And indeed he was ruined, after his death in twenty-eight propositions which might doubtless be found somewhere in him but which had none of his joy, his energy, his freedom.... Eckhart did not have the kind of mind that wasted time being cautious about every comma: he trusted men to recognize that what he saw was worth seeing because it brought obvious fruits of life and joy. For him, that was what mattered.

One senses Merton's outrage in almost every word of this critique. But before tracing further Merton's encounter with Eckhart, I will discuss my own encounters with that unique individual who, after all, was of my same Dominican family and whose fate at the hands of a corrupt papacy was not altogether unlike my own. At the time Merton was encountering Eckhart, I was a very young Dominican and priest in training. It would be about twenty years before Eckhart burst into my life. His work eventually led me to name the Four Paths of Creation Spirituality, which I feel describe Merton's spiritual journey from 1959 onward (as later chapters explore).

Myself and Meister Eckhart

In all my nine years of training as a Dominican, I never heard Meister Eckhart's name spoken once. I guess that is the price that one pays for being condemned, even by a vastly immoral papacy such as the one Eckhart lived through. As Merton put it, "he was ruined," that is to say, he was forgotten even by his own brothers. In my studies and readings on Christian spirituality at the Catho, I did hear some reference to him. The head of the spirituality department, historian and priest Louis Cognet, referred to how Eckhart boasted a "via negativa but no via positiva," and Cognet devoted two chapters to Eckhart in his book *Introduction aux Mystiques Rhéno-Flamands*. Yet as I learned during my own research into Eckhart, Cognet was simply wrong. Eckhart boasted a very rich Via Positiva, but scholars had often ignored it, choosing to focus on his Via Negativa almost exclusively.

In 1976, several years after returning to America, I first started looking seriously into Eckhart. I was inspired by Ananda Coomaraswamy's classic work *The Transformation of Nature in Art*. There, Coomaraswamy devoted a chapter to Eckhart, wherein he testified that reading Eckhart was like reading the Upanishads and that whole sentences read like they were translated from the Sanskrit. This certainly piqued my interest in Eckhart, but so did the fact that several of the sentences by Eckhart that Coomaraswamy translated were identical to sentences I had penned in an article I had recently published entitled "Sacred Space and Sacred Time."

More recently, I was bowled over to learn from Sister Therese Lentfoehr, a close friend of Thomas Merton, that Merton first encountered Eckhart through this same book by Coomaraswamy when Merton was a graduate student at Columbia University in 1938. Merton wrote a treatise on Coomaraswamy's book, in which he praised Eckhart as a "great medieval thinker."

Eckhart piqued my interest and curiosity because he answered an important question for me: "Am I crazy for how I see the spiritual journey or do I have a brother as well who sees it my way?" In addition, in 1978, I had a back operation to relieve problems from a serious car accident I had suffered in 1976. During the time I was under anesthesia, Meister Eckhart came to me, and we went walking together on a beach. No words were spoken between us, but I knew, upon waking from that dream, that Eckhart and I were destined to be companions for some time to come. It was the most transcendent dream of my life. That encounter birthed two books on Meister Eckhart in 1979: *Meditations* with *Meister Eckhart* and *Breakthrough: Meister Eckhart's Creation Spirituality in New Translation* (now retitled *Passion for Creation: The Earth-Honoring Spirituality of Meister Eckhart*). The second book included the first English translations of thirty-seven of Eckhart's sermons and treatises from critical German editions, along with my own commentary after each sermon. In addition, Eckhart was important to my book *A Spirituality Named Compassion*, as he was one of the few Christian theologians I could find who offered a substantive exegesis of the passage in Luke 6: "Be you compassionate as your Creator in heaven is compassionate." Compassion was a more important category for Eckhart than was "contemplation" — and that was unique among spiritual writers.

Merton, Heschel, and Western Spirituality

Also in 1979, the same year I published my Eckhart books, I edited a book entitled *Western Spirituality: Historical Roots, Ecumenical Routes*. I dedicated the book to both Thomas Merton and Rabbi Abraham Joshua Heschel, writing: "A catholic monk and a rabbinic prophet, two persons with the courage to explore their roots and worldwide routes. May we never forget them or their courage." I had not known at the time that the two of them were good friends. The book included articles by biblical scholar Helen A. Kenik, liberation theologian Jon Sobrino, feminist theologian Rosemary Radford Ruether, translations of two articles by M. D. Chenu (which he gave me permission to combine and translate), and essays by Nikolai Berdyaev, Native American teacher Sister Mary José Hobday, and more.

In the book's introduction, I invoked both Thomas Merton and Rabbi Heschel. As I commented on how E. F. Schumacher said that the West's experiment of trying to live without spirituality over the past few centuries had been a failure, I wrote:

Thomas Merton is equally harsh on what the West has made of its spiritual heritage. Speaking of how Christians should get back to an appreciation of history and become "as obsessed with history as" Marxists are, he comments: "The Marxian idea that the key to everything is found in history is, curiously enough, the basic Idea of the Bible. We, the Christians, have forgotten this. We have reduced our religious thought to the consideration of static essences and abstract moral values. We have lost the dynamic sense of God's revelation of himself in history."

I also raised Rabbi Heschel's distinction between the "God of the philosophers" involved "only with himself" versus "the God of the prophets emphatically involved in human affairs." Heschel believes that the philosophers prefer a God of sterile, static thought, while the Bible evokes a God who shows "active, dynamic concern for the human condition."

Thomas Merton and Rabbi Heschel — these two powerful voices of the West nourished by deep traditions of Christian and of Jewish spirituality respectively agree: The spirituality of our age will be biblical and Jewish instead of neoplatonic and Hellenistic. It will involve the Spirit in history and above all will be characterized by an "active, dynamic concern for the human condition." It is to these two biblical believers, who lived as well as reflected on their spiritualities that this volume is dedicated.

Clearly, I was calling upon Merton's later prophetic writings and his prophetic consciousness, which were developed during the sixties by both his reading of Eckhart and the basic teachings of the Second Vatican Council. This bifurcation in Merton — between the Merton of the fifties (which was so Augustinian based) and the Merton of the sixties (so Eckhartian based) — mirrored the larger one going on in the post–Vatican II church as a whole. I distinguished in the book between the Creation Spirituality tradition and the Augustine tradition:

> A modest purpose behind this volume, then, is to help *un*do the guilt that platonic dualisms via Augustine have heaped upon Christian spirituality. And thus to reveal that Christians do have options beyond Augustine. Biblical ones and historical ones. The Western spiritual tradition is far richer, far more diverse, far fuller of celebration and of socially involved compassion than we Westerners give it credit for being. There are traditions of our past where history and body are integral to and not separate from Christian spirituality. For, in Fr. Chenu's words, "to admit that God creates is implicitly to confess that matter is divinely willed and therefore good."

The Origin of the Four Paths

In *Western Spirituality*, I also published my first major essay on Meister Eckhart and my first writing on the Four Paths of Creation Spirituality, entitled "Meister Eckhart on the Fourfold Path of a Creation-Centered Spiritual Journey."

Just as, almost twenty years earlier, Thomas Merton had a significant, transformative encounter with Eckhart, so it was for me. Eckhart led me to the Four Paths of Creation Spirituality — the Via Positiva, Via Negativa, Via Creativa, and Via Transformativa. For several years, I had been conducting workshops and retreats where I took people through these paths. I invited them to respond with imaging and storytelling, and on each occasion the responses were deep and recognizable. Just like Eckhart predicted when he said, "The path of which I speak is beautiful and pleasant and joyful and familiar," people responded with a sense of familiarity — they recognized their own journeys almost intuitively and immediately, as they still do. In *Western Spirituality*, I took to task the presumptions that have existed since the sixteenth century that spirituality is about "exercises" or that it can properly be called "ascetic theology." That term was not employed until the year 1655, and Eckhart is not at home with either concept.

If one studies these paths in depth, one can recognize Thomas Merton's work named in all of them, as we shall see in the next chapters. Merton sheds light on each of them, and at the same time, the Four Paths assist us in grasping the depth of Merton's journey.

When I presented these paths at a lecture in Berkeley about this time, I received the following response from a Jewish scholar of Jewish mysticism who was visiting from Switzerland (and who had studied with the renowned Jewish mystical scholar Gershom Scholem). He said, "The four paths you speak of are truly the Jewish way. Now we have a bridge we can cross together with Christians — as well as your emphasis on Jesus and wisdom. It is so important to do what you have done and to discard those three paths — purgation, illumination, and union — which you have consciously done as they are in no way Jewish."

As we will see, this is what Merton was doing also. Eckhart triggered in Merton a deep spiritual awakening that led away from the three paths that define Christianity's Fall/redemption tradition. It was a movement away from platonic dualisms and Augustinian guilt and shame and toward the biblical spirituality of the Four Paths.

Merton and Eckhart: An Ongoing Relationship

Merton did not read Eckhart once and then walk away. He did not discuss Eckhart with Dr. Suzuki on one occasion and then drop him. Quite the opposite. Time and again, Merton refers to Eckhart. For example, Merton cites Eckhart in a diary entry in June 1959: "Opened a new translation of Eckhart, and immediately hit upon this: 'Obedience has no cares, it lacks no blessings. Being obedient, if a man purifies himself, God will come to him in course; for where he has no will of his own, then God will command for what God would command for Himself.... When I do not choose for myself, God chooses for me.'"

Then Merton applies this Eckhartian teaching to his status as a part-time hermit in the woods yearning for more solitude.

> I am sure now that it has been a temptation all along to think that by staying here where I like to pray in the woods I would be cuddling in self-love. Yes, I like it. But the important thing = it is what God has chosen for me. Hence I cannot really start off to go anywhere else unless it is clear that God wants it for me. And so far, no such thing is clear.
>
> "A pure heart is one that is unencumbered, unworried, uncommitted, and which does not want its own way about anything but which rather, is submerged in the loving will of God, having denied self."
>
> I cannot be loyal to that which is deepest and most genuine in my life if I am not first loyal to this principle.

In his essay "Buddhism and the Modern World," published in *Mystics & Zen Masters* in 1961, Merton invokes D. T. Suzuki who, when teaching of the "True Self" as the formless, original mind, "has explicitly compared this concept to that of the Godhead in Meister Eckhart and the Rhenish mystics." He explains Suzuki's use of the word *mind* in Zen as not meaning "the intellectual faculty as such but rather what the Rhenish mystics [including Eckhart] called the 'ground' of our soul or of our being, a 'ground' which is...enlightened and aware, because it is in immediate contact with God." Among other things, Merton credits Suzuki with "obviously thinking of Eckhart" when Suzuki talks of the light of *Prajna* penetrating "the ground nature of consciousness" and illuminating things inside and outside.

On July 20, 1963, Merton made the following entry in his journal: "In a sermon of Eckhart — God wants to give His greatest gifts. Love is the most noble and the most common of His gifts." I include this sermon (number twenty-nine) in my book *Passion for Creation*.

In 1967, in his prose poem *Cables to the Ace*, Merton cites Eckhart at least twice. He wrote: "No man can see God except he be blind, or know him except through ignorance, nor understand him except through folly (Eckhart)." And again, "The true word of eternity is spoken only in the spirit of that man who is himself a wilderness (Eckhart)."

Merton did not always explicitly acknowledge Eckhart's influence on him, but one can see the interaction between Merton and Eckhart. For example, an entry from December 19, 1967, shows how thoroughly Eckhart's mind-set had penetrated Merton's consciousness:

> Reading Basho again. Deeply moved by the purity and beauty of his travel notes and Haiku. "All who have achieved real excellence in any art, possess one thing in common, that is, a mind to obey nature, to be one with nature throughout the four seasons of the year.... The first lesson for the artist is therefore, to learn how to overcome such barbarism and animality, to follow nature, to be one with nature." I suspect that the Western language and vocabulary could be most misleading here. V.S. "one with nature" as a kind of foggy pantheism. The point: *not seeing something etc.* than what *is*. See it in its *isness* — and not interpreting it or dressing it up with "mind."

It is Eckhart who says "isness is God" and urges us to "live like the rose — without a why." Clearly, Merton has picked up on his teaching — to see the raw isness and behold. This entry was written less than a year before Merton's death.

In *Cables to the Ace*, he presents several clearly Eckhartian passages, such as this:

> The perfect act is empty. Who can see it? He who forgets form. Out of the formed, the unformed, the empty act proceeds with its own form.... Perfection and emptiness work together for they are the same: the coincidence of momentary form and eternal nothingness. Form: the flash of nothingness. Forget form and it suddenly appears.... Well, then: stop asking. Let it all happen. Let it come and go. What? Everything: i.e., nothing.

Here, he echoes Eckhart's language of the "unborn self" that we can all return to: "Follow the ways of no man, not even your own. The way that is most yours is no way. For where are you? Unborn! Your way therefore is unborn. Yet you travel. You do not become unborn by stopping a journey you have begun."

Further on in his prose poem is a lengthy passage entitled *Gelassenheit*, which is one of the key words in Eckhart's writings; I translate it as "letting be." Here is a portion of Merton's exegesis of the term:

> Desert and void. The Uncreated is waste and emptiness to the creature. Not even sand. Not even stone. Not even darkness and night.... The Uncreated is no something. Waste. Emptiness. Total poverty of the Creator: yet from this poverty springs *everything*. The waste is inexhaustible. Infinite Zero. Everything comes from this desert Nothing. Everything wants to return to it and cannot.... For each of us there is a point of nowhereness in the middle of movement, a point of nothingness in the midst of being: the incomparable point not to be discovered by insight. If you seek it you do not find it. If you stop seeking, it is there.

So much of this passage is pure Eckhart — indeed the last two sentences are found in Eckhart exactly as Merton utters them.

In February 1963, Merton talked about having "found fine things in the *Mirror of Simple Souls* today." This book was written by the French Beguine Marguerite Porete, who was burned at the stake and whom Eckhart cites in his own writings, but without giving her credit. However, Merton probably did not realize this connection, since Porete's authorship of this book and her influence on Eckhart have mostly come to light only more recently. I have described Eckhart's indebtedness to Porete and other Beguines in my recent book *Meister Eckhart*. The sermon of Eckhart's that most caught Merton's attention, what I call his "Sermon on the Mount" (sermon fifteen in *Passion for Creation*), contains much of Porete's ideas.

Merton, Suzuki, and Eckhart

Thus we can see that Eckhart permeates Merton's work and consciousness from 1959 onward. His encounters with Dr. Suzuki only confirm that. For example, Merton visited with Suzuki in New York City in 1964 — a very rare occurrence, since Merton was rarely allowed to travel outside his monastery at that time — and Merton recalled that Eckhart had been a big part of their conversation. He wrote, "Had two good long talks with Suzuki. He is now ninety-four, bent, slow, deaf, but lively and very responsive....He likes Eckhart, as I already know from the book I got at the University of Kentucky several years ago." Merton had been reading Suzuki, who has been called "the apostle of the West" for introducing Zen thinking to America. Later, Merton complimented Suzuki in the following way:

> I saw Dr. Suzuki only in two brief visits and I did not feel
> I ought to waste time exploring abstract, doctrinal explanations of his tradition. But I did feel that I was speaking
> to someone who, in a tradition completely different from
> my own, had matured, had become completed and found his

way. One cannot understand Buddhism until one meets it in this existential manner, in a person in whom it is alive.... This same existential quality is evident in another way in Dr. Suzuki's vast published work. An energetic, original and productive worker, granted the gift of a long life and tireless enthusiasm for his subject, he has left us a whole library of Zen in English.... His work remains with us as a great gift, as one of the unique spiritual and intellectual achievements of our time.

In Suzuki's classic work, *Mysticism: Christian and Buddhist*, not only is the first chapter on Meister Eckhart and Buddhism, but indeed the whole book is built on Eckhart's thinking as a basis for an East/West rapprochement. Suzuki begins the first chapter this way:

> In the following pages I attempt to call the reader's attention to the closeness of Meister Eckhart's way of thinking to that of Mahayana Buddhism, especially of Zen Buddhism.... When I first read — which was more than a half century ago — a little book containing a few of Meister Eckhart's sermons, they impressed me profoundly, for I never expected that any Christian thinker ancient or modern could or would cherish such daring thoughts as expressed in those sermons.

Suzuki goes on to take us through Eckhart's views on time and creation, on being, on life, on work, on detachment, on nameless nothingness, on emptying, on comparisons to the Tao, and more. He also defends Eckhart (and Buddhism) against charges of pantheism.

Merton's next-to-last book, *Zen and the Birds of Appetite*, published in 1968, shows that he remained steeped in Eckhart. The first essay in this collection, which was the last written, puts Meister Eckhart front and center. Merton points out that Suzuki considered Eckhart "the Christian mystic closest to Zen," and Merton agrees: "A fuller and truer expression of Zen in Christian experience is given by Meister Eckhart." And again, "Whatever Zen may be, however you define it, it is somehow there in Eckhart."

While praising Suzuki for latching on to Eckhart, Merton criticized him for seeing Eckhart as outside the mainstream of Christian mysticism — but how could Suzuki think otherwise, since he was condemned by the pope, ignored by mainstream Christianity and mysticism, and for the most part forgotten even by the Dominicans? However, Merton described what he felt was Eckhart's place within the Christian tradition.

> Although Dr. Suzuki accepted the current rather superficial Western idea of Eckhart as a unique and completely heretical phenomenon, we must admit, with more recent scholarship, that Eckhart does represent a profound, wide and largely orthodox current in Western religious thought: that which goes back to Plotinus and Pseudo-Dionysius and comes down in the West through Scotus Erigena and the medieval school of St. Victor, but also profoundly affected Eckhart's master, St. Thomas Aquinas.

I am pleased that Merton recognized that Eckhart is not a lone ranger and that he belongs to a Christian lineage. But I very much regret that in naming this lineage, Merton leaves out the Wisdom tradition of Israel, which in my opinion was far more formative to Eckhart than was Plotinus. This was also the tradition, as biblical scholarship since Merton has demonstrated, from which the historical Jesus derived. Merton is surely right about Thomas Aquinas's vast influence on Eckhart, but he also leaves out Benedict, Hildegard of Bingen, Francis of Assisi, and Mechtild of Magdeburg. Each of these was very much part of the Rhineland Creation Spirituality tradition, in spirit if not in geography.

Merton also correctly includes among Eckhart's influences Jo-hannes Tauler (who was Eckhart's Dominican student and brother) and also Jan van Ruysbroeck, who came shortly after Eckhart. The lineage then continues. Two others who were deeply influenced by Eckhart and whom Merton also admired were Julian of Norwich (in the fourteenth century) and Nicholas of Cusa (in the fifteenth century), whose library contained the transcripts of Eckhart's trial. About Cusa, Merton confessed that "he is someone to whom I am much attracted.... His manly idealism fascinates me."

Merton approved when Eckhart tells us about our deification: "Eckhart says in perfectly orthodox and traditional Christian terms, 'In giving us His love God has given us His Holy Ghost so that we can love Him with the love wherewith He loves Him-self. We love God with His own love; awareness of it deifies us.' D. T. Suzuki quotes this passage with approval, comparing it with *Prajna* wisdom of Zen."

Merton recognized the challenges Eckhart poses for church authorities: "His taste for paradox, his deliberate use of expressions which outraged conventional religious susceptibilities, in order to awaken his hearers to a new dimension of experience, left him open to the attacks of his enemies. Some of his teachings were officially condemned by the Church — and many of these are being reinterpreted today by scholars in a fully orthodox sense."

Still, Merton believed Eckhart is best understood as being outside any system of thought.

Eckhart can best be appreciated for what is really best in him: and this is not something that is to be found within the frame-work of a theological system but outside it. In all that he tried to say, whether in familiar or in startling terms, Eckhart was trying to point to something that cannot be structured and cannot be contained within the limits of any system. He... was trying to give expression to the great creative renewal of the mystical consciousness which was sweeping through the Rhineland and the Low Countries in his time.

There is in Eckhart's paradoxes and teachings "the same kind of consciousness as theirs [the Zen masters']." Merton cited these passages by Eckhart (using the Blakney translation), which so caught his attention:

> If it is the case that man is emptied of all things, creatures, himself and God, and if God could still find a place in him to act...this man is not poor with the most intimate poverty. For God does not intend that man should have a place reserved for him to work in since true poverty of spirit requires that man shall be emptied of god and all his works so that if God wants to act in the soul he himself must be the place in which he acts.

The final essay in *Zen and the Birds of Appetite* reproduces Merton's and Suzuki's dialogues from ten years earlier. At that time, Merton had attempted to explain the phrase "purity of heart" by way of Cassian, but Suzuki totally rejected this approach, insisting instead that Merton go deeper into Eckhart's thinking. This, to his credit, Merton did years later in the first essay of this book.

It is important to see the evolution in Merton's thinking that Suzuki and Eckhart brought about — an evolution that Suzuki very much endorsed and prodded Merton to undergo. To me this is evidence of how Suzuki and Buddhism itself, along with Eckhart, were necessary to prod Merton from a Fall / redemption stance to more fully embrace a creation-centered spirituality. The transformation did not happen overnight for Merton. In his lectures to novices in the mid-1950s, for example, Merton's main treatment of Eckhart was to caution against his so-called heresies. At that time, he had little positive to teach about Eckhart. It was only later, and with the help of Suzuki, that Merton truly entered into Eckhart's creation-centered worldview.

Merton evolved. His appreciation of Eckhart evolved, and his coming to grips with his prophetic vocation evolved, and Eckhart assisted him in all these evolutions. Indeed, Eckhart profoundly transformed Merton's thinking, and this "conversion" became almost a necessary prelude to his journey East — not only his physical journey but the intellectual and spiritual journeys that preceded it. Truly, Merton is indebted to Eckhart in a profound and explicit way. This is how Merton put it in an entry in his personal journal on June 30, 1966:

> "Blessed are the pure in heart who leave everything to God now as they did before they ever existed." Eckhart. This is what I have to get back to. It is coming to the surface again. As Eckhart was my life-raft in the hospital, so now also he seems the best link to restore continuity: my obedience to God begetting His love in me (which has never stopped!).

Merton's trip to Asia, which began in the fall of 1968, might be seen as a sort of culmination of the journey East that Suzuki and Eckhart initiated within him ten years previous. It is little wonder that, during his Asian journey, Merton frequently wrote in the margins of his journal, "Eckhart is my lifeboat, Eckhart is my lifeboat."

Eckhart's Importance to Merton

Why was Eckhart so important and so liberating to Thomas Merton? We have already seen how Eckhart was a supreme deep ecumenist long before that phrase was known (which, indeed, I coined in my 1988 book, *The Coming of the Cosmic Christ*). Eckhart is all about interfaith, so much so that Sufis claim him as a Sufi, Buddhists call him a Buddhist, Hindus say he reads like the Upanishads, and so on. Is there anyone else on this planet, dead or alive, about whom such things have been said? I think not. Since

Eckhart never met a Buddhist or a Hindu, nor did he read such works, how did he become so ecumenical? Because he plumbed his own soul and his own faith tradition and found in the depths of both the universal wisdom and experience that other traditions also champion. In other words, because he was so real and deep a mystic.

Merton was hungry in 1959 — after twenty years in the monastery, and eleven years after publishing his autobiography *Seven Storey Mountain*, which more or less subscribed to the reigning dualistic religion of the Fall/redemption tradition, and after the reign of Pope Pius XII ended in 1958 — to move beyond. He confessed in his book *New Seeds of Contemplation*, which he wrote in 1960, that his earlier book, *Seeds of Contemplation*, written twelve years previously, "was written in a kind of isolation, in which the author was alone with his own experience of the contemplative life," whereas this new book "is not merely a new edition of an old book. It is in many ways a completely new book." It was a completely new book because Merton had undergone an awakening in those twelve years and was evolving into a new person because of his widening contacts with others, including a new generation of novices and scholastics of his own community as well as people outside any monastery and people "outside the church." He acknowledged a greater debt to those who were "without formal religious affiliation" than to those in religion. He was already searching into avenues of deep ecumenism — why else would he have undertaken a dialogue with D. T. Suzuki, after all? But it was Eckhart — as Suzuki taught Merton — who could carry him to deeper encounters both with his Christian monastic experience and the wisdom of other traditions.

There is also in Eckhart, as there is in Merton, a great love of art and creativity as paths to the Divine. It has been said that one can "extract an almost complete philosophy of art from Eckhart's writings," and Merton was an artist in many spheres. We will consider his path of creativity further in chapter 6.

Another dimension to Eckhart's appeal and effect on Merton, I am sure, was his commitment to justice and compassion. Eckhart thoroughly weds the mystical life with the prophetic life and work, and Merton found not just a home there but a challenge. He took Eckhart up on that challenge in many of his works of the sixties, such as *Conjectures of a Guilty Bystander, Raids on the Unspeakable, Cold War Letters, Ishi Means Man*, and more wherein his political thought and his mystical teachings came together with power. In a culminating passage in a very important chapter in his book on monastic renewal called *Contemplation in a World of Action*, Merton offered Eckhart as a last word on the dualism of bad religious ideology that pits spirit or Christ against the world:

> If the deepest ground of my being is love, then in that very love itself and nowhere else will I find myself, and the world, and my brother and Christ. It is not a question of either-or but of all-in-one. It is not a matter of exclusivism and "purity" but of wholeness, wholeheartedness, unity and Meister Eckhart's *Gleichheit* (equality) which finds the same ground of love in everything.

The same combustible marriage is found in his journals from the sixties as well. He and Eckhart were truly on the same page even to the end. We will explore Merton's Via Transformativa more fully in chapter 7.

Another dimension both Eckhart and Merton emphasize is the role of the Cosmic Christ, which we will examine in chapter 11. Eckhart preached this Christology time and time again; it lies at the heart of his teachings (for instance, see sermon twenty-four in *Passion for Creation*). Not only are we other Christs but we are other Marys who are to give birth to the Christ in our work and in our persons and in our culture. We are all meant to be mothers of God, he preaches in a Christmas sermon, for "Christ is always needing to be born."

In all these ways, then, in Meister Eckhart's outreach in deep ecumenism or interfaith, his teaching of the Cosmic Christ and all of us as other Christs, his richly developed notions and practices of art as meditation, in the central place that compassion and justice came to play in his mysticism — one can see how Merton found in him a true brother.

CHAPTER FOUR

"Contemplation…is spiritual wonder"

Merton and the Via Positiva

Contemplation is the highest expression of man's intellectual and spiritual life. It is that life itself, fully awake, fully active, fully aware that it is alive. It is spiritual wonder. It is spontaneous awe at the sacredness of life, of being. It is gratitude for life, for awareness and for being.

— THOMAS MERTON

One difficulty in grasping Merton is that he wrote so voluminously and covered so many topics in both depth and breadth that one can get a little lost trying to grasp the entirety of his thought. I have found, however, that applying the Four Paths to Merton's work assists immensely. The Four Paths are clearly evident everywhere in the mature Merton, and they help us to see his profundity and aliveness. These paths are archetypal, and they do not fail to help us get to the real meat of Merton's life and his considerable body of work.

In this and the next three chapters we will explore the Four

Paths as found in Merton's writings. We will not exhaust the search but simply look for evidence that he was deeply immersed in all four ways of experiencing the Divine — and see that each path was a key element of his writing and teaching to others. The Four Paths lie at the heart of my work of moving Western spirituality from a dualistic, Fall/redemption foundation to the more ancient, more biblical, creation-centered or Wisdom-based foundation. Thus, to apply the Four Paths to Merton is to link Merton, myself, and Eckhart in the Creation Spirituality lineage.

Thomas Merton and the Four Paths of Creation Spirituality

What are the Four Paths of Creation Spirituality and how real were they to Merton? In September 1968, he shared a circular letter that succinctly summarized the spiritual journey that the Four Paths represent:

> Our real journey in life is interior; it is a matter of growth, deepening, and of an ever greater surrender to the creative action of love and grace in our hearts. Never was it more necessary for us to respond to that action.

How do we grow, deepen, and surrender to love and grace and action? That is where the Four Paths come in and assist us in naming our deepest journey.

VIA POSITIVA: This is the path of wonder and awe. Or as Merton begins: "Our real journey in life is interior; it is a matter of growth, deepening." Awe is an inner response, an opening to the beauty and wonder of life and God.

VIA NEGATIVA: This is the path of letting go and letting be, of solitude and silence, but also of undergoing grief and sorrow; it's an ongoing act of radical trust in the Divine. Eckhart calls it "sinking eternally into the One," and

Merton refers to it when he mentions "an ever greater surrender."

VIA CREATIVA: This is the path of celebration and creativity, of cocreating with the work of the Holy Spirit. Or as Merton says, it's "the creative action of love and grace in our hearts."

VIA TRANSFORMATIVA: This is the path of compassion and justice; it is the way of the prophet who calls us to action. The Holy Spirit moves us not just to contemplate Divine compassion, but to enact it in the world in order to help others. Merton voices this when he says, "Never was it more necessary for us to respond to that action."

There can be no question that Merton lives and writes a Creation Spirituality, and he dances through the Four Paths back and forth on a regular basis. His Creation Spirituality journey began about a decade before his death. In February 1958, he summarized the new path he felt he needed to take:

> The frustration of the American intellectual who can't get along without a Europe that can no longer sustain him. (Yet — he is sustained, without knowing it, by his own latent vitality.) This has been to a great extent my own frustration as a writer — from which I escaped temporarily "upward" — into spirituality — but that was not enough, because it is not a matter of escape, but of incarnation and transformation.

In this moment, Merton was on the cusp of moving away from the Augustinian and Neoplatonic "upwardness" of his early years. That same year, 1958, Pope Pius XII died and Pope John XXIII was elected, and within a few years, Pope John would call for a Second Vatican Council to redirect the church. With the help of Meister Eckhart and D. T. Suzuki, Merton learned to redefine spirituality in a way that was more ecumenical and more prophetic, more grounded and earthy. He no longer "escaped upward" away from matter, but he reimmersed himself in incarnation and transformation. He moved from a "Climbing Jacob's ladder" mentality so basic to patriarchy to a "Dancing Sara's Circle" mentality that was far more democratic and grounded and bodily and feminist. As a monk, Merton moved from contemplation alone to the vocation of the mystic as prophet, or the contemplative in action. Clearly, it was a Creation Spirituality journey.

Eckhart on the Via Positiva

The Via Positiva is about our falling in love with the beauty of existence. In it we undergo awe — Rabbi Heschel calls it "radical amazement." With this awakened sense of awe, a new depth of reverence and thanksgiving happens.

Eckhart teaches the Via Positiva when he talks about nature as grace, "the grace of creation" and "the gift of creation." He asserts that "isness is God" — thus when we encounter isness or existence in any form we are encountering God. He declares, "Every creature is full of God and is a book" about God. "Every creature is God's word" and thus a revelation of the Divine. For this reason we ought to "apprehend God in all things; for God is in all things." Eckhart gets ecstatic about isness. "Isness is so noble. No creature is so tiny that it lacks isness. When caterpillars fall off a tree, they climb up a wall, so that they may preserve their isness. So noble is isness." Whenever we talk about God the Creator, notes Eckhart, we are talking about goodness (or "blessing," since blessing is the theological word for "goodness"). "Goodness is the proper name of God the Creator," declares Eckhart.

Merton on the Via Positiva

Does Thomas Merton also teach about the Via Positiva? Consider this passage from *Conjectures of a Guilty Bystander*:

I stepped out of the north wing of the monastery and looked
out at the pasture where the calves usually are. It was empty
of calves. Instead, there was a small white colt, running
beautifully up the hill, and down, and around again, with
a long smooth stride and with the ease of flight. Yet in the
middle of it he would break into rough, delightful cavorting, hurling himself sideways at the wind and the hill and
instantly sliding back into the smooth canter. How beautiful
is life this spring!

How keenly Merton observed the beauty of the spring morning
in Kentucky on that day and how moved was he by the newborn
colt. Interestingly enough, Eckhart, too, offers a rich meditation
on horses in his keen love of nature at work when he compares
God's joy at observing us — God "finds joy and rapture in us"
— to our joy at observing a horse in a meadow. Just as the horse
would want "to pour forth its whole strength in leaping about
in the meadow, so too it is a joy to God to pour out the divine
nature and being completely into his likeness, since he is the
likeness himself." Just as Eckhart grew up in horse country in
Germany, and his ancestors were knights and horsemen and
-women, so too Merton, living in Kentucky, was surrounded by
horse country.

Merton actually understands contemplation as the Via Positiva, as "spontaneous awe" as he put it, in *New Seeds of Contemplation*.

Contemplation is the highest expression of man's intellectual and spiritual life. It is that life itself, fully awake, fully
active, fully aware that it is alive. It is spiritual wonder. It
is spontaneous awe at the sacredness of life, of being. It is
gratitude for life, for awareness and for being. It is a vivid
realization of the fact that life and being in us proceed from
an invisible, transcendent and infinitely abundant Source.

Contemplation is, above all, awareness of the reality of that
Source.

It was only the year of Merton's death, 1968, that science first
began to apply the evolutionary principle to the universe itself. I
think that had he lived to learn the new cosmology and its abundant teachings on the "sacredness of life" and of being, Merton's
sense of "spiritual wonder" would have been aroused even more
deeply, similar to the way it emerged in the work of Thomas
Berry. For example, Berry has this to say about recovering a sense
of "the sacredness of being":

> We will recover our sense of wonder and our sense of the sa-
> cred only if we appreciate the universe beyond ourselves as
> a revelatory experience of that numinous presence whence
> all things come into being. Indeed, the universe is the pri-
> mary sacred reality. We become sacred by our participation
> in this more sublime dimension of the world about us.

Further, Berry writes:

> The human venture depends absolutely on this quality of
> awe and reverence and joy in the Earth and all that lives and
> grows upon the Earth....In the end the universe can only
> be explained in terms of celebration. It is all an exuberant
> expression of existence itself....The feeling of presence to
> a sacred universe can appear once more to dynamize and
> sustain human affairs.
>
> We must feel that we are supported by that same power
> that brought the Earth into being, that power that spun the
> galaxies into space, that tilts the sun and brought the moon
> into its orbit.

Merton captured this "exuberant expression of existence itself" in his depiction of the young colt's "delightful cavorting."
Clearly, Merton, Eckhart, and Berry are looking at the same

universe — and responding to it with praise and joy and gratitude. This is all the Via Positiva at work.

Merton criticized the science of his day for being overly serious and too lacking in a sense of play (Thomas Aquinas says the
nearest word to "contemplation" is "play").

> The strictly scientific view of the universe needs this dimen-
> sion of love and play, which it sorely lacks. That is one thing
> I like about space flights: at last there is something of cos-
> mic play getting into the somber, unimaginative, and super-
> serious world of science. But what is a little play of astronauts
> against the great, gloomy, dogmatic seriousness of the death
> game, nuclear war? Can we recover from the titanic humor-
> lessness of our civilization?

Much science after Merton's day — including that of Thomas
Berry — has indeed brought in play and delight. I think of the
scientists who faced the TV cameras after the toy-like rover vehicle *Sojourner* successfully landed on Mars in 1997 and started
its journey on the red planet. They were giddy and laughing
like schoolchildren. Play was everywhere in abundance. I think
Merton would take delight in the postmodern science that makes
way for surprise and for play and that moves beyond humorlessness. Merton himself commented on the "end of conventional
nineteenth-century materialism" and how science has superseded
itself.

> Heisenberg's *Physics and Philosophy* is a very exciting book.
> The uncertainty principle is oddly like St. John of the Cross.
> As God in the highest eludes the grasp of concepts, being
> pure Act, so the ultimate constitution of matter cannot be
> reduced to conceptual terms. There is, logically speaking,
> nothing there that we can objectively know. (Unless you
> want to use the abstract concept of pure potency, but what
> does it mean?)

This seems to me to be the end of conventional nine-teenth-century materialism — which, funnily enough, now appears exactly for what it was: a "faith," and not science at all. To be more precise, let us say a "myth," which was accepted on faith in the "authority of science."

Thus the universe itself becomes a source for the Via Positiva in the many dimensions of that path, and Merton was anticipating that even before postmodern science truly got off the ground, so to speak.

The everyday beauty of things does not fail to catch Merton's eye (or on some occasions, his camera). He tells us of his "worship" in nature.

Warm sun. Perhaps these yellow wild-flowers have the minds of little girls. My worship is a blue sky and ten thousand crickets in the deep wet hay of the field. My vow is the silence under their song. I admire the woodpecker and the dove in simple mathematics of flights. Together we study practical norms. The plowed and planted field is red as a brick in the sun and says: *"Now my turn!"* Several of us begin to sing.

In *Woods, Shore, Desert*, he writes of his pilgrimage to the redwoods. "The worshipful cold spring light on the sandbanks of Eel River, the immense silent redwoods. Who can see such trees and bear to be away from them? I must go back. It is not right that I should die under lesser trees." On the same journey, upon alighting from the plane in Albuquerque for the first time, he observed:

"All blue is precious," said a friend of Gertrude Stein. There is very much of it here. A fortune in clear sky and the air...so good it almost knocked me down when I got off the plane in Albuquerque....Alone, amid red rocks, small pine and cedar, facing the high wall on the other side of the Chama canyon....Distant sound of muddy rushing water in the Chama River below me. I could use up rolls of film on nothing but these rocks. The whole canyon replete with emptiness.

Astutely, James Forest, a biographer of Merton, commented on this same journal that "the jottings and notes...well communicate the life of wonder." Yes, the Via Positiva, a life of wonder, indeed.

In *Asian Journal*, Merton commented on exiting Calcutta:

It is a city I love. Flying out today was beautiful...the subtle beauty of all the suburban ponds and groves, with men solemnly bathing in the early morning and white cranes standing lovely and still amid the lotuses and flying up in twos and threes against the fresh green of the coconut palms. Yet the city, too, its crumbling walls alive with Bengali inscriptions and palimpsests of old movie posters. And the occasional English spires, 18-century domes....I do not tire of Calcutta.

Or consider this meditation on the mountain named Kanchenjunga:

The clouds of the morning parted slightly and the mountain, the massif of attendant peaks, put on a great, slow, silent dorje dance of snow and mist, light and shadow, surface and sinew, sudden cloud towers spiraling up out of icy holes, blue expanses of half-revealed rock, peaks appearing and disappearing with the top of Kanchenjunga remaining the visible and constant president over the whole slow show. It went on for hours. Very stately and beautiful. Then toward evening the clouds cleared some more, except for a long apron of mist and shadow below the main peaks....O Tantric Mother Mountain! Yin-yang palace of opposites in unity! Palace of anicca, impermanence and patience, solidity and nonbeing, existence and wisdom.

And this observation of a woman and child: "I met a woman and child walking silently, the woman slowly spinning a prayer wheel — with great reverence and it was not at all absurd or routine — the child with a lovely smile." Or this encounter with a ten-year-old boy living up a mountain in a poor cottage:

> The boy was charming and I took some pictures of him as he was petulantly rolling down his sleeves to be more ceremonious. He went into his cell and sat cross-legged on his seat and received us with poise and formality.... Then we went down to the drama school where a girl was playing a lovely instrument, the name of which I forgot to ask — a string instrument laid out flat and played with two sticks. It had a charming sound — while around the corner was a radio playing popular Indian music — which I find pretty good!

Nature Is Grace

In his poem "Grace's House," Merton recognized the blessing that nature offers us. In doing so he echoed Eckhart's teaching that "nature is grace." In fact, Merton's poem is a response to the drawing of a house by a five-year-old artist named Grace.

> No blade of grass is not blessed
> On this archetypal, cosmic hill,
> This womb of mysteries.
> I must not omit to mention a rabbit
> And two birds, bathing in the stream...

Elsewhere, having said that every non-two-legged creature is a saint, Merton added:

> Every plant that stands in the light of the sun is a saint and an outlaw. Every tree that brings forth blossoms without the command of man is powerful in the sight of God. Every star

that man has not counted is a world of sanity and perfection. Every blade of grass is an angel singing in a shower of glory. These are worlds of themselves. No man can use or destroy them.

Merton learned to see the kingdom of God found in nature, writing: "The rain has stopped.... The quails begin their sweet whistling in the wet bushes. Their noise is absolutely useless, and so is the delight I take in it. There is nothing I would rather hear, not because it is a better noise than other noises, but because it is the voice of the present moment, the present festival." Yes, life is a festival. It is present. The kingdom/queendom of God *is* among us. "Isness is God" — provided we have been emptied enough to see it, smell it, and taste it. Merton spoke to his personal Via Positiva in the woods.

Here in this wilderness I have learned how to sleep again. Here I am not alien. The trees I know, the night I know, the rain I know. I close my eyes and instantly sink into the whole rainy world of which I am a part and the world goes on with me in it, for I am not alien to it. I am alien to the noises of cities, of people, to the greed of machinery that does not sleep, the hum of power that eats up the night.

Merton preached a profound and readily available Via Positiva. But we cannot be passive, we must respond. "Dance in this sun, you tepid idiot. Wake up and dance in the clarity of perfect contradiction. You fool, it is life that makes you dance: have you forgotten?"

On a brief visit to Alaska in May 1968, Merton commented on the mountains:

Most impressive mountains I've seen in Alaska: Drum and Wrangell and the third great massive one whose name I forget, rising out of the vast birchy plain of Copper Valley. They are sacred and majestic mountains, ominous, enormous, noble, stirring. You want to attend to them. I could not keep my eyes off them. Beauty and terror of the Chugac. Dangerous valleys. Points. Saws. Snowy nails.

Not only do we see Merton here as a keen observer and skilled raconteur, but he applies the word "sacred" to the beings of the natural world. To relate to them is a mystical experience. They are calling us. This is the Wisdom tradition in the Bible. This is the Via Positiva in action.

Merton described what flowers, light and shade, tell him even when they are cut and indoors:

> Beauty of the sunlight falling on a tall vase of red and white carnations and green leaves on the altar in the novitiate chapel. The light and shade of the red, especially the darkness in the fresh crinkled flower and the light warm red around the darkness, the same color as blood but not "red as blood," utterly unlike blood. Red as a carnation. This flower, this light, this moment, this silence = *Dominus est* [the Lord is here], eternity! Best because the flower is itself and the light is itself and the silence is itself and I am myself — all, perhaps, an illusion but no matter, for illusion is nevertheless shadow of reality and reality is the grace that under lays these lights, these colors, and this silence.

We can have Via Positiva experiences in nature even while indoors. Consider this meditation on a rainstorm at Merton's hermitage.

> Late afternoon — a good rainstorm began before supper and it is going on now as darkness falls. A moment ago there was a hawk up there flying against the wind in the dark and in the rain, with big black clouds flying and the pines bending. A beautiful storm, and it has filled my buckets with water for washing, and the house with cool winds. It is good and comforting to sit in a storm with all the winds in the

woods outside and rain on the roof and sit in a little circle of light and read and hear the clock tick on the table. And tomorrow's Gospel is the one about not serving two Masters, and letting the Lord provide. That is what I must do.

All this is the Via Positiva encountered in ordinary occurrences of nature and music and everyday people, young and old. None of it goes unnoticed by Merton. He is in no way immune to the everyday beauty of life, what Eckhart calls the Isness that is God. In fact, Merton is astutely vulnerable to it. One Merton scholar has counted over eighteen hundred references to nature in the corpus of Merton's journals alone — and they all reveal his rapture, wonder, and awe. A special burst of nature references occurred when he moved away from the larger monastery building and into the hermitage in the woods. Praise is what much of the Psalms are about, and in his years as a monk, like all the monks, Merton chanted the entire 150 psalms at least once per week. That, too, is a lot of praise. Merton wrote in the mid-1960s that "the Psalms then are the purest expression of the essence of life in this universe...*cantata*, *jubilate*, *exultate* [sing, rejoice, exult]." Lots of Via Positiva, both indoors and outdoors, for Merton.

Much of Merton's sensibility to the sacredness of nature no doubt comes from his Celtic roots. Both his parents were of Welsh ancestry. The same Celtic tradition settled all the way down the Rhineland and imbued Eckhart and Hildegard (raised in a Celtic monastery), as well as Saint Francis, with a respect for the sacredness of nature. It has been said that Merton "celebrated gratefully the Celtic spirit that coursed through his Welsh blood" and how in Celtic monasticism he "shared a similar spiritual temperament with these masters of natural contemplation (*theoria physike*) who sought God less in the ideal essences of things than in the physical hierophanic cosmos." This Celtic and creation-centered spirituality is a far cry from Augustine's morose teachings about "fallen nature" that were picked up by Protestant patriarchal theologians, such as Luther and Calvin.

It becomes readily clear that beginning with his move to the hermitage, a new part of Merton's Celtic soul opened up. "His engagement with nature as farmer and deforester was also tactile, athletic, even sensuous; like his father, he loved to walk barefoot in the woods, feeling the fragrant pine needles of Gethsemani beneath him." We are told that "the natural world played" a great significance "as the ecstatic ground of his own experience of God." This is how Merton put it:

> I live in the woods out of necessity. I get out of bed in the middle of the night because it is imperative that I hear the silence of the night, alone, and, with my face on the floor, say psalms, alone, in the silence of the night.
>
> .... The silence of the forest is my bride and the sweet dark warmth of the whole world is my love and out of the heart of that dark warmth comes the secret that is heard only in silence, but it is the root of all the secrets that are whispered by all the lovers in their beds all over the world.

Yes, nature is Merton's bride. Is this Creation Spirituality or what? The above passage demonstrates so clearly how Merton evolved from a darker spirituality to a creation-centered spirituality. As Kathleen Deignan writes, "In time...his unique subjectivity opened to the cosmos in wonder and awe, sounding a silent interval of praise in the rapturous hymn of creation." It did happen *in time*. This was the mature Merton; this was the Merton washed in the Creation Spirituality of Meister Eckhart and his Celtic forebears. This was the Merton on his later journey in life. He gives credit to his Celtic roots in his last poetic work, *The Geography of Lograire*, invoking the Welsh landscape and the dark sea and the harps that, one commentator said, "obviously symbolize the Celtic culture from which Merton stemmed and to which he always felt close."

A rightfully famous passage — among all of Merton's famous passages — emerges when he tells us of a mystical experience he underwent at Fourth and Walnut in downtown Louisville one afternoon. Today, a historic marker denotes the spot where he underwent his revelation, and I was informed by a local that this is the only historic marker in the country that marks a person's mystical experience. The passage is pure Via Positiva, and this breakthrough did not come to Merton in his monastic cell or choir stall or at the Sacred Liturgy, but on a busy street in downtown Louisville. Here is Merton's rendition of the event:

> Yesterday, in Louisville, at the corner of 4th and Walnut, I suddenly realized that I loved all the people and that none of them were, or could be, totally alien to me. As if waking from a dream — the dream of separateness of the "special" vocation to be different. My vocation does not really make me different from the rest of men or put me in a special category except artificially, juridically. I am still a member of the human race — and what more glorious destiny is there for man, since the Word was made flesh and became, too, a member of the Human Race!
>
> Thank God! Thank God! I am only another member of the human race, like all the rest of them. I have the immense joy of being a man! As if the sorrows of our condition could really matter, once we begin to realize who and what we are — as if we could ever begin to realize it on earth.

Here we have proof positive that Merton has moved beyond a monkish separateness to rejoin the human race — but in a more profound way, having tasted deeply of the deeper meaning of it all. He has left behind the "contempt of the world" that dominates so much of Fall/redemption religion.

So taken was I by Merton's well-developed sense of the Via Positiva that I wrote a reflection for *We Are Already One*, a 2015 essay collection celebrating the centenary of Thomas Merton. The title of the rich volume derives from a passage from Merton's *Asian Journal*, where he wrote:

> And the deepest level of communication is not communication but communion. It is wordless. It is beyond words, and it is beyond speech, and it is beyond concept. Not that we discover a new unity. We discover an older unity. My dear brothers and sisters, we are already one. But we imagine that we are not. So what we have to recover is our original unity. What we have to be is what we are.

I think my response to these words merits inclusion here. In it, I make the case of an "original blessing" awareness in Merton, an awareness at the heart of a nonanthropocentric spirituality and religion and a nonnarcissistic one (to borrow a phrase from Pope Francis).

> We all share what Merton calls an "original unity." And that original unity is not morally neutral, nor is it beauty-neutral. It is about shared goodness. It is an original unity *and* an original blessing. The original unity *is* an original blessing. Goodness is our origin ("blessing" is the theological word for "goodness") and it is our destiny. Consider Rabbi Heschel: "Just to be is a blessing, just to live is holy." Consider Eckhart: "Whenever we talk about God the Creator we are talking about goodness." If it is true that the essence of authentic religion is not buildings or structures or dogmas or ordained ones but rather *the virtue of giving thanks*, as Aquinas taught, then original grace and original blessing lie at the heart of all authentic religion. What does one give thanks for if not goodness?

Here is where we share an ancient and original origin and unity: In a place of gratitude and of praise. "Praise precedes faith," warns Rabbi Heschel. All our religions need to drop lots of faith concepts and dogmas to return to a shared oneness which has everything to do with praise and gratitude: The Via Positiva. It is there that our communion as humans will restart what we call religion. There lies our origin because, in Julian of Norwich's words, "we have been loved from before the beginning." Before the beginning of our religions, before the beginning of our earth, before the beginning of the Milky Way galaxy, way before the beginning there was love that brought us here. We ought to return kind for kind and blessing for blessing. We can and ought to restart our religions and put Praise and the Via Positiva out front and doing our work in the via negativa and the apophatic Divinity assists us in this task just as fasting assists one to appreciate water and food more fully after the fast.

In this way we "become who we truly are," in Merton's words. We become human beings again, late-comers in the universe with both larynx and consciousness for praise. As Thomas Berry put it, recounting what all the excitement is about, "When we see a flower, a butterfly, a tree, when we feel the evening breeze flow over us or wade in a stream of clear water, our natural response is immediate, intuitive, transforming, ecstatic. Everywhere we find ourselves invaded by the world of the sacred. Such was the experience of Thomas Merton. Such is the wonder that he is communicating to us." Or in Mary Oliver's words, "There is only one question: How to love the world."

CHAPTER FIVE

"I shall certainly have solitude...
beyond all 'where'"

Merton and the Via Negativa

What it all comes down to is that I shall certainly have solitude but only by miracle and not at all by my own contriving. Where? Here or there makes no difference. Somewhere, nowhere, beyond all "where." Solitude outside geography or in it. No matter.

— THOMAS MERTON

The Via Negativa is about many things. It is about silence, for example, and both Thomas Merton and Meister Eckhart are champions of silence.

Eckhart on Silence

Says Eckhart: "Nothing in all creation is so like God as silence." And again, "The best and noblest of all that one can come to in this life is to be silent and let God work and let God speak." The Word or true Christ is born in us through silence. "There is no question that the proper way to hear the word is in a stillness and a silence." Eckhart speaks to the practice of meditation and silence when he says: "The Word lies hidden in the soul, unknown and unheard unless room is made for it in the ground of hearing, otherwise it is not heard. All voices and sounds must cease and there must be pure stillness within, a still silence."

Great things happen in this place of silence, which Eckhart calls "the doorway of God's house" for "in the silence and peace ...there God speaks in the soul and utters Himself completely in the soul. There the Father begets His Son and has such delight in the Word and is so fond of it, that He never ceases to utter the Word all the time, that is to say beyond time." There one encounters, Eckhart says, "bare 'beingness' that has been stripped of all being and all beingness. There it takes hold of God as in the ground of His being, where He is beyond all being." In solitude the soul learns to "be alone as God is alone," and we encounter God's ground and our own. "To hear this Word in the Father (where all is stillness), a person must be quite quiet and wholly free from all images and from all forms."

Eckhart lays out a passage that any Buddhist would recognize as profoundly Buddhist — surely, Merton was moved deeply by this passage as he sought more and more a rapprochement with Buddhist wisdom, a journey that he alluded to in his initial letter to me but that came to a crashing culmination in his pilgrimage to Asia. Says Eckhart:

> How then should one love God? You should love God mindlessly, that is, so that your soul is without mind and free from all mental activities, for as long as your soul is operating like a mind, so long does it have images and representations. But as long as it has images...it has neither oneness nor simplicity. And therefore our soul should be bare of all mind and should stay there without mind. For if you love God

as God is God or mind or person or picture, all that must be dropped. How then shall you love him? You should love God as God is, a not-God, not-mind, not-person, not-image, even more, as God is a pure, clear One, separate from all twoness. And we should sink eternally from something to nothing into this One. May God help us to do this. Amen.

Notice how Eckhart talks of "sinking" into God, not climbing ladders *up* to God. This is part of his feminist consciousness and the return to Mother Earth and his appreciation of a God who is *below*, who is in the lower chakras and in the earth and not just up in the sky at the top of ladders. I deal with this in some depth in my book *A Spirituality Named Compassion*, where I devote a chapter to gender issues and identify the spiritual process as moving from "Climbing Jacob's ladder" to "Dancing Sara's Circle," which cannot take place climbing up ladders but only by staying close to Mother Earth.

Merton on Silence

What does Merton have to say about silence? A lot. Consider the following poem:

Be still
Listen to the stones of the wall
Be silent, they try
To speak your
Name.
Listen
To the living walls.
Who
Are you? Whose
Silence are you?

Such an invitation! To listen to the stones of the living walls and learn who one is, to whom one belongs. I cannot read this poem without thinking of a sweat lodge where, thanks to the ancient wisdom of the indigenous peoples, a ceremony is created wherein the rocks themselves, the oldest beings on earth and our elders, speak to us when they are heated up and glowing. I do not know if Merton ever experienced a sweat lodge, but I remain profoundly grateful for the numerous ones I have been blessed to attend. And in them all, silence is honored.

Another poem by Merton speaks to silence as well.

The whole
World is secretly on fire. The stones
Burn, even the stones
They burn me. How can a man be still or
Listen to all things burning? How can he dare
To sit with them when
All their silence
Is on fire?

Here, too, Merton evokes a sweat lodge. But he is also speaking to a profound truth revealed in postmodern science, which is that every atom in the universe contains photons or light waves. Thus, all atoms and all beings *are* on fire. All beings are a burning bush. One does not have to travel to Mount Sinai to encounter the Divine in a burning bush — every bush is a burning bush, every leaf, every stone, every fish, every bird, and every person. We are all on fire. But we have to "sit with them" and be receptive to them. We have to *dare* to sit and to listen. We have to *dare silence*. That is the contemplative way. Merton says: "Contemplation is essentially a listening in silence, an expectancy." All beings are, in Eckhart's words, "words of God and revelations of God." Merton knew this as well. But it takes silence to grasp it.

For Eckhart, emptying the mind is

the most powerful prayer, one almost omnipotent to gain all things, and the noblest work of all is that which proceeds from a bare mind.... A bare mind can do all things. What is a bare mind? A bare mind is one which is worried by nothing and is tied to nothing, which has not bound its best part to any modes, does not seek its own in anything, that is fully immersed in God's dearest will and goes out of its own.

A bare mind dwells in the now. Merton advises us to "love winter when the plant says nothing." Even nature enjoys darkness and solitude. Winter is that Via Negativa time of the year.

Merton on Solitude

Both Merton and Eckhart are keen on the experience of solitude. Indeed, it was no secret that toward the end of his life Merton was seriously considering leaving his monastery (while staying affiliated with it) and finding a place where solitude would be more readily available. From entries in his *Asian Journal*, it is clear that Alaska was his first choice, and the California redwoods were possibly a second choice. He wrote: "I still have the feeling that the lack of quiet and the general turbulence there [in Gethsemani], external and internal, last summer are indications that I ought to move. And so far the best indications seem to point to Alaska or to the area around the Redwoods." Solitude was not an abstract principle for Merton — he needed it and knew he needed it. No doubt some of his struggle was with the fame that had come his way from the success of his writings and the great number of persons he interacted with, some of whom were bent on meeting him in person.

Merton wrote a searing poem on solitude and lessons learned from it:

If you seek a heavenly light
I, Solitude, am your professor!
I go before you into emptiness,
Raise strange sounds for your new mornings,
Opening the windows
Of your innermost apartment....
For I, solitude, am thine own self:
I, Nothingness, am thy All.
I, Silence, am thy Amen!

As was quoted in chapter 4, Merton wrote in his *Asian Journal*: "The deepest level of communication is not communication but communion. It is wordless. It is beyond words, and it is beyond speech, and it is beyond concept." Merton also linked solitude to art and to nature when he wrote:

> In the interior life there should be moments of relaxation, freedom and "browsing." Perhaps the best way to do this is in the midst of nature, but also in literature. Perhaps also a certain amount of art is necessary, and music.... You also need a good garden, and you need access to the woods, or to the sea. Get out in those hills and really be in the midst of nature a little bit! That is not only legitimate, it is in a certain way necessary.... The woods and nature should be part of your solitude, and if it's not periodically part of your solitude I think the law should be changed.

For Merton as well as for the great psychologist Otto Rank, solitude is necessary for the artist, but it is often identified with being a "traitor" to the community, which in Rank's analysis projects an "artiste manqué" onto the artist. Merton believed that solitude is part of being a person of conscience, a prophet therefore. Prophets can be lonely at times and he invokes the writings of Ionesco to make his point.

There will always be a place, says Ionesco, "for those isolated consciences who have stood up for the universal conscience" as against the mass mind. But their place is solitude.
They have no other. Hence it is the solitary person (whether
in the city or in the desert) who does mankind the inestima-
ble favor of reminding it of its true capacity for maturity,
liberty and peace.

Merton extols the value of solitude when he discusses Ionesco's play *Rhinoceros*, saying Ionesco comes "very close to Zen and
to Christian eremitism." Why? Because, in Ionesco's own words,

> modern man is the man in a rush (i.e. a rhinoceros), man
> who has no time, who is a prisoner of necessity, who can-
> not understand that *a thing might perhaps be without use-
> fulness.*... If one does not understand the usefulness of the
> useless and the uselessness of the useful, one cannot under-
> stand art. And a country where art is not understood is a
> country of slaves and robots.

In my book *Prayer: A Radical Response to Life*, I end the first
chapter, entitled "What Prayer Is Not," with the observation: "In
reality, prayer is useless. To rediscover the useless yet valuable in
life is to recover prayer. Those who try to make use of prayer do
not respect prayer at all but manipulate it. Prayer is not a means
but a value in itself." As I cite, Karl Barth says the same.

Merton comments that rhinoceritis is "the sickness that lies
in wait 'for those who have lost the sense and the taste for solitude.'" This is an observation that Otto Rank makes in his classic work *Art and Artist*, where he argues that creativity requires
solitude in the struggle "against the community of living men
and against posterity." The artist, to bring something new to the
community, escapes "collectivizing influences by deliberate new

creations," and to do so the artist must withdraw from society on a regular basis. People and groups project onto others their immortality projects, and this is what underlies the struggle against fame that Merton and other artists often have to undergo. Jesus, too. Thus solitude is also a retreat from others' projections. I discuss this in my article "Otto Rank and the Artistic Journey as a Spiritual Journey," where I conclude that "true spiritual living includes the dialectic of solitude and social interaction that Jesus or any spiritual person lives." One needs "to escape the collective-immortality impulses of a community — impulses that may be expressed positively or negatively." Solitude (the Via Negativa) is an essential ingredient for birthing the prophet (the Via Transformativa) in us.

The Apophatic God and the Power of Silence

The Via Negativa is also about the Apophatic Divinity, that is to say, the God who is drawn to darkness rather than light (as is the case in the Via Positiva). Eckhart is very strong on the Apophatic Divinity. He says, "God is superessential darkness who has no name and will never be given a name." God is "without name and is the denial of all names and has never been given a name." God is hidden: "The prophet said: 'You are truly a hidden God' (Is. 45:15) who dwells in the ground of the soul where the ground of God and the ground of the soul are one ground." God talk takes us beyond language for "no one can really say what God is...the ineffable One has no name." God is "the Unnamable" and is both spoken (as in creatures who are God's word) and unspoken because creatures cannot fully express God. When we talk of God "we have to stammer," and thus it is best to "maintain total silence about that which is the source of all things." Indeed, "the most beautiful thing which a person can say about God consists in that person's being silent from the wisdom of an inner wealth. So be silent and do not flap your gums about God."

Merton, too, celebrates the Apophatic Divinity, as in the following prayer:

> My love is darkness!
> Only in the Void
> Are all ways one:
> Only in the night
> Are all the lost
> Found.
> In my ending is my meaning.

He does so again in this poem:

> Closer and clearer
> Than any wordy master,
> Thou inward Stranger
> Whom I have never seen,
> Deeper and cleaner
> Than the clamorous ocean,
> Seize up my silence
> Hold me in Thy Hand!

And he offers this admonition for the role of silence — even in church.

> Let there always be quiet, dark places in which people can take refuge. Places where they can kneel in silence. Houses of God, filled with God's silent presence. There, even when we do not know how to pray, at least we can be still and breathe easily…a place where your mind can be idle, and forget its concerns, descend into silence, and worship God in secret. There can be no contemplating where there is no secret.

The Via Negativa as Grief and Suffering

The darkness of the Via Negativa is also the darkness of grief and suffering, the darkness of the cross, the darkness of the dark night. Merton writes of "a flat impersonal song" and of "bleeding in a numbered bed / ... all my veins run / with Christ and with the stars' plasm."

> I have no more sweet home
> I doubt the bed here and the road there
> And WKLO I most abhor
> My head is rotten with the town's song.

He experiences within himself "man's enormous want" —

> Until the want itself is gone
> Nameless bloodless and alone
> The Cross comes and Eckhart's scandal
> The Holy Supper and the precise wrong.
> And the accurate little spark
> In emptiness in the jet stream
> ...
> A lost spark in Eckhart's Castle...
> Only the spark is now true
> Dancing in the empty room
> All around overhead
> While the frail body of Christ
> Sweats in a technical bed
> I am Christ's lost cell
> His childhood and desert age
> His descent into hell...
> And the spark without identity
> Circles the empty ceiling.

Merton wrote this poem from a hospital bed, and it is significant, surely, that he named what was left of him when he was stripped of so much in his hospital sojourn by invoking one of Eckhart's favorite images — that of the spark of the soul where the Christ is born in all of us and where the Holy Spirit's fire never goes out. Sister Lentfoehr calls this Merton's "most poignant and anguished poem." A return to nothingness where only the spark remains.

Merton addresses "Eckhart's Castle" in this poem. Eckhart talks about the soul as a castle, as in the biblical phrase "the kingdom of God." Kingdoms in Eckhart's day boasted castles, and Eckhart invokes the castle as an archetype for the soul and as the deepest part of the soul where our divinization occurs. "God glows and burns with all his wealth and all his bliss" in this castle. Jesus enters into this castle "in his being rather than in his acting, giving graciously to the mind the divine and deiform being. This regards the essence of being according to the words: 'By the grace of God I am what I am.'" This castle, however, "is free of all names and bare of all forms, totally free and void just as God is void and free in himself. It is totally one and simple just as God is one and simple, so that we can in no manner gaze into it." Indeed, it is in the "place" that "the Father begets his only begotten Son as truly as in himself." Here "with this part of itself the soul is equal to God and nothing else." The castle for Eckhart is the place/space where the Divine marries the human.

Merton composed another poem about the journey inward where one encounters silence and a "house of nothing."

> Fire, turn inward
> To your weak fort,
> To a burly infant spot,
> A house of nothing.
> O peace, bless this mad place:
> Silence, love this growth.
> O silence, golden zero

Unsetting sun
Love winter when the plant says nothing.

Both Eckhart and Merton are at home not only with the spark imagery (which Eckhart, by the way, attributed to the Muslim Avicenna at least thirteen times in his sermons), but with the naming of nothingness and the void. Sister Lentfoehr points out that

> Merton takes the Zen and Eckhartian approach, that of *kenosis*, variously described as "emptiness," "dark night," "perfect freedom," "poverty," to which he calls attention in *Zen and the Birds of Appetite*. This poem is explicitly based on Eckhart's Sermon 28 [number fifteen in *Passion for Creation*] on poverty of spirit, which speaks of God as "identical with the spirit and that is the most intimate poverty discoverable."

Sister Lentfoehr elaborates:

> It is when we lose the "self," according to Eckhart, "the persona that is the subject of virtues as well as visions, that perfects itself by good works, that advances in the practice of piety — that Christ is finally born in us in the highest sense." This is the pure, the perfect poverty, when one is no longer a "self," a concept that touches the "point of nowhereness, a point of nothingness in the midst of being."

Thus Merton is explicit about his deriving the language of nothingness from Eckhart, who said, "Everything which is created, in itself is nothing." Eckhart explains what he means this way: "The color of the wall depends on the wall and so the existence of creatures depends on the love of God. Separate the color from the wall and it would cease to be. So all creation would cease to exist if separated from the love that God is."

Eckhart talks about "returning to our unborn self," and Merton invokes this same language on several occasions. Eckhart talks about people being as free "as they were when they were not yet" and "in this poverty, people attain the eternal being that they once were, now are, and will eternally remain.... Therefore also I am unborn and following the way of my unborn being I can never die. Following the way of my unborn being I have always been, I am now, and shall remain eternally." Says Merton: "The way that is most yours is no way. For where are you? Unborn! Your way therefore is unborn."

Two words very important to Eckhart are *Gelassenheit* (letting be) and *Abgeschiedenheit* (letting go), and Merton also invokes the term *Gelassenheit*. According to Sister Therese Lentfoehr, Merton describes "the 'desert' and 'void' in the spirit akin to Eckhart's 'wilderness,' wherein the true word of eternity is spoken." In making her point, Sister Therese presents the following passage by Merton.

> But to each of us there is a point of nowhereness in the middle of movement, a point of nothingness in the midst of being: the incomparable point, not to be discovered by insight. If you seek it you do not find it. If you stop seeking, it is there. But you must not turn to it. Once you come aware of yourself as seeker, you are lost. But if you are content to be lost you will be found without knowing it, precisely because you are lost, for you are, at last, nowhere.

Eckhart has written: "The more you seek God, the less you will find God. If you do not seek God, you will find God." In his poem "The Fall," Merton put it this way:

To enter there is to become unnameable....
Whoever is nowhere is nobody, and therefore cannot
     Exist except as unborn:
No disguise will avail him anything
Such a one is neither lost nor found.

Merton wrote in his *Asian Journal* about a brief retreat he undertook on his travels. "This is a good retreat and I appreciate the quiet more than I can say. This quiet, with time to read, study, meditate, and *not talk to* anyone, is something essential in my life." On solitude, Eckhart says: "We must learn an inner solitude, wherever or with whomsoever we may be. One must learn to penetrate things and find God there." While in Northern California, Merton wrote in his journal:

> I am the utter poverty of God. I am His emptiness, littleness, nothingness, lostness. When this is understood, my life in His freedom, the self-emptying of God in me is the fullness of grace. A love for God that knows no reason because He is the fullness of grace. A love for God that knows no reason because He is God; a love without measure, a love for God as personal. The Ishvara appears as personal in order to inspire this love. Love for all, hatred of none is the fruit and manifestation of love for God — peace and satisfaction. Forgetfulness of worldly pleasure, selfishness, and so on in the love for God, channeling all passion and emotion into the love for God.

And so we see that Merton draws very heavily from Eckhart in his passages of the Via Negativa. They are companions on Eckhart's "wayless way." Nor does solitude have to interfere with engagement. Eckhart wrote: "When one has learned to let go and let be, then one is well disposed and is always in the right place whether in society or in solitude. Now one who is rightly disposed has God with one in actual fact in all places, just as much in the street and in the midst of many people as in church, or the desert, or a monastic cell." Merton, almost echoing Eckhart's words, wrote:

> As soon as a man is fully disposed to be alone with God, he is alone with God no matter where he may be — in the country, the monastery, the woods or the city. The lightning flashes from east to west, illuminating the whole horizon and

striking where it pleases and at the same instant the infinite liberty of God flashes in the depths of that man's soul and he is illumined. At that moment he sees that though he seems to be in the middle of his journey, he has already arrived at the end. For the life of grace on earth is the beginning of the life of glory. Although he is a traveler in time, he has opened his eyes, for a moment, in eternity.

For Merton, "the camera became in his hands, almost immediately, an instrument of contemplation."

CHAPTER SIX

"Something in my nature"

Merton and the Via Creativa

There is something in my nature that gets the keenest and sharpest pleasure out of achievement, out of work finished and printed and distributed and read.

— THOMAS MERTON

The Via Creativa, the path of creativity and the work of co-creating with the Holy Spirit, follows organically from the Via Positiva (our falling in love) and the Via Negativa (our learning to let go and be emptied). There is a sort of formula for creativity here, the vp + vn → vc. Creativity, we are learning from postmodern science, is intrinsic to the universe at large and always has been, from the very second of the original fireball. The cosmos has grown and developed — birthing beings that live, die, and resurrect — for all 13.8 billion years of its existence. We humans, late on the scene, are part of that richly fecund creative journey. Meister Eckhart grasped the reality of our universe well when he asked, "What does God do all day long? She lies on a maternity bed giving birth." If you substitute the word *universe* for *God*, Eckhart is speaking about postmodern science. We live in an always and ever busily creating universe. We humans have inherited a special gift of creativity from the universe, given our intellects and vast imaginations and powers for making things.

Merton understood this well. And he, like Eckhart, attributed our creativity to the work of the Holy Spirit:

> The theology of creativity will necessarily be the theology of the Holy Spirit re-forming us in the likeness of Christ, raising us from death to life with the very same power which raised Christ from the dead. The theology of creativity will also be a theology of the image and the likeness of God in [humanity].

Eckhart on the Via Creativa

For Eckhart, it is better to be a "wife" than a virgin, and by this he means that contemplation is meant to be a source for giving birth. He invokes language like "full fertility" and "becoming fruitful as a result of the gift is the only gratitude for the gift." Eckhart applies the word "virgin" to one who is practiced in letting go and is therefore "a person who is free of all false images, and who is as detached as if he or she did not yet exist." But he advises that we must not get stuck there; we need to move from "virgin" to "wife." For him, "the word 'wife' is the noblest term that we can attribute to the soul, it is far nobler than 'virgin.'" Why? Because "it is better for God to become fruitful within the person" than for someone simply to be in an emptied state. Indeed, the emptied state (the Via Negativa) is necessary as a prelude to birthing and creativity. Eckhart tells us he once had a dream that, even though he was a man, he was pregnant — "pregnant with nothingness. And out of that nothingness God was born." As we enter the Via

Creativa, we become "fruitful out of the most noble foundation of all." Indeed, we "bear out of the same foundation from which the Father begets his eternal Word."

Merton and the Role of Art in Spirituality

Art was to Merton as water is to fish. He swam in it from the first, since both of his parents were artists. Having settled in southern France, the family no doubt enjoyed artistic acceptance as their daily bread, for it was in the air in France especially at the turn of the twentieth century. Why were his parents — his father was from New Zealand and his mother from America — in Paris in the first place, except that both were artists and both felt at home there? Merton as a child drank this same nectar of artistic wonder and beauty, and might we say spirituality, that fed his parents, and he never forgot it. He wrote:

> All that has been said … of Christian mysticism about "dark contemplation" and "the night of sense" must not be misinterpreted to mean that the normal culture of the senses, of artistic taste, of imagination, and of intelligence should be formally renounced by anyone interested in a life of meditation and prayer. On the contrary, such culture is presupposed. One cannot go beyond what one has not yet attained, and normally the realization that God is "beyond images, symbols and ideas" dawns only on one who has previously made a good use of all these things.

This is strong language — that culture is presupposed for the contemplative journey, along with intelligence, imagination, artistic taste, and so forth. Merton makes a parallel point in his book *Contemplative Prayer*: "The function of image, symbol, poetry, music, change, and of ritual (remotely related to sacred dance) is to open up the inner self to the contemplative to incorporate the senses and the body in the totality of the self-orientation to God that is necessary for worship and for meditation." Thus ritual itself can come alive, and ought to, by way of "the senses and the body," and this is part of meditation as well as worship.

Merton responded very favorably to a tape he heard of an African liturgy:

> Yesterday Fr. Chrysogamus played in chapter a tape recording of a Mass sung in Africa with native drums and music. Some of it was very impressive, especially a rather complex and sophisticated Agnus Dei. The drums were splendid, and the voices were full of power and life, raw, fresh, and wonderful. It was not all first class African music, but very authentic, very moving.

Merton's attitudes here could be taken as a great endorsement of our Cosmic Mass, which I have been developing for twenty years, ever since I became an Episcopal priest. In a Cosmic Mass, multiple generations of worshippers, but especially young adults, come together and dance their prayers, using their whole bodies in worship. The experience incorporates postmodern art forms and requires the work of many people, from VJs and DJs to rappers and computer experts and altar builders and more. Above all, this kind of worship is profoundly participatory, since "the posse is the priest," and everyone, by the energy they put into their dancing and prayer and meditation on the visuals offered, is a "midwife of grace" (my definition of the archetypal meaning of priesthood). A Cosmic Mass is *not* about one ordained person but about the community at work, "the work of the people" (which is the etymological meaning of the word *liturgy*).

This intersects with something else that Merton called for: a complete overhaul of the priesthood and its meaning. Here was his candid assessment:

I think the whole thing needs to be changed; the whole idea of the priesthood needs to be changed. I think we need to develop a whole new style of worship in which there is no need for one hierarchical person to have a big central place, a form of worship in which everyone is involved.

Indeed, a Cosmic Mass is worship in which "everyone is involved." We need a lot more of such rituals that are also very interfaith and ecumenical and welcoming to persons of diverse spiritual tribes.

The Via Creativa as the Work of the Holy Spirit

In emphasizing the role of the body, the senses, imagination, and art, Merton has a bold ally in Meister Eckhart, for whom the Via Creativa is central to the entire spiritual journey. For Eckhart, creativity is the very work of the Holy Spirit, who is creating still and cocreating through all of us. He invokes the story of the Annunciation, the promise to Mary from the angel that the Holy Spirit will come over you, and applies it to all of us:

> Then the angel said: "The Holy Ghost shall come upon thee from above." ... The work that is "with," "outside," and "above" the artist must become the work that is "in" him, taking form within him, in other words, to the end that he may produce a work of art, in accordance with the verse "The Holy Spirit shall come upon thee" (Lk. 1:35), that is, so that the "above" may become "in."

What a rich affirmation of the creative and artistic process! But Eckhart does not stop as he continues his teaching of the Holy and Creative Spirit at work in all of us.

> What help is it to me if Mary is full of grace, if I am not also full of grace? And what help is it to me that the Father gives birth to his Son unless I also give birth to him? It is for this reason that God gives birth to his Son in a perfect soul and

lies in the maternity bed so that he can give birth to him again in all his works.

Eckhart speaks of the "living water" of the Holy Spirit that "springs," "rises," "presses," and "leaps" in us when we are in a creative state. Through this "the Son comes into being in us." We birth the Cosmic Christ who is "always needing to be born." We humans are heirs of the "fearful creative power" of God, and that is one reason that art is a rich and necessary sort of meditation. "Whatever can be truly expressed in its proper meaning must emerge from inside a person and pass through the inner form. It cannot come from outside to inside of a person, but must emerge from within."

Merton, like Eckhart, sees the Holy Spirit at work birthing the soul and God in the soul. And he recognizes that true art leads us to the Divine Silence, writing, "Let us be proud of the words which are given to us for nothing, not to teach anyone, not to prove anyone absurd, but to point beyond all objects into the silence where nothing can be said." Merton invokes Eckhart's teaching on the divine birth, comparing it to a thunderbolt that entices one to turn, "without realizing, completely toward it."

Merton on Art as Meditation

Was Merton himself familiar with art as meditation? Of course he was. First, as a writer, he no doubt experienced moments of ecstasy and union/communion in his research and finding of truth and in sharing it. This is the joyful vocation of a writer. This is surely why he was so fecund a writer, leaving behind dozens of books and hundreds of articles and essays.

We also know that Merton was a very serious photographer, and we can see in his photography much spiritual depth and insight along with skill and discipline. His friend and official biographer, John Howard Griffin, introduced Merton to his first camera. Griffin subsequently wrote an entire book on Merton's photography, *A Hidden Wholeness: The Visual World of Thomas Merton*. He observed that for Merton, "the camera became in his hands, almost immediately, an instrument of contemplation." He points out how Merton included the Via Negativa in his picture-taking for "his concept of aesthetic beauty differed from that of most men. Most would pass by dead roots in search of a rose. Merton photographed the dead tree root or the texture of wood or whatever crossed his path…seeking not to alter their life but to preserve it in his emulsions." For Merton, said a friend, "photography is a way of framing wholes so that suchness reveals itself." But *suchness*, as Dr. Suzuki put it, is the Cosmic Christ in Christian parlance. For it is about how every being is an image of God. Said Suzuki: "In Christian terms [suchness] is to see God in an angel as angel, to see God in a flea as flea."

Indeed, on his final journey, Merton was often taking pictures, and he shared with us his philosophy of photography: "The best photography is aware, mindful of illusion and uses illusion, permitting and encouraging it — especially unconscious and powerful illusions that are not normally admitted on the scene." For Merton it is not the camera that does the taking for "the camera does not know what it takes: it captures materials with which you reconstruct, not so much what you saw as what you thought you saw." A friend comments that Merton "was not a 'photographer.' For him, the camera was merely another tool 'for dealing with things everybody knows about but isn't attending to,'" as Susan Sontag put it.

Three days before he died, on December 7, Merton recorded in his journal, "I sent contact prints to John Griffin with a few marked for enlargement. Took nine rolls of Pan X to the Borneo Studio on Silom Road, hoping they will not be ruined." John

Griffin wrote the Borneo Studio after Merton's death and acquired these last photos from Merton, including them in his book *A Hidden Wholeness*. Thus, they were not ruined. So right up to the end, Merton was engaged with his photographic vocation — art as meditation, indeed! Griffin described his last meeting with Merton before he left for his Asian trip, which included a telling description of the *joy* that Merton found in art as meditation:

> On my last visit with him before his trip to Asia, we went out together to photograph. He had now developed a photographer's eye. He became excited by almost everything he saw — the peeling paint on window facings, plants, weeds, the arrangement of a stack of wood chips.... I photographed him in the act of photographing, an activity in which his joy was unblemished and which added a special aura of happiness to his features.

Yes, art as meditation does bring joy, and it brought joy to Merton right up to the end.

Psychologist and ex-Benedictine Thomas Moore had this to say about Merton's love of photography:

> I am also inspired by Merton's practice of photography. Notice that I connect his art with his spiritual life as he did in his writing. It makes complete sense that he would have discovered an art that smoothly connected his contemplative life with the world around him in a form analogous to his writing.... he wrote his books and his casual writing, if you can call it that, as an artist careful with his style, even though he was such a master at it that it seems easy and natural. Most artists move from a primary art to a secondary or complementary one, and Merton's turn to photography was a major movement in his life.

Moore names Merton's discovery of photography as an art and prayer form "a major movement" in his life. Moore elaborates on the role of art as meditation in Merton's vocation:

Merton's photographs inspire me to connect the arts to the spiritual life as integrally and as tightly as possible. When I encourage people to engage an art as spiritual practice I often remind them how in history and around the world religions and the arts have been linked so closely that it's difficult to imagine one without the other. But Merton refines that idea. He invites us to zoom in on it and notice that our meditations are complete when we can use the lens of a camera to see the interiority or the art forms of the world around us. The camera frames our world so that we can transform it into an image that speaks to the soul and spirit and is an object of contemplation.

Merton admired the Hindu tradition in which all artistic work is recognized as a form of yoga. In this way, he commented, "there ceases to be any distinction between sacred and secular art. All art is Yoga, and even the art of making a table or a bed, or building a house, proceeds from the craftsman's Yoga and from his spiritual discipline of meditation." This is a fine way to name the process of art as meditation, and Merton does so word for word. Indeed, by embracing a "craftsman's Yoga," Merton endorses a broader spirituality of work. He wrote: "Your work is your yoga and it can lead to a sense of being one with God.... Basically, Hinduism says that your everyday work can lead you to union with God. No matter who you are, no matter how material the work is, it can unite you with God." This parallels my theology, and my teaching of the "priesthood of all workers," as laid out in my book *The Reinvention of Work*, which was the basis of the unique doctorate of ministry I created at the University of Creation Spirituality.

Merton also turned to calligraphy as an art and meditation experience. Griffin wrote, "Thomas Merton referred to his calligraphic drawings in a variety of terms...he called them abstractions, abstract writings, marks, signatures, signs, and sometimes calligraphies." Griffin cautioned: "No need to categorize these marks. It is better if they remain unidentified vestiges, signatures of someone who is not around." Merton held some public exhibitions of these drawings as well. Griffin wrote that Merton

> trusted in the "connections" that would somehow be made between the observer and the images, particularly if the observer could see them simply as what they are: Free expressions, signs executed without preplanning, having their own reality. Merton hoped that this reality would not be obscured by undue explanations or analyses...abandon all attempts to decipher "what they mean" or "how to interpret them."...They ask nothing at all. They demand nothing at all. They just are and that is all. "Does there always have to be a reason for everything?" Merton asked again and again in his writings.

Griffin concluded, "The drawings are free and they leave the viewer free."

Merton also liked music. He was so in love with jazz that almost every time he could leave the monastery and go into the nearby city of Louisville, he would gravitate to what was then the segregated, black area of town and hang out in the jazz clubs. To this day, many local African Americans, now old, tell stories of hanging out and talking jazz with Merton when they were young. He could play the piano, and he admired the music of Joan Baez and Bob Dylan. Once, with a third party present, Merton and Baez had a picnic on the monastery grounds, in which Baez reported that Merton got a bit tipsy from too much champagne. When French philosopher Jacques Maritain visited Merton in 1966, Merton described Bob Dylan to him as "the American Villon" and said he was preparing a study of Dylan's poetry and songs. Merton put on a recording of some of Dylan's songs and played them at full volume. "The Dylan songs blasted the still atmosphere of Trappist lands with the wang-wang of guitars and voice at high amplification."

Merton was not the only one who was impacted by Baez and Dylan; I was, too, and during the same time period. In the mid-1960s, while the Second Vatican Council was in session, the strict rules were relaxed in our Dominican training, and we were allowed to listen to recordings of folk singers, of which Joan Baez made a special impression on me. My first encounter with Dylan occurred when a sort of traveling minstrel, a young hippie troubadour walking the country, showed up at our studium in Dubuque, Iowa, and played Dylan's "The Times They Are a-Changin'" at the picnic table behind our priory. I was deeply moved. In the 1970s, after I returned to Dubuque after my Parisian sojourn, Peter, Paul, and Mary became the most influential mystic-prophet troubadours among my young Dominican brothers studying for the priesthood.

Merton was also a serious poet. We can feel his soul in his poems, such as in this tribute to the grace one feels while chanting the psalms, a practice that his monastic community undertook several times a day and in the middle of the night:

> When psalms surprise me with their music
> And antiphons turn to rum
> The Spirit sings: the bottom drops out of my soul
> And from the center of my cellar Love, louder than thunder
> Opens a heave of naked air.

Merton said, "Poetry is not ordinary speech, nor is poetic experience ordinary experience. It is closer to religious experience. Rasa is above all santa: contemplative peace." In a discussion with Dr. V. Raghavan on rasa and Indian aesthetics, Merton reported that together they "discussed the difference between aesthetic experience and religious experience: the aesthetic lasts only as long as the object is present. Religious knowledge does not require the presence of 'an object.' Once one has known Brahman one's life is permanently transformed from within. I spoke of William

Blake and his fourfold vision." Among Merton's jottings in his *Asian Journal* are passages from many writers, which he wrote down possibly for meditation or for future commentary. One such passage from G. B. Mohan's book *The Response to Poetry* reads as follows:

> Aestheticism which fails to integrate art with life and crude moralism which reduces poetry to sermons perpetuate the end-means conflict. Aesthetic experience is both an end in itself and a means for a fuller realization of human values....
> By pointing out unsuspected affinities between apparently dissimilar things, by establishing meaningful relations between apparently unrelated phenomena, poetry extends the range of our awareness.

One can presume that Mohan is in some way speaking for Merton's appreciation of poetry and its capacity to "extend the range of our awareness."

Merton was also keen about visual art, and he wrote movingly about cave art and iconography, such as in the following story:

> No art form stirs or moves me more deeply, perhaps, than Paleolithic cave painting — that and Byzantine or Russian icons. (I admit this may be really inconsistent!)
> The cave painters were concerned not with composition, not with "beauty," but with the peculiar immediacy of the most direct vision. The bison they paint is not a mere representation of an animal, it is a sign, a *gestalt*, a presence of the unique and peculiar life force incarnated in this animal — in terms of Banta philosophy, its *muntu*. This is anything but an "abstract essence." It is dynamic power, vitality, the self-realization of life in act, something that flashes out in a split second, is seen, yet is not accessible to mere reflection, still less to analysis.
> Cave art is a sign of pure seeing, nothing else.

While traveling in India with friend Amiya Chakravarty, Merton visited the home of painter Jamini Roy, "a warm, saintly old man," where Merton described encountering "simple, formalized little icons with a marvelous sort of folk and Coptic quality absolutely alive and full of charm, many Christian themes, the most lovely modern treatment of Christian subjects I have ever seen." Merton concluded, "All the faces glowing with humanity and peace. Great religious artists. It was a great experience."

Merton had a powerful experience in meditation at the large sacred statues of the Buddha at Polonnaruwa, Ceylon.

> I am able to approach the Buddhas barefoot and undisturbed, my feet in wet grass, wet sand. Then the silence of the extraordinary faces. The great smiles. Huge and yet subtle. Filled with every possibility, questioning nothing, knowing nothing, knowing everything, rejecting nothing, the peace not of emotional resignation but of Madhyamika, of sunyata, that has seen through every question without trying to discredit anyone or anything — without refutation — without establishing some other argument.

He explains how it hit him so hard, becoming a breakthrough event:

> I was knocked over with a rush of relief and thankfulness at the obvious clarity of the figures, the metal bodies composed into the rock shape and landscape, figure, rock and tree. And the sweep of bare rock sloping away on the other side of the hills, where you can go back and see different aspects of the figures.
>
> Looking at these figures I was suddenly, almost forcibly, jerked clean out of the habitual, half-tied vision of things, and an inner clearness, clarity, as if exploding from the rocks themselves, became evident and obvious.... The rock, all matter, all life, is charged with dharmakaya...

everything is emptiness and everything is compassion. I don't know when in my life I have ever had such a sense of beauty and spiritual validity running together on one aesthetic illumination.

He tells us that this mystical/aesthetic experience with the Buddha statues was the culmination of his pilgrimage to the East. "My Asian pilgrimage has come clear and purified itself. I mean, I know and have seen what I was obscurely looking for. I don't know what else remains but I have now seen and have pierced through the surface and have got beyond the shadow and the disguise. This is Asia in its purity."

Sister Lentfoehr said that, in a Chilean magazine interview in 1967, Merton "named himself not only the author of 'many books of prose and poetry' but also an artist, and though living 'as a hermit, solitary in the forest in contact with groups of poets radicals, pacifists, hippies, artists, etc. in all parts of the world.'" It is true, Lentfoehr observed, that "Merton considered himself a poet, and he was that, and it is highly interesting to trace his poetic development over the years — from the early poems which he chose to keep, to his latest, so-called antipoetry, strongly marked by sociological concern and a richly orchestrated neo-surrealist technique." Ross Labrie, in *The Art of Thomas Merton*, concluded that Merton is

recognized as an important figure in recent American poetry. The range of his work strikes one in retrospect as impressive — from the austerely beautiful religious lyrics of the early period to the inventiveness and structural complexity of the later style. In the late 1960s he had finally come to feel that the poet and the contemplative in him were one, and this confidence gives the later poems an attractive energy and buoyancy that seem in hindsight to have been full of promise.

Merton was a poet, an essayist, a diarist, a narrative writer, and a spiritual author. He told his friend Robert Lax that his poems helped his calligraphies, his calligraphies helped his poems, and his calligraphies helped his manifestos. He identified himself as a writer, confiding to a friend, "There is something in my nature that gets the keenest and sharpest pleasure out of achievement, out of work finished and printed and distributed and read." The Via Creativa, indeed!

As we have seen, Merton was also a photographer, a lover of visual art and music, and he drew as well. He was also very outspoken and very much practiced in the *art of friendship* — an art form that is often quite rare in American society, especially among men. Indeed, this was driven home to me when I was living on a Basque farm in the foothills of the Pyrenees in southwestern France (Merton was born in Prades, France, in the southeastern Pyrenees). One night in the local family-run inn where I ate my dinners, we watched the first moon landing on a black-and-white television. Afterward, an unknown visitor came to see me, a ninety-year-old Basque priest who came limping through the door on a cane. He approached me, shook my hand excitedly, and extended his congratulations: "Bravo!" he said. "Who but the Americans could land someone on the moon? Congratulations!" Then he added, "But when it comes to friendship, you Americans are morons." And with that he turned around and left the room.

Merton was not a moron. His friends and friendship were important to him. Sister Lentfoehr reminds us that in September 1968, just three months before his death, Merton wrote an article entitled "The Monastic Theology of St. Aelred," a saint and English Cistercian. Merton had studied St. Aelred in depth as a young monk, especially Aelred's well-known treatise on friendship. Merton wrote, "The natural basis for this theology of friendship is of course the indestructible inclination to love which is the divine image in us." He employed the phrase "an apostolate of friendship" — and he practiced it. In just one collection of Merton's letters, the great range of individuals he wrote to included people in Argentina, Austria, Belgium, Brazil, Canada, England, Japan, and Pakistan. As one person put it, this testifies "to the ever-widening circle of friendships he built through his correspondence." Of course, this was decades before email! Among his friends by correspondence were peace activists such as Dorothy Day, James Forest, Jean and Hildegard Goss-Mayr, Dan and Philip Berrigan, and Gordon Zahn; writers such as Lawrence Ferlinghetti, Wendell Berry (who visited him in his hermitage), Boris Pasternak, Czeslaw Milosz, Bill Everson (Brother Antoninus, who visited him in his hermitage), and Henry Miller; psychologists and psychoanalysts such as Erich Fromm, Karl Stern, and Joost Meerloo; scientists like Leo Szilard, and more.

John Howard Griffin, one of his closest friends, said that Merton had a "genius for friendship." Griffin wrote:

> Thomas Merton found no inconsistency in seeming opposites. He was a hermit, with a true vocation for solitude and at the same time he had such a boundless affective nature that he made and cherished deep friendships. He counted as friends the famous and the unknown of the world. Many who never met him except through correspondence were authentic friends. He had a genius for friendship in that he gave of himself without demanding anything. His closest friends reflected that genius, never intruding unduly, leaving him free as he left others free.

One friend Merton made on his final trip to Asia was Chögyam Trungpa Rinpoche, who was only thirty-one years old at the time and made a deep impression on him. Merton considered him "a good friend of mine — a very interesting person indeed…who got the complete reincarnation treatment: a thorough formation in Tibetan science monasticism, and everything," and who had to escape from Tibet "to save his life, like most other abbots." Chögyam Trungpa Rinpoche later started the Naropa Institute (which became Naropa University). After his death, Naropa University linked up with my University of Creation Spirituality and accredited our master's program in Creation Spirituality in Oakland for seven fruitful years.

Merton as Teacher and Intellectual

Merton saw his vocation as that of teacher and student as well as writer. For instance, after reading William of Conche's *Philosophy of the World*, he commented:

> Beautiful little chapter on the Teacher. I was very moved by it. I usually ignore this element in my own vocation, but obviously I am a writer, a student and a teacher as well as a contemplative of sorts, and my solitude etc. is that of a writer and teacher, not of a pure hermit. And the great thing in my life is, or should be, love of truth. I know there is nothing more precious than the body of charity created by communicating and sharing the truth. This is really my whole life.

Here I see the "Dominican" in Merton, since the motto of the Dominican Order is "Veritas" or "Truth," and the solitude promoted in contemplation constitutes a prelude to sharing by way of writing and teaching, as Eckhart knew well.

Merton applied art as meditation in his teaching of the novices. He wrote, "I want as many of the novices as possible to learn how to weave baskets," and he called on an old monk to instruct the young ones. Merton cared about education — he was a teacher, after all, and part of the monastic tradition is the *lectio divina* and study. He wrote sarcastically about a brother monk

who had recently returned from two years of study in Rome:
Father Baldwin "has a degree but has learned nothing dangerous.
In fact he has learned a philosophy which, he avers, is useless for
his spiritual life and cannot be meditated on ('being' is in his way
of thinking an unreality). This is excellent! He has been away for
two years and comes back without ideas and indeed with a repug-
nance for thought." Thus for Merton learning has something of
the "dangerous" to it. Elsewhere, Merton commented on the state
of education in the West in general and how we need to reach out
to other cultures and to emphasize *wisdom*:

> Christopher Dawson has remarked on the "religious vac-
> uum" in our education. It is absolutely essential to intro-
> duce into our study of the humanities a dimension of *wisdom*
> oriented to contemplation as well as to wise action. For this,
> it is no longer sufficient merely to go back over the Chris-
> tian and European cultural traditions. The horizons of the
> world are no longer confined to Europe and America. We
> have to gain new perspectives, and on this our spiritual and
> even our physical survival may depend.

I think Merton would be at home with my efforts at alternative pedagogy over the years, which have employed art as meditation to train the intuition or right brain along with the analytic
and left brain and that have reached out to other traditions and to
a diversity of professions in order to put wisdom before knowledge. The fact that we have taught inner city youth as well (in my
YELLAWE program) would please him also. Its philosophy of
values — the "ten C's" — are described in my book *The A.W.E.
Project: Reinventing Education, Reinventing the Human*.

Merton talked in his *Asian Journal* about picking up books
along his trip and throwing some away because they were "stupid." For me the very meaning of being an intellectual is about
being creative with ideas; it is about mixing and matching ideas

and birthing a third thing from such marriages. Truly Merton, with his passion for learning, was an intellectual. This is, to me, a far cry from an academician, which is often a career that is anything but a practice of the Via Creativa. Merton was not an academician; he was a bona fide intellectual who was at home with other creative thinkers of many stripes. Recall Merton's interest in and critique of the science of his day (in chapter 4). On the one hand, he called Heisenberg's *Physics and Philosophy* "a very exciting book" and compared it to St. John of the Cross. Yet he also criticized a "strictly scientific view of the universe" and our culture's "titanic humorlessness," while embracing the sheer wonder of space flight and "cosmic play."

Eckhart teaches about the cocreation that humans accomplish in company with God when we and God are giving birth together. "God does this: he begets his only begotten Son in the highest part of the soul. At the same time as he begets his only begotten Son in me, I beget him again in the Father."

Eckhart notes: "God and this humble man are entirely one and not two; for what God works, he also works, and what God wills, he also wills, and what God is, he also is: one life and one being.... Under these circumstances this person is a divine being, a divine being is this person, for her the kiss is exchanged between the unity of God and the humble person." The work that we give birth to is nothing less than the Christ for "this is the fullness of time, when the son of God is begotten in you."

It seems that Merton very much lived this spirituality of fruitfulness and birthing. The immense breadth and depth of his work is proof of that. His generativity could not be diminished; even his final journey was an act of imagination. His search for the essence that connected East and West and that brought together the contemplative life with a considered critique of culture formed the very subject of his final talk, "Karl Marx and Monasticism."

Imaginative? Creative? Dangerous? Remember, the Vietnam War was ostensibly being fought to combat the spread of communism. Here, in the Via Creativa, is where the personal and the social come together, the mystic and the prophet.

During his Asian journey, Merton referred to the books he was reading: authors include Ruth Benedict, Anaïs Nin, Denise Levertov, William Blake, and many others. An isolated thinker Merton was not. In his final talk, Merton made reference to the following thinkers: Dom Jean Leclercq, Herbert Marcuse, Roger Garaudy, St. Teresa of Avila, Ludwig Feuerbach, Teilhard de Chardin, Carl Jung, St. Bernard, Adam of Perseigne, St. Augustine, Karl Marx, Erich Fromm, St. Paul, the Dalai Lama, St. Benedict, Chögyam Trungpa Rinpoche, John Cassian, Sartre, Karl Jaspers, Rilke, Jacques Maritain, and many more. No, his intellectual life was neither staid nor frozen. He brought medieval wisdom and Western and Eastern wisdom together with today's wisdom. His mind danced the creative dance of a real thinker, an authentic intellectual, an artist of ideas who was not playing competitive games of sophistry or of selfhood but was bent on truth seeking.

Author and Merton scholar Michael Higgins also recognized in Merton "a public Catholic intellectual distinguished by a rigorous self-scrutiny, possessed of a literary voice of singular virtuosity and bold eclecticism. He was a contemplative, restless, chronically unsure, posed at many a liminal point — spiritual and emotional — ever aching into holiness." Higgins credits Merton with introducing him to "a genuine ecumenicity of mind, an unfettered Catholic way of being in the world, an intellectual vulnerability that eschewed certitude in favor of exploration — humble, tentative, and fearless." Calling Merton a "truly visionary" thinker, he praises him for his "essentially universalist sensibility, his capacity to transcend narrow and constrictive modes of thinking, his openness to the risks of disruptive insights, his embrace of the wondrous and luminous in all traditions of faith, his very temerity of mind and spirit. I think these are genuinely Blakean qualities and Merton was his astute, critical and discerning disciple."

Part of Merton's artistry was birthing himself anew on several occasions. In his final talk, he warned that today we can no longer rely on institutions as we have in the past. Thomas Moore observes that Merton "was a person in motion, always thinking his way to the next step, re-inventing himself within the limits of his chosen monastic lifestyle, stretching the limits when he had to." In this sense and also in his willingness to bring premodern wisdom to his times — mixing the past with the present, Cassian with Karl Marx — Merton was very much a postmodern thinker and actor.

I think it is clear that Merton suffered and struggled mightily with his work as an artist. From the mid-1950s on, he was eager to get his own hermitage in order to withdraw not only from daily community life but also from the many pressures coming his way due to the success of his writings. Hundreds of letters came in every week and countless invitations to talk — most of which of course his abbot refused him to attend. This irked Merton on many occasions. I think Merton might have been helped considerably by the teaching of psychologist Otto Rank who, in his classic work *Art and Artist*, pays heed to the suffering and struggles of the artist. One point Rank makes that truly speaks to Merton's situation is that the greatest danger to the artist is success. The success that Merton had with his autobiography and the renown that followed from his many writings, along with the pressure he was under as the monastery demanded more work of him, was something Merton had to wrestle with interiorly as well as regards his schedule and commitments. Was it pride to keep on writing? Was he experiencing the freedom that allured him to the monastery in the first place? Was he being used by the monastery as, to use Merton's own words, a "cash cow"? Could he ever escape all the demands coming his way? One observer put it this way: "Instead of blending into the monastic community as he had hoped, Merton had in essence become 'the chosen one,' the famous monk who was making Gethsemani famous."

I think it is impressive how Merton did indeed deal with his success eventually, by finding space and time in what might be called a semi-hermitage. He was able to stay true to his vocation as a writer and cultural critic as well as a monk who managed to keep his interior life alive. Plus, add in his outreach to Eastern practice, and of course his final pilgrimage East, and it's not a big surprise that it drove him to a certain "neurosis." His abbot, with whom Merton had plenty of misgivings, called him a "harebrained neurotic" — and it drove him also to plenty of contradictions (including his affair with a nurse). The good news is that he landed on his feet.

Otto Rank observes that the artistic vocation is itself a deep calling, so much so that this "calling is not a means of livelihood, but life itself. . . . The artist does not practice his calling but *is* it. . . . The artist needs his calling for his spiritual existence." These words apply aptly to Merton both as a writer/artist and as a monk. He married the two vocations, and neither was easy.

Ross Labrie, summarizing Merton's artistic vocation, believes that it took Merton quite a while as a monk "to accept the artist in himself as a viable agent of the contemplative life." In other words, the Via Creativa was not named for him as an authentic dimension to the spiritual journey — he had to find it pretty much on his own. In this regard he needed the Creation Spirituality tradition to assist that naming, and he spent years in some turmoil because it was not named for him. He did find support in the writings of the Russian Orthodox lay theologian Nikolai

Berdyaev and especially his distinction between an "ethics of law" and an "ethics of creativeness." Merton writes in his journal that this teaching

> is a very good one for me now. So good, perhaps, that it is a temptation.... Yes, sneers the ethics of law — you have put your nose in Dostoevsky and Berdyaev and Zen Buddhism and now where are you? On the road to heresy.
>
> Well, what about St. Paul, and all the saints? What about the gospel? Certainly, it is a dangerous problem, and I *am* in danger. Thank God for it. I beg Him to protect me and bring me through the danger. And I still do not know what to do.
>
> Berdyaev says under the ethic of law the future is determined by a fixed duty to realize a set purpose — the ethic of law is teleological. The ethic of creativity leaves the future *immanent to ourselves* and we to its nearness.

Meister Eckhart assists immeasurably in the task of honoring creativity, but I am not sure that Merton saw this in Eckhart. I present ten rich and profound sermons that are essentially committed to the Via Creativa in *Passion for Creation*. Among these sermons is one that truly creates a bridge between the Via Negativa and solitude and the Via Creativa. Yet it is quite clear that Merton devotes more of his attention with Eckhart on the Via Negativa (perhaps to lead him into Buddhism and because Suzuki does that also) than on the Via Creativa.

The story is told that when French philosopher Jacques Maritain visited Merton in his hermitage, they agreed that because of the current state of chaos in theology and philosophy, it might be best to approach theological and philosophical problems through "creative writing and literary criticism." Merton wrote explicitly that, to get to the depths of our spiritual crises today, insights "are to be sought less in the tracts of theologians than in the meditations of the existentialists and in the Theater of the Absurd." Further, when Merton was once denied the right to publish his article on Boris Pasternak (author of *Doctor Zhivago*), he complained: "No one seems to suspect that there might be, in Pasternak, something of deeper spiritual value and significance. Something perhaps spiritually *more* significant than anything that has yet manifested itself in any of our monasteries."

This is striking to me because I came to a similar conclusion while writing my doctoral thesis in the late 1960s at the Institut Catholique de Paris. I later published my thesis as a book entitled *Religion USA: An Inquiry into Religion and Culture by Way of "Time" Magazine*, in which I wrote that the artist and musician and writer "will prove to be the staunchest allies of those in search of a critically understood religion." My study aimed to develop a critical methodology for critiquing culture and the media by examining religious expression in *Time* magazine as representative of American middle class culture. To do that, in part, I compared articles between *Time*'s "Religion" section and its "Art" and "Book Review" sections. In the "Religion" section, I found 53 percent of the articles were taken up with what I termed "ethnic religion," or religion as mere group identification and institutional structures. Meanwhile, in the "Book Review" section, only 19 percent of the articles dealt with "ethnic religion," while 60.4 percent dealt with religion as a deep spiritual engagement that included elements of mysticism and prophecy. One of the conclusions of my doctoral thesis was that the "Art" and "Book Review" sections of *Time* magazine contained more about authentic religion or spirituality than the section titled "Religion" ever did, which was invariably about religion's institutions alone. I concluded, "This reveals what we have seen elsewhere, that religion is disassociating itself from former cultural patterns — even those of religion." This might shed light on the last encounter I had with my mentor, Pere

Chenu, when he was ninety-one years old. He said to me, "Never forget! The greatest tragedy in theology of the last three hundred years has been the divorce of the theologian from the dancer, the musician, the potter, the poet, the artist, and the filmmaker."

Thus we can see that Merton, Maritain, M. D. Chenu, and I all turned — as is the French way — to the artist in us all for healthy spirituality in dark times. I did it very early in my theological career and that path has never ceased for me. It is a "Way." Now I have a name for it: the Via Creativa.

CHAPTER SEVEN

"The prophetic struggle with the world"

Merton and the Via Transformativa

In the conflict between law and freedom God is on the side of freedom. That is a scandalous statement! But it is the New Testament! How are we going to affirm to the modern world the scandal of the New Testament? It is here that we confront the seriousness of our prophetic as distinct from our contemplative calling.

— THOMAS MERTON

These words from Thomas Merton frame well the biblical basis for the many positions he took on behalf of justice and freedom. He reminds us that we have both a contemplative and a prophetic calling. Merton was often controversial in his day, but he derived his passion for justice and the strength to ground his courage from the scriptures themselves. He was fully aware of the potential of our species to misuse its divine powers of creativity. Creativity does not stand alone cut off from values and priorities. We can use our creativity, after all, to build gas ovens to kill enemies more efficiently, or we can use our creativity to build community and to restore health and to heal. Creativity needs direction and parameters. Justice and compassion provide that testing ground for our creativity. Thus, the Via Creativa, along with the Via Positiva and Via Negativa, leads to the Via Transformativa.

Creativity and the Prophet

There was never a prophet who was not also an artist — what I call a "social artist" or an artist at organizing and awakening the people. Biblical scholar Walter Brueggemann established this in his classic work *The Prophetic Imagination*, writing: "Every totalitarian regime is frightened of the artist. It is the vocation of the prophet to keep alive the ministry of imagination, to keep on conjuring and proposing alternative futures to the single one the king wants to urge as the only thinkable one." Merton knew the prophetic tradition — in fact, he once wrote a letter to a rabbi saying that he often sat on his front porch in his hermitage and shouted the poetry of Isaiah and others into the air about him. The artist, as Rabbi Heschel says, is one who "interferes." Merton did a lot of interfering in his life, most of it by way of his writing.

As Ross Labrie commented, "Merton saw the prophetic role of the artist as a natural one for the contemporary artist to assume amidst the decline in the authority of religion." This is a significant observation — that Merton was attuned to the lesser role that religion was playing in contemporary culture. Merton pointed to Faulkner and Camus as two examples of prophetic artists, and he wrote to poet Nicanor Parra in 1965 that contemporary artists tended to fulfill many of the functions that were once the monopoly of monks. Thus, Labrie commented that for Merton, "a writer like Faulkner could be profoundly biblical in his work without being a churchgoer or a conventional believer. It was the artist, 'facing the problems of life without the routine consolations of conventional religion,' who experienced in depth the 'existential dimensions of these problems.'"

According to Labrie, for Merton, solitude was necessary for the artist to do his or her prophetic work, which includes anticipating "the struggles and the general consciousness of later generations." Among the artist's important role as prophet is to, as Labrie wrote, "show finally 'where everything connects,' a reflection of Merton's own passionate role as a unifier of different kinds of experience....Merton saw the artist's creation as both analogous to the freshness of paradise and a sign of its possible recovery." As Merton put it, "Here the world gets another chance. Here man, here the reader discovers himself getting another start in life, in hope, in imagination."

Here, too, in the question of artist as prophet, Merton and my work in Creation Spirituality very much coincide. In my first book (now called *Prayer: A Radical Response to Life*), I speak about "the artist as a spiritual guru" and cite Santayana who says "art is more spiritual than dogma." I continue:

> The poets, the painters, the musicians, the script writers — these are frequently those who lead the struggle with the demons of life in our day. The artist calls up our common roots so that we all might examine, enjoy, and criticize them. Artists are the "monks" of a lay culture not asking to be imitated in lifestyle or morality (cf. Tolstoy: "The poet skims off the best of life and puts it in his work. That is why his work is beautiful and his life bad"), but of inviting others to plummet their recognition of the spiritual, of life. The artist is a listener to life.

I cite Tolstoy, who says:

> An artist's mission must not be to produce an irrefutable solution to a problem, but to compel us to love life in all its countless and inexhaustible manifestations. If I were told I

might write a book in which I should demonstrate beyond any doubt the correctness of my opinions on every social problem I should not waste two hours at it; but if I were told that what I wrote would be read twenty years from now by people who are children today and that they would read and laugh over my book and love life more because of it, then I should devote all my life and strength to such a work.

Merton was a great lover of Russian literature, iconography, and theology. One scholar, Nicholas Zernov, proposes that "one must look to Russian literature to find the sort of religious expression usually found in the musings of theologians.... Dostoevsky and Tolstoy, for example, are among the most important theological writers in the Russian language."

In February 1964, Merton wrote "Message to Poets," which he sent to a gathering in Mexico City of the "new" Latin American poets and some young North American ones. He said: "Let us obey life, and the Spirit of Life that calls us to be poets, and we shall harvest many new fruits for which the world hungers — fruits of hope that have never been seen before. With these fruits we shall calm the resentments and the rage of man." Surely this is an affirmation of the prophetic role of the artist and the artist's "radical response to life." He further elaborated on the process of the Via Negativa, Via Creativa, and Via Transformativa working in tandem:

> Let us be proud of the words that are given to us for nothing; not to teach anyone, not to confute anyone, not to prove anyone absurd, but to point beyond all objects into the silence where nothing can be said.
>
> We are not persuaders. We are the children of the Unknown. We are the ministers of silence that is needed to cure all victims of absurdity who lie dying of a contrived joy. Let us then recognize ourselves for who we are: dervishes mad

with secret therapeutic love which cannot be bought or sold,
and which the politician fears more than violent revolution,
for violence changes nothing. But love changes everything.
We are stronger than the bomb.
Let us then say "yes" to our own nobility by embracing
the insecurity and abjection that a dervish existence entails.

In the same message Merton explicitly takes up the issue of
prophecy and the poet, and he offers his own definition of prophecy: "To prophesy is not to predict, but to seize on reality in its
moment of highest expectation and tension toward the new. This
tension is discovered not in hypnotic elation but in the light of
everyday existence." By stressing "everyday existence," Merton
is teaching that prophecy is for all of us. Does his definition of
prophecy correspond to Rabbi Heschel's, who says the primary
work of the prophet is "to interfere"? I think it does. "Highest
expectation and tension toward the new" is always a kind of inter-
ference, isn't it? It interferes with the status quo, and it interferes
with despair. It is a road, therefore, to hope and possibility born
of great expectations.

Ever since my first book, I have written about the artist's prophetic contribution. In music, one example is Gustav Mahler, who
"sensed in the early years of our century the immanent upheavals
in Western civilization." Mahler himself said of his music: "What
is the purpose of suffering? How can I understand cruelty and
malice in the creation of a kind God? Will the meaning of life finally be revealed in death?" In that book I also treat the prophetic
role of the "Negro spiritual" and the prophets of the sixties, including Bob Dylan, Joan Baez, Peter, Paul, and Mary, and more.

Through over thirty years of pedagogy, I have taken up the
role of the artist as prophet in designing curricula for master's degrees and then doctor of ministry degrees in Creation Spirituality.
An essential part of our curriculum is always "art as meditation"

classes, since it is through the Via Creativa (preceded by the Via Positiva and the Via Negativa) that the prophet is born and nurtured. I laid this out many years ago in an article called "Art as Meditation," and I invoked Thomas Merton in my book *Original Blessing*: "Art enables us to find ourselves and lose ourselves at the same time. The mind that responds to the intellectual and spiritual values that lie hidden in a poem, a painting, or a piece of music, discovers a spiritual vitality that lifts it above itself, takes it out of itself, and makes it present to itself on a level of being that it did not know it could ever achieve."

Meister Eckhart on the Via Transformativa

Eckhart does not countenance running away from the world. He says that spirituality "is not to be learned by world-flight turning away from things, turning solitary, and going apart from the world. Rather, one must learn an inner solitude, wherever or with whomsoever he may be. One must learn to penetrate things and find God there." Since all beings are interconnected, it follows that our work of compassion flows from the relationship of all things. "You should love all people as yourself, esteeming and consider them alike. What happens to another, whether it be evil or good, should be the same to you as if it had happened to you." For Eckhart, following in the footsteps of the Hebrew prophets, "compassion means justice." Justice is so central to Eckhart that he dares say that "whoever understands my teaching on justice understands everything I have to say." He declares that "God is justice" and God is born from our work of justice.

> God will be born in this just person and the just person is born into God; and therefore God will be born through every virtue of the just person and will rejoice through every virtue of the just person. And not only at every virtue will

God rejoice but especially at every work of the just person, however small it is. When this work is done through justice and results in justice, God will rejoice at it, indeed God will rejoice through and through; for nothing remains in his ground which does not tickle him through and through out of joy.

Justice and compassion are the high point of the spiritual journey for Eckhart — but it does not stop there. For the goal of justice is to re-create our world so that God might find a home here and so that the gifts of life may be shared by all. The Via Transformativa returns to the Via Positiva therefore — the table is set for ever more people to undergo the joy of living because justice accomplishes that. Justice and compassion are not only the test of healthy creativity, they are also the result of healthy creativity. Indeed, compassion is the "best name" for God, according to Eckhart.

In his commentary on the Our Father prayer, Eckhart applies lessons of our interconnectivity and the imperative of justice to the words "Give us this day our daily bread":

Bread is given to us not in order that we eat it alone but that others who are indigent might be participants, lest anyone say "my bread given to me for me" but "*our*," as if it were given for me and for others through me and to me through others. Still, however bread and all similar necessities of the present life are for us with others and on account of others and given for others in us. He who does not give to another what belongs to another, does not eat his own bread but another's at the same time with his own....For everything which we have unjustly is not ours.

Other consequences follow. "What do the poor people do, who undergo the same or much worse sickness and suffering without anyone to give them even some cold water? They are forced to seek their dry bread in rain, snow and cold, from house to house. Therefore, if you will be comforted, forget those who are better off and think about those who are less fortunate."

Eckhart, in Dominican fashion, did not think contemplation and action were at odds but that one flowed into the other. "In contemplation you serve only yourself; in good works you serve many people," he wrote. And again, "St. Thomas says that the active life is better than the contemplative, for in it one pours out the love he has received in contemplation. Yet it is all one: For what we plant in the soul of contemplation we shall reap in the harvest of action...but it is all a single process with one end in view — that God is....In all he does, man has only his one vision of God."

Merton on Our Prophetic Calling

Thomas Merton came very much to the same conclusion, especially in the sixties when so many of his works were either outreach to Asian wisdom or treatises on justice and injustice. He was explicit about our "prophetic as distinct from our contemplative calling," writing: "In the conflict between law and freedom God is on the side of freedom. That is a scandalous statement! But it is the New Testament! How are we going to affirm to the modern world the scandal of the New Testament? It is here that we confront the seriousness of our *prophetic* as distinct from our *contemplative* calling." He learned much from Rabbi Heschel who, Merton tells us, sent him a personal copy of his book *The Prophets* when it was first published. This book is still recognized as a classic. Merton wrote on January 5, 1963: "Began reading Heschel's new book, which he sent, on the *Prophets*. Exactly the kind of approach with which I am in sympathy and which makes sense to me. The kind of deep reflection leading to insights which enable us to 'be' the prophet we are reading — while yet remaining in all our proper distribution."

Merton wrestled with how to balance the prophetic and contemplative callings, at one point asking: "Supposing that the only authentic Christian experience is that of the first Christians, can this be recovered and reconstructed in any way whatever? And if so, is it to be 'mystical' or 'prophetic'? And in any case, *what is it?*" For me, these words truly strike home and strike deep because all my work in spirituality, beginning with my first book, has been addressing the question Merton raises here and in the same language: What shall it be? Mysticism or prophecy (that is, the struggle for social justice)? I have answered that question with a both/and, not an either/or, and Merton eventually did the same. He was both, and he advised being both. Addressing the original Benedictine charism, Merton pointed out: "The true vocation of the monks of the Benedictine family is not to fight for contemplation against action, but to restore the ancient, harmonious and organic balance between the two. Both are necessary."

Merton tells us that "the prophetic struggle with the world is the struggle of the Cross against worldly power." He wrote: "To live prophetically, you've got to be questioning and looking at factors behind the facts. You've got to be aware that there are contradictions. In a certain sense, our prophetic vocation consists in hurting from the contradictions in society. This is a real cross in our lives today. For we ourselves are partly responsible." The prophetic consciousness then is not one of us versus them but of sorting out evil wherever it is to be found, since evil, like reality itself, is interdependent. Franciscan friar Daniel P. Horan, in his essay "Seeing the World as It Really Is: The Prophetic Legacy of Thomas Merton," says that Merton left us a "prophetic legacy" and that many Merton students have recognized that.

From Gerald Twomey's tellingly titled 1978 collection of essays, *Thomas Merton: Prophet in the Belly of a Paradox*, to the more recent volumes including Paul Dekar's *Thomas Merton: Twentieth-Century Wisdom for Twenty-First-Century Living* (2011) and Mario Aguilar's *Thomas Merton: Contemplation and Political Action* (2011) scholars and enthusiasts of Merton's life and work have identified the threads of prophetic intuition and proclamation that continue to speak to the pressing concerns and unsettling times of our own day.

Merton, Horan says, "could not help but cry out and call attention to the problems…of systemic sin in our time ranging from racial inequality, international threats of violence and war, economic disparity, etc." Monica Weis agrees and captures some of Merton's Via Transformativa stances that he took:

> His critique of the Vietnam war, and war itself, his caution about the dangers of technology, his defense of the rights of indigenous people, his censure of racial injustice, his challenge to America to develop an ecological conscience — all were prophetic words whose deep meaning we are just discovering — words that we now know to be true on multiple levels.

On March 21, 1968, the *New York Times* reported that some six thousand sheep had been struck down by "some mysterious killing agent.…Suspicion was pointed tonight at nerve gas being tested at the Army's Dugway Proving Ground (Utah)." The army refused to comment, but two days later the head of a special investigating team said, "We are as positive as medical science can ever be" that nerve gas from army tests had killed sixty-four hundred sheep in western Utah's Skull Valley. Merton comments on this incident in his May journal as he flies over the state. "Utah? It's dry. Far down, a bright nosed armed jet goes by very fast. *Six thousand dead sheep*. Utah. 'New secret poison gas harms no one but the enemy.' *Six thousand dead sheep*."

Merton on Ecology

Merton spoke bluntly about the eco-devastation our species is engaged in:

> What a miserable bundle of foolish idiots we are! We kill everything around us even when we think we love and respect nature and life. This sudden power to deal death all around us *simply by the way we live*, and in total "innocence" and ignorance, is by far the most disturbing symptom of our time....A phenomenal number of species of animals and birds have become extinct in the last fifty years — due of course to man's irruption into ecology. There was still a covey of quail around here in early fall. Now I don't hear a single whistle or hear a wing beat.

Merton sees eco-justice as a Christian imperative and he redefines "obedience" in that context.

> Perhaps the most crucial aspect of Christian obedience to God today concerns the responsibility of the Christian, in a technological society, toward creation and God's creation and God's will for creation. Obedience to God's will for nature and for man — respect for nature and love for man — in the awareness of our power to frustrate God's designs for nature and for man — to radically corrupt and destroy natural goods by misuse and blind exploitation, especially by criminal waste.

He speaks to the Western philosophical tradition's failures that contribute to our being cut off from nature. "How absolutely true, and how central a truth, that we are purely and simply *part of nature*, though we are the part which recognizes God. It is not Christianity, indeed, but post-Cartesian technologism that separates man from the world and makes him a kind of little god in his own right, with his clear ideas; all by himself."

These observations are not old or obsolete. One wonders where we would be today if they had been heeded when Merton wrote them back in the sixties. Indeed, they are integral to Pope Francis's encyclical on ecology and sustainability, which appeared on Earth Day, 2015.

In a move very telling about Merton's spiritual instincts and his cultural alertness, Merton responded in his journal in late 1962 to ecological prophet Rachel Carson very soon after her wake-up call, the soon-to-be-classic *Silent Spring*, was published. He wrote:

> I have been shocked at a notice of a new book, by Rachel Carson, on what is happening to birds as a result of the in-discriminate use of poisons (which do not manage to kill all the insects they intend to kill). Some will say: you worry about birds: why not worry about people? I worry about *both* birds and people. We are in the world and part of it and we are destroying everything because we are destroying ourselves, spiritually, morally and in every way. It is all part of the same sickness, and it all hangs together.

This is veritable Creation Spirituality. To worry *both* about non-two-legged creation (birds) *and* about the two-legged ones. He also notices that the cause of this destruction of creation around us is to be found in our self-destruction, "spiritually, morally and in every way."

On January 12, 1963, Merton was moved to write a two-page letter to Rachel Carson. The immediate response to her book had been fiercely negative from many scientists, corporations, media moguls, and others. One commentator wrote of this: "Carson's writing and scientific career seemed to be at an end. Targeted in a vicious and financially underwritten campaign to discredit her scientific integrity, Carson was vilified as a 'hysterical female,' a 'pseudo-scientist,' 'probably a communist,' a 'bird and bunny lover,' and a charlatan researcher." In his letter Merton thanked

Carson for her awareness of the "interdependence" of all things; he told her that from now on DDT would not be employed at the monastery; and he elaborated on the "sickness" that he alluded to in his journal above. "I would almost dare to say that the sickness is perhaps a very real and very dreadful hatred of life."

I find this language very powerful, for if prayer is "a radical response to life" and we are carrying a "very real and very dreadful hatred of life" within our culture, where are we? This resonates for me with poet Adrienne Rich's observation that many men carry a "fatalistic self-hatred" within them — and therefore, I would propose, within cultural institutions. Does patriarchy hate life? Is it driven to offer its own substitutes for life — from empires to pyramids to other idols as well? Many mystics whom Merton knew well — Hildegard of Bingen, Thomas Aquinas, and Meister Eckhart, to name a few — talk about God as "life." And Merton himself offers this comment on his being stretched from a narrow understanding of contemplation to life being at its center when rewriting his book *What Is Contemplation?* In July 1959, he wrote, "A lot of water has gone under the bridge since 1948. How poor were all my oversimplified ideas — and how mistaken I was to make contemplation only *part* of a man's life. For a contemplative his whole life is contemplation." How like my definition of prayer as a radical response to *life* is this comment. Is a dreadful hatred of life also a dreadful hatred of God? No matter the sentimental talk of God all around us.

Merton scholar Monica Weis writes, "January 12 marked a turning point in the ecological consciousness of Thomas Merton — a day of revelation and revolution, when a significant spiritual insight effected a dramatic and permanent change in his attitude and behavior." She calls Merton's reading of *Silent Spring* "an epiphanic event akin to other well-known and powerful moments of spiritual insight in his life." This conversion or *metanoia* provides more powerful evidence that he was moving from anthropocentric and Fall/redemption spirituality into a creation-centered one. Weis interprets his letter to Carson as "a revelation of his long-held incarnational vision that acknowledges the divine spark in all creation, making each creature holy and worthy of respect."

The reference to the "divine spark" in all creation is a reference to Eckhart, the Kabbalah, and the Muslim tradition, since Eckhart on many occasions credits the Muslim philosopher Avicenna with the image of the "divine spark" that is so meaningful to Eckhart (as it was also to Merton). Weis concludes that Merton enlarged his vision to embrace the rest of creation. "Having focused his social justice writing on right relationship among people — topics of racism, the rights of indigenous people, the dangers of atomic energy and technology, as well as the moral imperative for making peace through nonviolent means — Merton is now articulating a new insight: responsibility for the Earth." In the tradition of the Desert Fathers, the divine spark in humanity needs attending and nurturing for it to come to its ripe completion — and this completion concerns our work of transformation. Says Merton: "It is written: Our God is a consuming fire. Hence we ought to light the divine fire in ourselves with labor and with tears."

Technology: The Great Problem of the Day

Merton saw in technology "the great problem of the day."

> The problem of getting technology back into the power of man so that it may be used for man's own good is by all odds the great problem of the day. And one of the things that is demanded is a real iconoclastic attack on the ambiguities and confusion surrounding the misuse of technology....A naïve optimism about technology is a source of great problems.

The technology issue was a personal one for Merton because when he arrived at Gethsemani in 1940 the place was essentially a peasant-like farm operated not by machines but by the hands of the monks. Gradually, however, the place evolved and machinery was introduced by the abbot, who saw a more efficiently run farm in the offing. Yet the machinery interrupted the monastic silence and meditation. "The machines bothered Merton — the thought of them as much as the noise they produced," comments Merton scholar Ross Labrie. Merton felt machinery could replace the love of life that ought to lie at the heart of the spiritual journey:

> Met a brother leading a young Holstein bull by the bull's nose. Had this thought: 'thank God here is a living thing and not a machine, something big and warm and alive and unpredictable, with fears and angers and appetites.' And I was glad of all this and reassured by it because of the value that is in life itself. So the second thought won out over the first [that the bull could easily kill me]. I am willing to trust life more than machinery.

Merton's "life first" spirituality emerges strongly in his resistance to machines. Merton's suspicions about technology rose anew after *Sputnik* launched in 1957 and the 1960s' space race began. In response to space travel, he asked: "What is wrong with their humanism? It is a humanism of termites, because without God man becomes an insect, a worm in the wood, and even if he can fly, so what? There are flying ants. Even if man flies all over the universe, he is still nothing but a flying ant until he recovers a human center and a human spirit in the depth of his own being." It is that center and depth that Merton insists must undergird all technology. Referring to the efforts to land the first person on the moon, Merton asked: "What can we gain by sailing to the moon if we are not able to cross the abyss that separates us from ourselves. This is the most important of all voyages of discovery, and without it all the rest are not only useless but disastrous." This "most important of all voyages" is an inner journey into our deepest selves to see what is holding us back from our best self.

Larry Dossey raised a similar warning while commenting on my recent book *Meister Eckhart*: "Whether our species has a future on Earth does not depend on the development of more gee-whiz technologies, but on whether we are willing to move into the psycho-spiritual dimension proclaimed by Meister Eckhart and elucidated by Matthew Fox in this important book." Dossey, like Merton and myself, finds Eckhart to be a very reliable guide into our inner psycho-spiritual selves. Technologies that are roaming outer space on our behalf or are appearing as tools in our hands must not be allowed to distract from that all-important journey. Without this journey, our inner demons can remain unattended, and all our creativity can easily go to war, death, and destruction, serving only ego power, nationalism, or other idols. With it, we might harness our creative technology to serve the earth, the children, the future, and ourselves.

Merton complains about the "fiery chariots" of technocracy —

Grand machines, all flame,
With supernatural wings...

He tells us he much prefers the

old trailer ("My chariot")....
Bring me
My old chariot of broken-down rain.

Merton was also suspect of technology because, as Labrie puts it, "the right arm of technocracy is war." Merton reacted sarcastically to warocracy when he wrote:

I hear they are working on a bomb that will destroy nothing but life. Men, animals, birds, perhaps also vegetation. But it will leave buildings, factories, railways, natural resources.

Only one further step, and the weapon will be one of absolute perfection. It should destroy books, works of art, musical instruments, toys, tools and gardens, but not destroy flags, weapons, gallows, electric chairs, gas chambers, instruments of torture or plenty of strait jackets in case someone should accidentally survive. Then the era of love can finally begin. Atheistic humanism can take over.

He sees insanity ruling in a purely technocratic response to life. Of course, Merton lived during the height of the Cold War and witnessed the most severe standoffs between the United States and the Soviet Union, which he referred to when writing: "That is why we must not be deceived by the giants and by their thunderous denunciations of one another, their preparations for mutual destruction. The fact that they are powerful does not mean that they are sane, and the fact that they speak with intense conviction does not mean that they speak the truth." He mocked the technology of the ovens used in the Holocaust and composed a "Chant to be used in processions around a site with furnaces," which ends with this warning: "Do not think yourself better because you burn up friends and enemies with long-range missiles without ever seeing what you have done."

Very near to the monastery of Gethsemani is the large military base Fort Knox. The irony of this did not go unremarked upon by Merton. He often observed giant planes flying low overhead en route to landing at the military base while he was out working or meditating in the fields. It was in this context that Merton wrote the poem "The Guns of Fort Knox."

Guns at the camp (I hear them suddenly)
Guns make the little houses jump. I feel
Explosions in my feet, through boards.
Wars work under the floor. Wars
Dance in the foundations. Trees

Must also feel the guns they do not want
Even in their core.

Here Merton contrasts war technology with nature (the trees).
Technology can be the enemy of nature — and of hermits, since
the roar of the planes shakes the floor of his hermitage.

Merton composed a modern morality play called *The Tower of
Babel* wherein the tower symbolizes the arrogance of technology
and the victimization of language that follows inevitably in a culture in which communication is primarily mechanical. Language
becomes, he writes, an "instrument of war. Words of the clocks
and devils. Words of the wheels and machines. Steel words stronger than flesh or spirit. Secret words which divide the essence of
things." Is another word for "secret words" the esoteric and privileged language of the professionals of a culture who alone know
the secrets behind their professional and elitist craft?

Merton's suspicion toward technology was in great part fu-
eled by World War II and its many atrocities, especially those
suffered by civilian populations. He faults the Allies as well as
the Axis powers on this score. The atomic bomb is on his mind
continuously. But so, too, is the Holocaust and the demonic way
in which technology was employed on behalf of that project of
genocide. In a journal entry reflecting on French philosopher
Gabriel Marcel and what he calls "Eschatological Conscience,"
Merton talks of the "refusal to accept mass-mind, technological
'unity' etc." and an "awareness of concentration camp as figures
of the world to come (under technology)."

No doubt, today, Merton would have a field day with current "advancements" in technology, from computers and iPhones
to drones for surveillance and killing at a distance, and more. In
his study on the Desert Fathers he tells us why he admires them.
Their wisdom is "at once primitive and timeless, and...enables
us to reopen the sources that have been polluted or blocked up

altogether by the accumulated mental and spiritual refuse of our technological barbarism. Our time is in desperate need of this kind of simplicity.... The word to emphasize is *experience*." Calling technology "barbarism" is strong criticism indeed.

Late in his life, Merton learned something of the advantageous side of technology. He had a back problem that was relieved by a surgical intervention that inserted a piece of metal near his cervical disc. In 1967 he published a poem commemorating that experience entitled "With the World in My Bloodstream," in which he celebrated "the technical community of men."

In his letters to Rosemary Ruether, Merton addressed the use of technology in a slightly more nuanced way. Technology, he wrote, "is not evil, but it is not beyond all criticism either. If used cynically and opportunistically for power and wealth, it becomes a disastrous weapon *against* humanity and is the instrument by which the demons crush and humiliate and destroy humanity. Witness the Vietnam war." In a 1965 article, he cautioned that "the mere rejection of modern technology as an absolute and irremediable evil will not solve any problems. The harm done by technology is attributable more to its excessive and inordinately hasty development then to technology itself. It is possible that in the future a technological society *might* conceivably be a tranquil and contemplative one." He then called for "a wisdom appropriate to our own predicament: and such wisdom cannot help but begin in sorrow."

Merton often critiqued technology, which was a very important issue for him. In fact, one of the papers he mailed me a few months before he died was titled "Technology," and in it he made the following notes:

> When the acceleration becomes such that efficiency and progress become ends rather than means — then you have the technological revolution.... This results in a climate of

practicality for its own sake and a contempt for value and for principle.... The questions asked are not "is this right," "is this good," but "will this work," and "will it pay off?" "Will it increase our profits?"

Note effect of this mentality for example in mass media — results in giving the public what it wants in order to get the public's money.

Merton sees a need "to restore to technological man a true contact with his own human and spiritual ground, his own neglected inner resources: to help awake in others their creative and personal potential...helping modern man to develop an inner awareness, not in terms of knowledge of doctrines, but in terms of personal inner experience." He reproduces ample quotes from US Navy admiral H. G. Rickover's article "A Humanistic Technology," which includes observations about the price we pay for anthropocentrism. Writes Rickover:

I can find no evidence that man contributes anything to the balance of nature — anything at all. On the strength of his knowledge of nature, he sets himself above nature; he presumes to change the natural environment for *all* the living creatures of this earth. Do we, who are transient and not overly wise, really believe we have the right to upset the order of nature, an order established by a power higher than man?

It cannot be said too often that government has as much a duty to protect the land, the air, the water, the natural environment of man against such damage, as it has to protect the country against foreign enemies and the individual agent against criminals.

It is striking to see this military man stand up for the environment as much as against ideological foes. Merton observes that the "important principle" is this: "The true renewal of the world must spring from God's love and from the new creation, not from Faustian love of power."

Merton on Racism

The closeness of Merton to his friend John Howard Griffin is evidence of his keen interest in issues of racism in American culture. Griffin wrote the classic work *Black Like Me*, in which he described how, after taking a drug that darkened his skin, he traveled through the South to learn how people of color were treated. Griffin frequently visited Gethsemani to spend time with Merton. Griffin spent much of his life in France, was a member of the French resistance during World War II, and studied with the Catholic philosopher Jacques Maritain. After Merton's death, the board of trustees of the Merton Center chose Griffin to be his official biographer, though Griffin died before he could complete the assignment.

In a journal entry in July 1961, Merton cited Protestant theologian Reinhold Niebuhr: "Race pride is revealed today as man's primary *collective* [double underlined] sin" (brackets in original). Merton spoke out on Dr. Martin Luther King Jr., who was, in Merton's day, still very much a controversial figure.

> Martin Luther King, who is no fanatic but a true Christian, writes a damning letter from Birmingham jail, saying that the churches have utterly failed the Negro. In the end, that is what the Black Muslims are saying too. And there is truth in it. Not that there is not a certain amount of liberal and sincere concern for civil rights among Christians, even among ministers, priests, and bishops. But what is this sincerity worth? What does this "good will" amount to? Is it anything more than a spiritual luxury to calm the conscience of those who cultivate it? What good does it do the Negro? What good does it do the country? Is it a pure evasion of reality?

Sometimes, Merton warned, sincerity alone is not enough. It can be

> so subjective and so ineffectual as to be worse than mean-
> ingless. It is a personal luxury, which enables the individual
> to feel concern — without doing anything.

Merton commented on the news in May 1963:

> Much trouble in the South, Alabama. Negroes demonstrat-
> ing, cops turning fire hoses on them, getting after them with
> police dogs. The character of the Negro demonstrations is
> religious and non-violent, concerns mostly their right to
> vote or rather the right to use their right to vote. Pictures of
> fat-arsed police, grin[ning], stupid and "efficient," arresting
> Negroes, dragging them off. Three of them after a Negro
> woman whom they have flat on her back one with a knee in
> her neck. She was, it is alleged, "pushing" the police.

The story evokes déjà vu even fifty-two years later.

Merton on Sanity and Social Conformity

In *Raids on the Unspeakable*, Merton commented on the 1961 trial
of Nazi officer Adolf Eichmann for his role in the Holocaust.
Merton used the occasion to criticize the notion of "sanity" in our
time and culture and the obedience that so-called sanity requires.
"It all comes under the heading of duty, self-sacrifice, and obedience. Eichmann was devoted to duty, and proud of his job. The
sanity of Eichmann is disturbing. We equate sanity with a sense
of justice, with humaneness, with prudence, with the capacity to
love and understand other people.... Now it begins to dawn on
us that it is precisely the *sane* ones who are the most dangerous."
    Merton then turned from Eichmann and the atrocities of the
Holocaust to identify a similar definition of "sanity" in modern
culture:

It is the sane ones, the well-adapted ones, who can without qualms and without nausea aim the missiles and press the buttons that will initiate the great festival of destruction that they, *the sane ones*, have prepared.... No one suspects the sane, and the sane ones will have *perfectly good reasons*, logical, well-adjusted reasons, for firing the shot. They will be obeying sane orders that have come sanely down the chain of command.

What then is sanity?

We can no longer assume that because a man is "sane" he is therefore in his "right mind." The whole concept of sanity in a society where spiritual values have lost their meaning is itself meaningless.... And so I ask myself: what is the meaning of a concept of sanity that excludes love, considers it irrelevant, and destroys our capacity to love other human beings, to respond to their needs and their sufferings, to recognize them also as persons, to apprehend their pain as one's own? Evidently this is not necessary for "sanity" at all.

Merton did not elevate obedience as a cardinal virtue. Consider this passage from his book *Conjectures of a Guilty Bystander*: "A Spirituality that preaches resignation under official brutalities, servile acquiescence in frustration and sterility, and total submission to organized injustice is one which has lost interest in holiness and remains concerned only with a spurious notion of 'order.'" Say good-bye to fascism, he is saying, which is a "spurious notion of order," indeed.

In the same vein, Merton critiqued the social conformity and culture of denial that was promoted by the media, warning that those who read *Time* and "fit in painlessly" are usually "one-dimensional," in the sense that Marcuse writes about in *One-Dimensional Man*. Merton warned about the "New Lords of

Things as They Are" who "possess and control the major means of mass communication." This alert seems to parallel the study I was undertaking in Paris on Henry Luce and his media empire. Merton gave notice to educators in the following letter:

> A Christian must be seriously concerned with the ruthlessness and indifference to ruthlessness that are possible in an advanced technological society when the major means of mass communication are monopolized by a small group representing similar economic, political and social interests. . . . Mass media is presently being consciously employed to hide the lot of the nations' victims behind a glittering Niagara of Trivia.

Has the "glittering Niagara of Trivia" diminished since Merton wrote these words in the midsixties? Hardly. Today we live in an avalanche of trivia fed by the Murdoch empire, Twitter, the internet, and more.

Merton on Living Marginally

To be a champion of interfaith in Merton's day was not an easy thing. As he wrote in his *Asian Journal*, "My interest in Buddhism has disturbed some of the Catholics, clergy and religious. They wonder what there can be in it." He tells the story of how, when he visited the great Buddhist shrine in Ceylon where he had his deep experience of enlightenment, the vicar general with whom he was traveling chose to sit under a tree and read a guidebook rather than join him at the shrine because he shied away from "paganism." No doubt Merton was breaking new ground in 1968, as was Dom Aelred Graham, whose book *Zen Catholicism* was a breakthrough ecumenical book in the sixties and which I read during my training as a Dominican. Several times Merton gives credit to Graham for his mentorship, and indeed, Graham helped Merton make several contacts on his Asia trip.

It was not just his ecumenism or interfaith stance that put Merton at the edge, but he was explicit that he felt that being an outsider was part and parcel of the monastic vocation. In an informal talk in Calcutta in October 1968, he said:

> In speaking for monks I am really speaking for a very strange kind of person, a marginal person, because the monk in the modern world is no longer an established person with an established place in society. We realize very keenly in America today that the monk is essentially outside of all establishments. He does not belong to an establishment. He is a marginal person who withdraws deliberately to the margin of society with a view to deepening fundamental human experience.

The mature Merton did not separate the Via Negativa (solitude) from the Via Transformativa. He wrote that the contemplative life

> must not be construed as an escape from time and matter, from social responsibility and from the life of sense, but rather, as an advance into solitude and the desert, a confrontation with poverty and the void, a renunciation of the empirical self, in the presence of death, and nothingness, in order to overcome the ignorance and error that spring from the fear of "being nothing." The man who dares to be alone can come to see that the "emptiness" and "uselessness" which the collective mind fears and condemns are necessary conditions for the encounter with truth.

The language here is pure Eckhartian, as are the concepts and the teachings. Merton is, at heart, a Dominican, for he insists on the marriage of contemplation and action and also on the deep emptying and poverty and kenosis of the Via Negativa that monks know about. Laypeople know about this, too.

Merton compared the monastic vocation to that of hippies and poets.

I find myself representing perhaps hippies among you, poets, people of this kind who are seeking in all sorts of ways and have absolutely no established status whatever.... Are monks and hippies and poets relevant? No, we are deliberately irrelevant. We live with an ingrained irrelevance which is proper to every human being. The marginal man accepts the basic irrelevance of the human condition, an irrelevance which is manifested above all by the fact of death. The marginal person, the monk, the displaced person, the prisoner, all these people live in the presence of death, which calls into question the meaning of life.

The work of all these people is "to go beyond death even in this life, to go beyond the dichotomy of life and death and to be, therefore, a witness to life." Connecting the monastic vocation to that of poets and hippies in the late sixties was not a sure way to make friends and influence people among the, shall we say, establishment types. Merton was, once again, sticking his neck out. He acknowledged that part of his vocation as a monk was to offer "iconoclastic criticism" of how culture was operating. This is a way of talking about the prophetic dimension to his vocation.

Merton's talk on "Karl Marx and Monasticism" proved to be his last talk ever, since he died a few hours after delivering the lecture. In it he defined compassion this way: "The whole idea of compassion is based on a keen awareness of the interdependence of all these living beings, which are all part of one another and all involved in one another." I was so taken with this definition of compassion and its ground in interdependence that I chose this sentence as the frontispiece for my book *A Spirituality Named Compassion*, which was first published in 1979. It flows from Eckhart's statement that "what happens to another, whether it be a joy or a sorrow, happens to me." Eckhart, too, speaks of interdependence as the basis of compassion.

In the same talk, Merton invoked Herbert Marcuse's book *One-Dimensional Man*. He urged the monks to read it, and he acknowledged the student riots happening in the 1960s and how much they were due to the crisis of values that Marcuse names. "Marcuse's theory is that all highly organized technological societies, as we have them now, all so-called managerial societies, as found both in the United States and in the Soviet Union, end up by being equally totalitarian in one way or another." He admitted that he "agrees with it somewhat," and he invoked the rioting students themselves. "Marcuse and the students who are revolting in the universities contend that, in fact, significant choices can no longer be made in the kind of organized society you have either under capitalism or under soviet socialism. The choices that are really important have all been made before you get around to trying it yourself." Merton told the story of running into university students at the Center for the Study of Democratic Institutions at the University of California at Santa Barbara on his journey to Asia. During a break in the proceedings, Merton introduced himself as a monk. To which "one of the French revolutionary student leaders immediately said: 'We are monks also.'"

Merton did not react defensively to this surprise assertion from the student rebels. Rather, he later remarked to a room full of monks that "the monk is essentially someone who takes up a critical attitude toward the world and its structures, just as these students identify themselves essentially as people who have taken up a critical attitude toward the contemporary world and its structures.... The monk is somebody who says, in one way or another, that the claims of the world are fraudulent." This story is especially meaningful to me, since at this very time, during my studies in Paris, I too was meeting such revolutionary students and finding common ground with them and their fight over cultural values. They and I were also studying Herbert Marcuse.

Indeed, in 1968, student riots were happening worldwide, from Berkeley, California, to Madison, Wisconsin, and from Santa Barbara to Paris and Berlin. But not every teacher or monk who witnessed them was sympathetic to the voices and concerns of youth. One who wasn't was Joseph Ratzinger. When students broke into a faculty meeting in Tübingen, Germany, and ranted and raved about the need for reform in education, all but one of the faculty members stayed to listen to the young people vent. Ratzinger was the only one to leave, and the next time he was seen he had become an arch conservative (a "conversion" that I discuss in my book *The Pope's War*). What is clear is that Merton did not fear the young. Nor did my mentor, Pere Chenu, who that spring urged us students in Paris not to come to class the next week but instead to "join the revolution and come back in two weeks and tell me what you have contributed." This was a chance, he said, "to make history and not just study it." He was seventy-five years old at the time; Ratzinger was forty-two.

Thomas Merton, Meister Eckhart, and Karl Marx

Not only did Thomas Merton dare to speak at the height of the Vietnam War in Southeast Asia about Karl Marx, but there is also a deep connection between Karl Marx and Meister Eckhart (which I write about in some depth in *Wrestling with the Prophets*). Marxist psychiatrist Erich Fromm observed that "Eckhart has described and analyzed the difference between the having and being modes of existence with a penetration and clarity not surpassed by any teacher." Meanwhile, Eckhartian scholar Reiner Schurmann said, "To a healthy number of Marxists, Meister Eckhart appears as the theoretician of the class struggle in the Middle Ages." His is a "mysticism of the left" that "would designate the appropriation of man of his authentic good when he is alienated by the dogma of an inaccessible heaven." Marxist philosopher Ernst Bloch wrote, "In Eckhart the heretical, antiecclesiastical lay movement of the late Middle ages became articulate in German, which is a decisive factor in any socialist evaluation." Bloch credits Eckhart with demystifying the economic and political facts of life for the "common people" he inspired "in the revolutions of the next two centuries," including the Hussites and Thomas Müntzer in the German Peasants' War.

Eckhart was the first major intellectual to preach in the vernacular German, which was a series of peasant dialects at the time — he spoke clearly and consciously to the poor and about their "nobility" on a regular basis. He also supported the Beguines, who were the women's movement of his day. Pope John XXII was so threatened by the Beguine movement that he condemned it seventeen times (he was the same pope who condemned Eckhart after he died). Interestingly enough, Merton mentioned the Beguines in a cryptic note in his journal: "Nazareth, Beguines, mystics of the Rhineland, beginning of the modern consciousness." How are Jesus, the Beguines, and the mystics of the Rhineland (Eckhart included) the beginning of modern consciousness? Merton does not elaborate. But in the same piece he also spoke out on the dangers of power: "The promise of God to the poor or the promises of the beast to the rich? Judgment of power. Ecclesiastical power. Power prevents renewal. Power prevents real change."

At the heart of Eckhart's Marxist-like critique of society are seven of Eckhart's principles: 1) a realized eschatology. That is, the idea that we are not here to barter our way to heaven in an afterlife but to live out eternal life here and now. This principle was also very important to Merton, who wrote: "I am coming to see clearly the great importance of the concept of 'realized eschatology' — the transformation of life and of human relations by Christ now.... Realized eschatology is the heart of genuine Christian humanism and hence its tremendous importance for the Christian peace effort for example." 2) The spiritual journey culminates in a return to the world, not a flight from it. Or in Eckhart's words, "in contemplation you serve only yourself, in good works you serve many people." 3) Salvation is a we, not an I, concept, as Eckhart wrote: "God has been the common Savior of the entire world, and for this I am indebted to him with much more thanks than if he had saved only me." 4) By championing an Apophatic Divinity and our capacity for letting go — even of our names for God — Eckhart encourages radical starting over. "I pray God to rid me of God," he says. 5) The "Kingdom of God" theme is personalized with Eckhart — we are all to undergo it — and he does not confuse church with Kingdom of God. 6) Eckhart rejects dualisms and displaces theism with political panentheism. 7) Marx objected to philosophers who contemplate and gaze at the world as an object, but he instead insisted that we must change the world. Eckhart also rejected contemplation as mere gazing at. Reiner Schurmann wrote that Eckhart's is not "a theoretical dogma of what man is, but...a practical guide to what he must become." His spirituality "is not oriented towards contemplation. It produces a new birth: the birth of the Son." It is oriented therefore toward a creativity that brings about a real birth of justice and compassion.

Three of Eckhart's teachings deal with social and economic injustice, which Marx was to address in his fashion five centuries later. The first is Eckhart's teaching on "the merchant mentality." We all become "mere merchants" in Eckhart's understanding if we do even pious works in order to get "something in return" from God. A mercenary or a serf is one who "seeks something with their works" and works "for a Why or Wherefore." He adds: "Truth needs no huckstering. God does not seek His own ends; in all His works He is free and untrammeled, and performed them from true love. So does the person who is united with God: Such a one is free and untrammeled in all his or her actions and performs them to the glory of God alone." He castigates those who relate to God as they do to a cow — "for the milk and cheese and profit it makes them. This is how it is with people who love God for the sake of outward wealth or inward comfort."

A merchant mentality leads us down a false path of ownership, whereas in fact all in life is on loan. "Whether they are body and soul, sense, strength, external goods or honors, friends, relations, house, hall, everything in fact," Eckhart wrote. Eckhart introduced a concept that Marx was later to build on — that of alienation — when he warned: "If a person's work is to live, it must come from the depths of him — not from alien sources outside himself — but from within." Instead of grabbing, hoarding, possessing, clinging, Eckhart teaches letting go (*Abgeschiedenheit*) and letting be (*Gelassenheit*). When we learn these practices, we move beyond materialistic addiction and ego aggrandizement.

Merton speaks against the merchandising mentality when he talks about people selling us the rain.

> Let me say this before rain becomes a utility that they can plan and distribute for money. By "they" I mean the people who cannot understand that rain is a festival, who do not appreciate its gratuity, who think that what has no price has no value, that what cannot be sold is not real so that the only way to make something *actual* is to place it on the market. The time will come when they will sell you even your rain. At the moment it is still free and I am in it. I celebrate its gratuity and its meaninglessness.

Here Merton certainly echoes Eckhart's teaching of living and loving "without a why."

In a second teaching, Eckhart speaks to the nobility of us all. He tells us, "Everyone is an Aristocrat." In everyone is an "inward person, whom the Scriptures call the new person, the heavenly person, the young person, the friend, and the noble person."

In Eckhart's day and place, everyone knew who an "aristocrat" was — they had "von" before their name. So Eckhart directly challenged that societal status of privilege by saying, in the vernacular dialect no less, that we are all aristocrats and noble people. In one teaching he turned peasants into nobles to point out that "no one is nobler than you"; that is, all people are equal because all are equally noble. "How nobly man is constituted by nature, and how divine is the state to which he can come by grace." After all, "What our Lord calls a nobleman the prophet calls a great eagle. Who then is nobler than he who is born, on one hand of the highest and the best that the creature has, and on the other hand from the inmost ground of the Divine nature and of His desert?" In the original, Eckhart uses word play, since in German the word for "eagle" (*Adler*) and for "noble" (*Edler*) are very similar. We all carry the seed of the Divine within us. "The seed of God is in us.... The seed of a pear tree grows into a pear tree, a hazel seed into a hazel tree, a seed of God into God." Ernst Bloch noted the profound political implications of this teaching:

> One thing is certain: Eckhart's sermon does not intend to snuff man out for the sake of an Otherworld beyond him:...
> The revolutionary Anabaptists, those disciples of Eckhart and Tauler, showed afterwards in practice exactly how highly and how uncomfortably for every tyrant. A subject who thought himself to be in personal union with the Lord of Lords provided, when things got serious, a very poor example indeed of serfhood.

Like Merton, Eckhart speaks of the interdependence of all things that lies at the heart of compassion. "All creatures are interdependent," Eckhart declared. Thus Bloch says that "*anima mea anima nostra* [my soul is our soul] has seldom or never been so highly thought of" as in Meister Eckhart's mysticism. The redemption of one is the redemption of all.

This summary of Eckhart's influence on Marx shows how thoroughly present Eckhart is in Merton's final talk, where he cites Herbert Marcuse and Ludwig Feuerbach (who also influenced Marx on religion) and others. Once again, Merton and Eckhart are at work together — even in Merton's last words — this time in the Via Transformativa.

Further underscoring Thomas Merton's commitment to the Via Transformativa are his relationships with Daniel and Philip Berrigan, protesters of the Vietnam War, and Dorothy Day, another Catholic activist. Both Day and the Berrigan brothers made many trips to jail as a result of their public protest, and all cherished their relationship with Thomas Merton. They found strong support and inspiration in his writings and in his person to walk their talk no matter where it led them. The fact that Peter Marin, the cofounder of the Catholic Worker Movement with Dorothy Day, was a Frenchman probably also played no small part in the Day/Merton relationship. In May 1968, Merton wrote in his journal:

> Somewhere, when I was in some plane or in some canyon, Dan and Phil Berrigan and some others took A-1 draft files from a draft center in a Baltimore suburb and burned them in a parking lot. Somewhere I heard they were arrested but I've seen no paper and don't know anything, but an envelope came from Dan with a text of a preface to his new book, evidently on the Hanoi trip, saying he was going to do this. It was mailed from Baltimore, May 17th, and had scrawled on it, "Wish us luck."

Did Merton Die a Martyr?

I cannot in conscience speak of Merton's witness to the Via Transformativa without discussing his death. To put this delicate subject bluntly: Was Merton murdered by the American government?

There is, in my opinion, considerable circumstantial evidence that this was so, in which case Merton died a martyr to the peace cause.

Merton was the first religious figure in America to come out strongly against the Vietnam War. Martin Luther King spoke out against the war, but after Merton. I am told that many of Merton's monks, on hearing of his sudden death, felt he was assassinated. Why? Because they knew that Merton, like King, had been getting hate mail from government agencies for years. After their burning of draft records in Baltimore in 1968, the Berrigan brothers were also pursued by the FBI, and Merton's mentorship to the Berrigans was no secret.

Journalist and Merton aficionado Robert Grip, using a request through the Freedom of Information Act, found that "the FBI did indeed have a file on Merton, complete with anonymous tips and reports on his letter of recommendation to a young man requesting conscientious objector status from the military draft." The CIA intercepted a letter Merton wrote to Russian author Boris Pasternak, "an intercept that was illegal at the time." So both the FBI and the CIA were on Merton's trail.

Then, there is the incident itself. Supposedly, Merton stepped out of a shower in the retreat center in Bangkok, and while still soaking wet, he plugged a fan into the wall and was electrocuted. Who would be that careless? People who knew Merton told me his personality most resembled that of a "New York taxi driver." Merton was not some abstract professor lost in the clouds. Merton's fellow monk Brother Patrick tells us that someone came onto the scene after the fact, plugged in the fan, and got a shock; the fan had a short in it. Fine. But how did the fan get a short in it? Presumably, Merton had used the fan before and it hadn't shocked him. Some say: "Oh, but it was a third-world building. Anything could happen." But I have seen the television program produced by Dutch television of Merton's last speech. The retreat center building was practically brand new and solidly constructed of concrete blocks.

Furthermore, and most importantly, I asked a CIA agent who was in Southeast Asia at the time: "Did you guys kill Thomas Merton?" His answer: "I will neither affirm it nor deny it." Why didn't he just say, "No, of course not"? I then asked: "Could you have?" His reply: "A piece of cake. The retreat center had no security to speak of." A friend of mine asked another CIA agent who was operating in Southeast Asia at the time if they killed Merton. The agent responded that he did not know, but since the CIA in Southeast Asia was "flooded with cash" at that time, and they were very much without supervision or accountability, a CIA agent who felt Merton was a threat to the American cause could have easily had him eliminated with no questions asked.

Merton died on December 10, 1968: at this time, things were at their hottest in the anti–Vietnam War protests in the United States, Paris, Germany, and around the world. Earlier that summer, during the famous riots at the Democratic National Convention in Chicago, police freely beat war protesters (including many priests and nuns). That same year, Dr. Martin Luther King Jr., who had also come out against the Vietnam War, had been murdered on April 4, and Robert Kennedy had been assassinated on June 6. These assassinations followed those of Malcolm X in 1965 and President John F. Kennedy in 1963. Plus, in what I would call a rather naïve monkish fashion, Merton was traveling through Southeast Asia asking people *in English*, "I am giving a talk on Karl Marx and monasticism. Have any ideas?" Since Karl Marx is considered the "father of communism," and the whole rationale for the Vietnam War was to prevent the spread of communism in Southeast Asia, Merton was clearly on another side of the fence from the US government.

Merton's opinions about the CIA were pretty clear. He called them "strange," "stupid," "fools," and "idiots," as in this journal entry from September 1965:

> It is said that the war in Kashmir is due in part to some machinations of the CIA. This is a very strange outfit from what I hear, and in some ways typical of what is ill about America. It appears to be monumentally stupid in the first place! What this country has to suffer from fools in government! But since it is the most powerful country in the world the whole world is endangered by the folly of these idiots.

No autopsy was done on Merton's body. And, strange to tell, his body was flown back to the United States on a CIA plane along with deceased American soldiers. In Oakland, California, his body was transferred to a commercial jet liner for the trip home to Kentucky. The irony of this was caught by Merton himself. In his last work, *The Geography of Lograire*, he wrote:

> Same is the Ziggurat of everywhere
> I am one same burned Indian
> Purple of my rivers is the same shed blood
> All is flooded
> All is my Vietnam charred.

Given all this circumstantial evidence, I think it is naïve not to be asking the question. Perhaps we will never know whether or not Merton died a martyr at the hands of the American government. But it is very possible he did. I believe he did.

CHAPTER EIGHT

"A *readable* theologian is dangerous"

Merton on the "Heresies" of Feminism

I sometimes wonder why Rahner is considered so dangerous. Perhaps because he is too clear and not involved in the technical mumbo jumbo that makes others unreadable. In a word: a readable *theologian is dangerous.*

— THOMAS MERTON

I n the 1980s, when Cardinal Joseph Ratzinger was head of the Congregation of the Faith — and before he became Pope Benedict XVI in 2005 — he called my work "dangerous and deviant" and listed seven objections to my theology. Eventually, conflicts over these seven so-called heresies and other disagreements with the Catholic Church led to my expulsion from the Dominican Order in 1993. Needless to say, I do not see Cardinal Ratzinger's seven objections as heresies at all. Rather, to me, they became a sort of Rorschach test of what the Vatican, quite ignorant of the Creation Spirituality tradition under the previous two popes, was misbelieving and projecting onto myself and others.

However, in the context of this book, this raises an interesting question: What would Thomas Merton have said about these so-called heresies? And what would he have done if he had lived long enough to undergo the return of the Inquisition that occurred under Pope John Paul II with Cardinal Ratzinger as its head? Might similar objections have been brought against Merton's teachings?

To answer this question I will put Merton in the inquisitorial docket with me in the next two chapters, since as we've seen, in the last decade of his life, Thomas Merton espoused a creation-centered spirituality himself. If he had lived, he might very well have faced censure over certain views from the Catholic Church. So, in this and the next chapter, I will address these seven so-called heresies, and I will bring Merton, and Meister Eckhart, into the conversation to consider how they would have responded.

By the early 1960s, German Jesuit priest Karl Rahner also drew the ire of the Vatican fundamentalists over some of his "radical" teachings, though he, like so many theologians prior to the Second Vatican Council, was eventually a theological leader at that very council, which was called by Pope John XXIII from 1962 to 1965. In July 1963, Merton offered his take on the heresy hunters who were going after the very respected German Jesuit theologian Karl Rahner: "I am reading Karl Rahner's essays on grace.... They seem clear and obvious. I sometimes wonder why Rahner is considered so dangerous. Perhaps because he is too clear and not involved in the technical mumbo jumbo that makes others unreadable. In a word: a *readable* theologian is dangerous."

Heresy #1: "Matthew Fox Is a Feminist Theologian"

I did not know then and I do not believe now that being a feminist theologian — or any other kind of feminist — is a heresy. In fact, I would propose that Jesus in his day was a feminist. He shocked the world and the religion of his time by the sense of equality that characterized his interactions with women. He was far from patriarchal attitudes and thinking. He came out of the Wisdom tradition, which meant that he sought the God experience primarily in nature. As feminist anthropologist Marija Gimbutas put it, the whole meaning of the Divine Feminine is that "the Goddess in all her manifestations was a symbol of the unity of all life in Nature." Furthermore, the word *wisdom* in the Bible in both Greek and Hebrew is feminine. Paul, the first Christian theologian and the first writer in the Christian Bible, calls Christ "Sophia" or "Lady Wisdom" on several occasions. Biblical scholars of our time (many of them women, but not all) have pointed out how much of Jesus's teachings were of a feminist philosophy, which is a non-dualist philosophy. Some of these teachings were downright subversive toward patriarchy and its institutions, such as his teaching that Torah is to be taught to women.

In the earliest generation of the Christian movement, women held positions of leadership, as is clear in Paul's letters, among other places. In addition, New Testament scholar Bruce Chilton, in his important book *Mary Magdalene: A Biography*, argues strongly that the closeness of Jesus and Mary and her gifts of a healing ministry gave birth to Jesus's decision to leave the tradition of healing and anointing in Mary's hands. He concludes therefore that Mary Magdalene was the source of the entire sacramental system that unfolded and developed as the church evolved.

Feminism Equals Compassion and Nondualism

What does feminism mean? Some see feminism as a philosophy of nondualism; others as a philosophy of relationship (Eckhart says relation is the "essence" of everything that exists); and others as nonviolence. I would add that feminism is the opposite of the reptilian brain, which sees life as win/lose and thus others as objects.

Feminism also includes nonsentimental compassion — I believe there is a reason that the words for *compassion* in both Hebrew and Arabic derive from the root word for *womb*. This is now supported by contemporary science, which tells us we possess both a 420-million-year-old reptilian brain along with a 210-million-year-old mammalian brain. Our mammalian brain stands out as a source of our kin- and family-oriented compassion, but of course it needs cultivating, and this is the work of authentic religion. It cannot be done without balancing the masculine and feminine energies. I treat the "sacred marriage" of the Divine Feminine and the Sacred Masculine in my book *The Hidden Spirituality of Men: Ten Metaphors to Awaken the Sacred Masculine*.

When Jesus says, "Be you compassionate as your Creator in heaven is compassionate" (Luke 6:36), he is teaching what the Buddha taught. As the Dalai Lama has put it, "We can do away with all religion but we can't do away with compassion. Compassion is my religion." It is no small thing that Buddhism, Taoism, Hinduism, Judaism, Islam, Christianity, and more speak regularly about bringing the compassionate brain alive. The history of religion, like the history of the rest of the human story, can be analyzed from the point of view of whether the reptilian brain (fight or flight) or the mammalian brain (compassion) is at work. It is clear which is dominant in today's world, in which the human species spends $58,000 per second on war and militarism, and we are destroying our Mother Earth. Says feminist theologian Dorothee Soelle: "To feed the hungry means to do away with militarism. To bless the children means to leave the trees standing for them." When patriarchal religion — as embodied by Cardinal Ratzinger's charge of heresy — denies feminism, it is denying the central message of Jesus's teaching, which is all about compassion. It is also denying justice (and "compassion means justice," as Eckhart says). Women have rights equal to men — or ought to.

A feminist philosophy offers a different attitude toward life
— and even toward dying — than does patriarchal philosophy.
A fine example of this is found in a poem by M. C. Richards, the
potter, painter, poet, and philosopher who is best known for her
classic work *Centering*, which is a treatise on how centering clay
on the wheel is not unlike the spiritual process of centering and
meditation. M. C. was on my faculty both at ICCS and later at the
University of Creation Spirituality for many years, and she was
a dearly beloved teacher to all of her students. When she learned
she was dying, she wrote a poem entitled "I Am Dying." I think
this poem movingly captures the difference between patriarchal
and feminist attitudes toward death.

> Four children are singing "ring around the rosy" here
> where I am drinking my morning coffee with hot milk.
> I was an English major in school —
> so many famous lines about death:
> "Death be not proud"!
> Such a masculine presence —
> part of our paternalistic culture — and religion.
> I relax into someone's arms.
> I feel a softness as of sleep,
> a gentleness that is friendly.
> The children are riding their bicycles through my room,
> They do not see me or the walls.
> I think of Eliot's Hollow Men
> "Is it like this," they ask
>   "In death's other kingdom —
>   walking alone when we are
>   trembling with tenderness,
>   lips that would kiss, form prayers to broken stone."
> Those lines brim with self-pity
>   and accusation —
> Like Thomas Hardy's "The terrible antilogy of

Making figments feel."
Oh no, now is not then.
I do not feel betrayed or bereft,
    it's more like the Chattanooga Choo Choo:
the great traffic of evolution
and I am carrying my bit of being
free of agenda —
            open to a future
Ready to experiment, be creative, serve
be beautiful, be real,
be nowhere
be no one I already know
be birthing myself
            waves and particles
backpacking in the hereafter.

Notice how M. C. takes on patriarchy and its levels of self-pity and reptilian-brain "accusations" amid feelings of betrayal and bereftness. Instead she is substituting a cosmic awareness — joining the caravan of evolution and cosmology, including waves and particles on a unique journey in the hereafter. Death is more familiar than hostile — much like relaxing, softness, gentleness. In many ways this is a poem about the mammalian brain versus the reptilian brain, and it is not just for women — it is for the womanly side of the male soul as well. I think Tom Merton and M. C. Richards would have gotten along famously. He would have especially enjoyed *Centering*, which names so well the reality of art as meditation.

Merton and Feminism

How did Thomas Merton treat the topic of feminism? Since he died in 1968, he had very little time to develop a fully coherent discourse on the subject — but that did not mean he was not fully engaged. He had a strong friendship with Sister Therese Lentfoehr and great respect for Rachel Carson; he sat at Carson's feet, so to speak, listening to her prophetic take on the eco-crisis as soon as her book came out. In his last journal, he refers to the "feminine mystique," so he was obviously aware of the emerging women's movement. He praised Flannery O'Connor's work to the skies. "When I read Flannery I don't think of Hemingway, or Katherine Anne Porter, or Sartre but rather of someone like Sophocles. What more can be said of a writer? I write her name with honor, for all the truth and all the craft with which she shows man's fall and his dishonor."

He criticized those who put women on a pedestal or stereotyped women as "passive" and "mysterious." Why? Because "everybody is mysterious and sometimes passive." And he applied this critique to contemplative nuns, since "women take an awful beating and have a very tough time in the Church." He said the nuns have "an absolute duty to rebel, for the good of the Church itself."

In his essay on the two versions of Prometheus, that of Hesiod and that of Aeschylus, Merton rejected the former and embraced the latter. Why? He felt Hesiod offered a "strange, ponderous fantasy of an aggressively male society! Woman comes from Zeus as a *punishment*, for in her 'everything is good but her heart.' Woman, the culminating penance in a life of labor and sorrow!" He wrote that in Hesiod "we find this darkness, this oppressive and guilty view that life and love are somehow a punishment. That nothing can ever be really good in it. That life is slavery and sorrow...nothing but a wheel upon which man is broken like a slave." This language comes very close to the terms I use when distinguishing the Fall/redemption religion versus Creation Spirituality. Merton concluded: "Hesiod is a great poet and yet his view of life is cold, negative and odious. In any case I hate it."

In contrast, "the Prometheus of Aeschylus is the exact opposite of the Prometheus of Hesiod." Prometheus, the Earth Mother, and the Ocean have a good relationship, but Zeus tries to destroy it. Prometheus's rebellion "is the rebellion of life against inertia and death, of mercy and love against tyranny, of humanity against cruelty and arbitrary violence. And he calls upon the feminine, the wordless, the timelessly moving element to witness his sufferings. Earth hears him." Here Merton presents a feminist philosophy in opposition to a patriarchal one.

Merton also developed a very rich correspondence with a young and budding feminist theologian. I am speaking of Rosemary Ruether, whom I hired to be on my faculty both at Barat College and at the Institute in Culture and Creation Spirituality at Mundelein College in Chicago. Their correspondence took place over an eighteen-month period and started when Rosemary was a twenty-nine-year-old teacher at Howard University, a black theological seminary, in Washington, DC. The last letter from Merton was written on February 28, 1968, ten months before his death.

The exchange is quite remarkable for a number of reasons. One is the difference in age (Merton was then fifty-two and Ruether twenty-nine) and the difference in settings — Merton lived in a wooded hermitage and monastery, and Ruether worked in urban churches. The issues they discussed included race, poverty, and militarism. In a recent reflection on the correspondence, Ruether remarks that she felt Merton was facing the "next stage of his life" and that he was conflicted by the demands of his abbot and his order. She comments:

> What comes across in these letters is that, although we were
> separated by more than twenty years in age, he as a sea-
> soned thinker and I as a neophyte, Merton from the begin-
> ning addressed me as an equal. (This did not surprise me
> at the time since I saw myself as an equal, but it is more

impressive in retrospect.) Occasionally he assumed the stance of subordinate asking me to be his teacher or even confessor. But never did he take the paternalistic stance as the father addressing the child which is more typical of the cleric, especially in relation to women.

Ruether tells us that her intention in entering the dialogue with Merton was to discover "whether it was in fact, actually possible to be a Roman Catholic and to be a person of integrity." She admits to a kind of "ruthless questioning of Merton's own integrity." Ruether confronted Merton on a number of occasions; he was clearly engaged and willing to learn from this younger woman. Ruether once wrote to him: "I am really kind of disappointed in you. Do you realize how defensive you are, how you are forever proving, proving how good your life is, etc. You really won't hear the kind of balance that I am trying to establish in my letters, but immediately distort it into your own caricatures, so that you can again have the riposte. I'm not interested in any of that." Elsewhere, she addressed one of his points about the wilderness: "We do not bring paradise out of the wilderness by taking off to the hills, but by struggling with the principalities and powers where they really are, and it is only in this way that paradise is brought out of the wilderness, the real and not the figurative wilderness." But Merton became feisty, too. He stood up to her seeming putdown of rural people: "This is not 'sub-human nature' out here, it is farm country, and farmers are people with the same crucial twentieth century problems as everybody else. Also tree planting and reforestation are not simply sentimental gestures in a region that has been ravaged by the coal and lumber companies."

Merton invoked his monastic experience as a creation-centered one, writing: "I am so far from being 'an ascetic' that I am in many ways an anti-ascetic humanist." By calling himself an "anti-ascetic," Merton has traveled quite far. It also calls into question his suggestion to me in 1967 that I should study ascetic theology, a piece of advice that I did not take to heart.

In the letter, Merton further explained his monastic life:

One of the things in monasticism that has always meant most to me is that monastic life is in closer contact with God's good creation and is in many ways simpler, saner, and more human than life in the supposedly comfortable, pleasurable world. One of the things I love about my life, and therefore, one of the reasons why I would not change it for anything, is the fact that I live in the woods and according to a tempo of sun and moon and season in which it is naturally easy and possible to walk in God's light, so to speak, in and through his creation.... Monks are, and I am, in my own mind, the remnant of desperate conservationists. You ought to know what hundreds of pine saplings I have planted, myself and with the novices, only to see them bulldozed by some ass a year later.... This loving care for natural creatures becomes, in some sense, a warrant of his [the monk's] theological mission and ministry as a man of contemplation, I refuse in practice to accept any theory or method of contemplation that simply divides soul against body, interior against exterior, and then tries to transcend itself by pushing creatures out into the dark. What dark? As soon as the split is made the dark is abysmal in everything and the only way to get back into the light is to be once again a normal human being who likes to smell the flowers and look at girls, if they are around, and who likes the clouds, etc.

Merton's critique of asceticism is much in the vein of my own in *Original Blessing*, where I put "aesthetic" ahead of "ascetic" in a creation-centered spirituality. Rabbi Heschel reinforces this, since he did not believe that the prophets were ascetic. How then can we develop a prophetic awareness and action out of asceticism? In the prophet's work, much asceticism is built in — when you make enemies with the powers that be, there is plenty of inner discipline required. As Gandhi put it, prepare yourself for mountains of suffering. The suffering, however, is inflicted from the outside and not the inside. One prepares one's inside for converting violence to fruitfulness amid nonviolence. Meister Eckhart also dismissed asceticism:

> Asceticism is of no great importance. There is a better way to treat one's passions than to pile on oneself ascetic practices which so often reveal a great ego and create more instead of less self-consciousness. If you wish to discipline the flesh and make it a thousand times more subject, then place on it the bridle of love. Whoever has accepted this sweet burden of the bridle of love will attain more and come much further than all the penitential practices and mortifications that all the people in the world acting together could ever carry out. Whoever has found this way needs no other.

In his letter to Ruether, Merton echoes Eckhart and directly addresses asceticism:

> On the other hand, the real purpose of asceticism is not cutting off one's relation to created things and other people, but normalizing and healing it. The contemplative life, in my way of thinking (with Greek Fathers, etc.), is simply the restoration of man, in Christ, to the state in which he was originally intended to live.... The monk here and now is supposed to be living the life of the new creation in which the right relation to all the rest of God's creatures is fully restored.

Dorothee Soelle was a solid feminist and liberation theologian who was also deeply grounded in Meister Eckhart's theology. She reminds us that feminism and mysticism go hand in hand and that mysticism is in fundamental opposition to patriarchy by its very nature. She writes:

The language of religion, by which I do not mean the stolen language in which a male God ordains and imperial power radiates forth, is the language of mysticism: I am completely and utterly in God, I cannot fall out of God, I am imperishable. "Who shall separate us from the love of God?" we can then ask with Paul the mystic: "neither death nor life, height nor depth, neither present nor future" (Romans 8:35 and 38).

We must approach mysticism, which comes closest to overcoming the hierarchical masculine concept of God.... The mystical certainty that nothing can separate us from the love of God grows when we ourselves become one with love by placing ourselves freely and without guarantee of success on the side of love.

Soelle teaches that the word *transcendence* does not any longer mean a rugged independence that is "ruling over everything else, but rather as being bound up in the web of life.... That means that we move from God-above-us to God-within-us and overcome false transcendence hierarchically conceived." It follows — and Cardinal Ratzinger should make note of this — that those who condemn feminism are condemning mysticism. This in turn helps to explain why the patriarchal church is so mystically illiterate and keeps others mystically ignorant even at this sad and dangerous point in history. True mysticism empowers.

Merton and Women Thinkers

Merton was very high on Julian of Norwich. He wrote about her in a letter to Sister Mary Madeleva, president of St. Mary's College in Notre Dame, Indiana, who had just inaugurated the first advanced degree program in theology for women.

Julian is without any doubt one of the most wonderful of all Christian voices. She gets greater and greater in my eyes as

I grow older and whereas in the old days I used to be crazy about St. John of the Cross, I would not exchange him now for Julian if you gave me the world and the Indies and all the Spanish mystics rolled up in one bundle. I think that Julian of Norwich is with Newman the greatest English theologian. She is really that. For she reasons from her experience of the substantial center of the great Christian mystery of Redemption. She gives her experience and her deductions clearly, separating the two. And the experience is of course nothing merely subjective. It is the objective mystery of Christ as apprehended by her with the mind and formation of a fourteenth-century English woman.

This is amazing praise, calling Julian "the greatest English theologian" (along with recently canonized John Henry Newman) and saying that she supplants John of the Cross and other Spanish mystics — and I wholeheartedly agree with this powerful endorsement. Not only did Merton confess he preferred Julian to John of the Cross, he also grew to prefer her to Teresa of Avila. Why? "She is a true theologian with greater clarity, depth, and order than St. Theresa: she really elaborates, theologically, the content of her revelations. She first experienced, then thought, and the thoughtful deepening of experience worked it back into her life, deeper and deeper, until her whole life as a recluse at Norwich was simply a matter of getting completely saturated in the light she had received all at once, in the 'shewings,' when she thought she was about to die." For me Julian is very much an heir of Eckhart's creation-centered spirituality. Clearly, there is no put-down of women or women intellectuals in Merton's consciousness.

Merton also tells us that he read Marguerite Porete's book *The Mirror of Simple Souls*. Porete was a Beguine who was burned at the stake in 1310 by the Inquisition for having written that book, and today's scholarship reveals that Meister Eckhart not only read her work but preached from it after her cruel death. I tell this important story in *Meister Eckhart: Mystic-Warrior for Our Times*.

Thomas Merton's relationship with Dorothy Day was one of mutual respect. It is said that her "prophetic witness to nonviolence and pacifism disturbed many in the Catholic Church" but "challenged and inspired others, including Merton." Merton was so in league with Day that he often published in their magazine, *The Catholic Worker*, including his essay "The Root of War Is Fear" in October 1961. They exchanged letters and reading materials frequently, and he wrote: I "think it is a scandal that most Christians are not solidly lined up with you. I certainly am." There is not the slightest hint of Merton "talking down" to Day. Rather, they exchanged profound spiritual as well as cultural observations. For example, in one letter he wrote, "I think the evil in us all has reached the point of overflowing. May the Holy Spirit give us compunction and inner truth and humility and love, that we may be a leaven in this world. And that we may help and bring light to those who need it most: and the Lord alone knows who they are for the need of all is desperate."

In the 1960s, Valerie Delacorte organized a movement called "Women Strike for Peace," and Merton wrote her a letter in May 1962, where he laid out some of his feminist consciousness.

> Woman has been "used" shamelessly in our commercial society, and in this "misuse" has been deeply involved in falsity. Think for instance of advertising, in which woman is constantly used as bait. And along with that, the mentality that is created for woman, and forced on her complacently, by the commercial world. She becomes herself a commodity. In a way the symbol of all commodities. In the false image of woman, life itself is turned into a commodity in its very source. Woman too has been used to create a kind

of spiritual smokescreen behind which the "reality" of the power struggle evolves. Give the soldiers enough pin up girls and they will go gladly into battle.... Refuse any longer to be part of the image of woman that is created by the commercial world. I leave you to meditate on the implications of that. Your refusal to remain passive in the fantastic nonsense of the big campaign to sell shelters has been providential. You have reacted against one of the more ultimate commercial perversions of the sacred reality of the family.... The springs of thought have been poisoned. Thank you for trying to help purify them.

Merton exhibited a critical approach not only to the abuse of women but to the power games behind it, including that of advertising, consumer capitalism, and militarism. He also genuinely encouraged women in leadership roles, praising their "refusal to remain passive."

Clearly, Merton was on the side of the women's awakening from its beginning stages in the early 1960s onward. He can be called a "feminist theologian," and I think he would have taken the epitaph as a compliment, not a charge of heresy.

Heresy #2: "Matthew Fox Calls God 'Mother'"

Indeed, I do! By deliberate choice and not by chance. I have laid out in my writings how all the medieval mystics whom I respect so much — from Hildegard of Bingen to Mechtild of Magdeburg and Meister Eckhart and Julian of Norwich — call God "Mother," directly or indirectly. This was common practice in the Middle Ages. Thomas Merton also cites Julian's teachings on the Motherhood of God, and clearly he was on my side in this argument also. Why was Cardinal Ratzinger — and his boss Pope John Paul II — so threatened by this aspect of the Christian mystical tradition that they considered it a heresy? After he became Pope Benedict XVI,

Ratzinger declared Hildegard of Bingen a "doctor of the church," and it is ironic that he did so, since Hildegard also speaks to the feminine side of God. As I put it in my 2012 book *Hildegard of Bingen: A Saint for Our Times*, Hildegard has become a "Trojan horse" inside the Vatican precisely because she supports a feminine side to God and a Mother of God dimension to our God talk.

Merton on the Motherhood of God

Julian of Norwich developed the theme of the "Motherhood of God" more fully than any theologian up to the late twentieth century — and Merton knew that. He too talked of the "Motherhood of God." Merton not only approved of Julian's theology with gusto, he also developed his own teaching on the subject of the Motherhood of God. "God," he wrote, "is at once Father and Mother. As Father He stands in solitary might surrounded by darkness. As Mother His shining is diffused, embracing all His creatures with merciful tenderness and light. The Diffuse Shining of God is Hagia Sophia. We call her His 'glory.' In Sophia His power is experienced only as mercy and as love." Elaborating on the Divine Feminine, Merton went on to suggest a Quarternity rather than just a Trinity in the Godhead:

> Perhaps in a certain very primitive aspect Sophia [Sophia is Wisdom and is feminine] is the unknown, the dark, the nameless Ousia. Perhaps she is even the Divine Nature, One in Father, Son and Holy Ghost. And perhaps she is in infinite light unmanifest, not even waiting to be known as Light. This I do not know. Out of the silence Light is spoken.... In the Nameless Beginning, without beginning, was the Light. We have not seen this Beginning. I do not know where she is, in this Beginning. I do not speak of her as a Beginning, but as a manifestation.

Mechtild of Magdeburg, a thirteenth-century Beguine and Creation Spirituality mystic, spoke of God as Mother one hundred years before Julian, and Merton knew and respected Mechtild. She wrote: "God is not only fatherly. God is also mother who lifts her loved child from the ground to her knee." And again: "The Trinity is like a mother's cloak wherein the child finds a home and lays its head on the maternal breast." As I have indicated elsewhere, both Hildegard of Bingen and Meister Eckhart also spoke of God in maternal and feminine imagery.

Why does it matter whether we talk of God exclusively as "Father" or as "Mother/Father" God? It matters a lot. Ask any mother or father of girls. I recall speaking years ago at a conference on women and spirituality in Portland, Oregon (Rosemary Ruether also presented at this event). I showed Hildegard's mandalas and paintings, based on her visions, and shared the story of her life and accomplishments. After my presentation, a woman came up to me and said: "I have three teenaged daughters at home, and I am dashing home to tell them about this lady Hildegard. I am Catholic, but the only model I have had of holy womanhood to share with my daughters is Mary, and Mary did not do all that much. But this woman was a healer and a painter and a musician and a scientist and a prophet who stood up to power in the church and beyond. I can hardly wait to run home and tell my girls about Hildegard!"

Meister Eckhart says that "all the names we give to God come from an understanding of ourselves." So if our religious instruction leaves out the feminine side of God, it is feeding a patriarchal culture that also leaves out the feminine side of life. How dangerous is that? Father Bede Griffiths put it this way: "The suppression of women in the Church is but one of the many signs of this masculine domination.... Reason has to be 'married' to intuition; it has to learn to surrender itself for the deeper intuitions of the spirit. These intuitions come, as we have seen, from the presence of the Spirit in the depths of the soul." Father Bede talked about a "fundamental defect in Western man," which was a lack of balance of the masculine and the feminine. He felt this was the great gift the East had to give the West. "It is an encounter ultimately between the two fundamental dimensions of human nature: the male and the female — the masculine, rational, active, dominating power of the mind, and the feminine, intuitive, passive and receptive power." This marriage needs to take place "at the deepest level of the human consciousness." I think Merton would be 100 percent in agreement. As a monk, he spent hours every day and night feeding that intuitive side through prayer and chanting and meditation and quiet, both alone and in communal ritual and ceremony.

Carl Jung says that creativity comes "from the realm of the mothers." An antiwomen theology, one that leaves out the feminine side of divinity, is anticreativity. Indeed, the best scholarship I know on this topic comes from the mathematician Ralph Abraham, who is one of the founders of chaos theory. In his important book *Chaos, Gaia, Eros*, Abraham makes clear that the goddess Chaos was honored and incorporated in the cultures that preceded patriarchy — cultures that have left behind no evidence of war, by the way. Fundamentalism in all its forms is a supreme effort to control the goddess of chaos and therefore to control creativity. Merton would be at home in "the realm of the mothers," since creativity meant so much to him. Art as meditation was everywhere in his spiritual practice, as we have seen. There was no hint of control addictions or of fundamentalism of any stripe in Merton's work or life.

How at home was Thomas Merton with "God as Mother" language? In a long prose poem entitled "Hagia Sophia" (Holy Wisdom), Merton reminds us of the "feminine principle" in the universe. He reminds us that within the biblical and Western mystical tradition, the Divine Feminine has been recognized and honored. Interestingly, the poem is arranged according to the hours that the Divine Office is sung each day in the monastery — Lauds, Prime, Tierce, and Compline. In this way Merton emphasizes the *Wisdom tradition* that is honored in the daily prayers of chanting the Psalms in the church and the monastery. Yet one fact rarely gets the attention it deserves: Wisdom is feminine in the Bible, and in both Latin and Hebrew, *and* as current scholarship has reminded us, *the historical Jesus himself comes from the Wisdom tradition.* The Psalms are a large part of the Wisdom tradition of the Hebrew Bible. To sing the Psalms daily in prayer, as the monastic tradition does, reminds us of our relationship to the journey of the sun and moon each day; the cosmos is attended to, and thereby we are assisted to move beyond anthropocentrism. Time does not come from the clock; it comes from the movement of the sun, which the clock merely records.

Merton tells us that he finished the poem "at Pentecost, 1961," and that "it became a prose poem in honor of Sophia." Originally born as a response to a friend's painting of Mary crowning her Son, Merton tells us how his poem evolved. "*Hagia Sophia* (Holy Wisdom) is God Himself. God is not only a Father but a Mother. He is both at the same time, and it is this 'feminine principle' in the divinity that is the *Hagia Sophia....* The Three Divine Persons each at the same time are Sophia and Manifest her." Merton compares Sophia, the wisdom of God, to "the Tao, the nameless pivot of all being and nature." (The Tao is feminine and the Great Mother in the Chinese tradition.) Furthermore, Merton brings up the black Madonna and the darkness that the Divine Feminine represents: "*Hagia Sofia* is the dark, nameless *Ousia* [being] of the Father, the Son and the Holy Ghost, the incomprehensible, 'primordial' darkness which is infinite light.... Hence, Sophia is the feminine, dark, yielding, tender part of the power, justice, creative dynamism of the Father."

This is not the only reference to the dark Mother in Merton's life. There is a rather untold story about his conversion: In 1940 when Merton was recuperating from an illness, he visited the shrine of the black Madonna in Cobre, Cuba. There he made a vow to Nuestra Señora de la Caridad (Our Lady of Charity), who is recognized as a special protector and emancipator of slaves in the New World. It is a well-known shrine even to this day. While there, he prayed: "There you are, Caridad del Cobre! It is you that I have come to see. You will ask Christ to make me His priest... and I will give you my heart, Lady." So meaningful was this experience to Merton that when, eight years later, he celebrated his first mass as a priest in the Trappist Order, he dedicated it to the black Madonna!

Merton wrote a poem called "Song for Our Lady of Cobre," in which he celebrated the likeness and the difference of "the white girls" who "lift their heads like trees" and "the black girls" who "close their eyes like wings." Thus the black Madonna gives him eyes to see a new marriage of black and white and the celebration of both. He ends the poem with images of the Cosmic Mother.

> Because the heavenly stars
> Stand in a ring:
> And all the pieces of the mosaic, earth,
> Get up and fly away like birds.

The black Madonna also represents to Merton the contemplative rest and tenderness of the night and of the "nameless God."

> The shadows fall. The stars appear. The birds begin to
> sleep. Night embraces the silent half of the earth. A vagrant,
> a destitute wanderer with dusty feet, finds his way down a
> new road. A homeless God, lost in the night, without papers, without identification, without even a number, a frail

expendable exile lies down in desolation under the sweet stars of the world and entrusts Himself to sleep.

Merton presents his Mariology in the same letter that accompanied his "Hagia Sophia" poem: "Now the Blessed Virgin is the one created being who in herself realizes perfectly all that is hidden in Sophia. She is a kind of personal manifestation of Sophia." In the poem he links her to waking up in the morning to Wisdom and to a man being born again when Wisdom "touched his spirit. . . . I am indeed this man lying asleep. . . . I am like all humankind awakening from all the dreams that ever were dreamed in all the nights of the world." There exists a universal slumbering — and a universal awakening brought about by the feminine: "It is like being awakened by Eve. It is like being awakened by the blessed Virgin. It is like coming forth from primordial nothingness and standing in clarity, in Paradise." He compares it to a sick person in a hospital being awakened by gentleness and mercy. It is a cosmic awakening: "All that is sweet in her tenderness will speak to him on all sides in everything, without ceasing, and he will never be the same again. He will have awakened not to conquest and dark pleasure but to the impeccable pure simplicity of One consciousness in all and through all: one Wisdom, one Child, one Meaning, one Sister."

Merton invokes the medieval teaching of "Jesus our Mother," saying that there, too, "Sophia had awakened in their childlike hearts."

Sister Lentfoehr comments that "the theological substrata of the prose poem is rooted in an ancient intuition of reality which goes back to the oldest Oriental thought: the masculine-feminine relationship basic to all being, since all being mirrors God." Merton derives his passion for the Divine Feminine from this and from the Wisdom scriptures where Sophia is amply celebrated.

I think it is clear that Merton and I both celebrate the Divine

Feminine. It is a pity that Cardinal Ratzinger and inquisitors in general have been so ignorant of this rich tradition and so over-reacted to the good news that the feminine can and needs to return and bring balance back to an excessively patriarchal and indeed reptilian brain–driven culture and religion.

CHAPTER NINE

"Every non two-legged creature is a saint"

Merton on Original Blessing and Other So-Called Heresies

The saint knows that the world and everything made by God is good while those who are not saints either think that created things are unholy, or else they don't bother about the question one way or the other because they are only interested in themselves.

— THOMAS MERTON

Chapter 8 examined the first two so-called heresies of Creation Spirituality as named by Cardinal Ratzinger, and in this chapter, we take up the remaining five accusations. If Thomas Merton had been in the defendant's box with me, what might he have said?

Heresy #3: "Matthew Fox Calls God 'Child'"

That is true. Isn't that what the birth narratives and the Christmas story are all about?

And consider Meister Eckhart, who is especially keen on the youthfulness of God. He says that God is *novissiumus*, which means "most new" or "the newest thing in the universe" — and you can't get any younger than that. Eckhart says that God is "forever young," and of course, God invites us into our neoteny, our newness. Scientists tell us that neoteny, our ability as humans to play, is what distinguishes us from primates — they play as children but less so as they grow older. Not so humans — unless we choose to let play go as we grow old. Eckhart notes that both Bibles — the Hebrew Bible and the Christian Bible (John's Gospel) — begin with the phrase "In the beginning." Why is that? Because, says Eckhart, God is always "in the beginning," and when we return to our beginnings we are "in God."

So it strikes me that institutional men who are threatened by the newness of God are telling us how profoundly fear and tiredness and the negative senex, the "old goat syndrome," have taken over their souls. They may be tired of life, but God is not. Life experience may have rendered them cynical, but God is not cynical. Too bad that Christmas means so little to them. God is always young, and we should be also. Eckhart says:

> Every action of God is new and "he makes all things new" (Ws. 7:27). Existence...does not grow old, nor is it changed.... The psalmist says: "Your youth will be renewed like an eagle's." ...Thus God, who always operates and always is new. Therefore every being is new insofar as it is from God and has newness from no other thing. By ascending to God, by drawing near to God, by running back to God, by returning to God — all things are made new, all things become good, are purged, cleansed, made holy. On the other hand, by receding from God they grow old, they perish, they sin as Paul says: "The wages of sin are death." (Rm. 6:23)

God is young and so is the soul — indeed, Eckhart says, "The soul is as young as it was when it was created. Old age concerns only the soul's use of the bodily senses....My soul is as young as it was when It was created, Yes, and much younger! I tell you, it would not surprise me if it were younger tomorrow than it is today!"

Merton on Youthfulness

I think Merton would agree with Eckhart. He, too, was committed to constantly renewing himself, as we've seen. Sister Lentfoehr made this clear when she compared his sixth collection of poems, *Emblems of a Season of Fury*, published in 1963, to his 1957 poem collection *The Strange Islands*: "Merton's attitude had changed, and that immeasurably, toward the so-called 'world.' He now found relevance in all that touches his fellow man, with whom he closely identified living in the aftermath of two world wars — a season of social and political unrest and of a deep emptiness of spirit." Merton was constantly learning — and unlearning. Even his final trip East was a quest to learn, and it required a youthful and humble attitude to be always learning — and yearning.

Merton speaks of the childlikeness of the Divine when he discusses Holy Wisdom, reminding us of the teachings in Proverbs 8 — "the feminine child" playing before God, the Creator of the universe, "playing before Him at all times, playing in the world...playing in the world, obvious and unseen, playing at all times before the Creator." According to Proverbs, Wisdom is "delighting God day after day, ever at play in the divine presence, at play everywhere in God's world, delighting to be with the sons and daughters of the human race."

In addition, Merton's poem "Grace's House" was inspired by a five-year-old child's drawing (the poem is quoted in chapter 4). "What a drawing, what a house, what suns and birds," Merton exclaimed to Mark Van Doren about the drawing. "If we choose we can let loose in the circle of paradise the very wrath of God...but children can, if they still will, give us the lie and show us our folly. We are now more and more persistent in refusing to see any such thing. All we will see is the image, the image, the absurd image, the mask over our own emptiness." Merton not only invokes the child, but he writes a commentary on a child's drawing. Would that inquisitors could learn similar lessons.

Heresy #4: "Matthew Fox Prefers Original Blessing to Original Sin"

Amen. I do. I certainly do. I cannot lie. I am guilty. Original blessing is part of a nonanthropocentric consciousness, since sin came along only with humans. As Merton wrote, "Every non two-legged animal is a saint." Anthropocentrism leaves out 13.8 billion years of God's handiwork, a rather substantial lacuna, I would suggest. That handiwork, the unfolding of the cosmos from the original fireball to today, is pre-sinful. But neither is it aesthetically or morally neutral. It is good, even "very good" (Genesis 1). And the theological word for "goodness" is *blessing*. Yes, the universe is, the Earth is, the soil and sun and rain and trees and forests and oceans and rivers and rocks and animals and finned ones and winged ones — they are all *blessings*. Haven't we noticed? If we haven't noticed, that may be one reason we are so busy destroying it all. Because an original sin ideology, rooted in anthropocentrism ("humans first!") as well as in pessimism ("woe is we — we are all sinners and can do nothing about our sin"), creates a self-fulfilling prophecy of disempowerment and there-fore of do-nothing and care-for-nothing idleness and acedia and couch-potatoitis.

An original sin ideology is terrible psychology. It feeds masochism and self-hatred and perfectionism and addictions, and it reinforces any abuse we might have undergone as children. It is also terrible sociology; it feeds racism, sexism, homophobia, and more. It is terrible theology, since Jesus, supposedly the founder of Christianity, *never heard of original sin*. *No Jew has*. In fact, author and Holocaust survivor Elie Wiesel says that the idea of original sin "is alien to Jewish thinking." Why would the church invest so fully in a doctrine that is alien to the very way that Jesus himself lived and thought? Most likely because it served political interests, empire-building interests, that came along just at the time that St. Augustine developed his ideas about original sin. It came along in the fourth century when the Roman Empire became a Christian empire.

Merton on Original Blessing

Does Thomas Merton address original blessing and original sin? Indeed, he does, but in his own language. I first used the term "original blessing" in my book of that name, which came out in 1983, or some fifteen years after Merton's death.

On the concept of original blessing, Merton said this:

> There is in all visible things an invisible fecundity, a dimmed light, a meek namelessness, a hidden wholeness. This mysterious Unity and Integrity is Wisdom, the Mother of all, *Natura naturans*. There is in all things an inexhaustible sweetness and purity, a silence that is a fount of action and joy. It rises up in wordless gentleness and flows out to me from the unseen roots of all created being welcoming me tenderly, saluting me with indescribable humility. This is at once my own being, my own nature, and the Gift of my Creator's Thought and Art within me, speaking as Hagia Sophia, speaking as my sister, Wisdom.

If this is not a description of original blessing, I don't know what is. Merton also said elsewhere: "Yet despite the innate tendency toward sin and the degree of evil imposed or freely chosen, each person is created good, in the image of God, and one can never presume that the spark of goodness has been extinguished in anyone, that anyone is beyond the reach of divine grace." Passages abound in Merton about the holiness and even saintliness of all things natural. He declares that "Everything That Is, Is Holy" (capitalization in original). He declares, "The saint knows that the world and everything made by God is good while those who are not saints either think that created things are unholy, or else they don't bother about the question one way or the other because they are only interested in themselves." He writes:

> The forms and individual characters of living and growing things, of inanimate beings, of animals and flowers and all nature, constitute their holiness in the sight of God.
>
> The special clumsy beauty of this particular colt on this April day in this field under these clouds is a holiness consecrated to God by His own creative wisdom and it declares the glory of God.
>
> The plain flowers of the dogwood outside this window are saints. The little yellow flowers that nobody notices on the edge of that road are saints looking up into the face of God.
>
> This leaf has its own texture and its own pattern of veins and its own holy shape, and the bass and trout hiding in the deep pools of the river are canonized by their beauty and their strength.
>
> The lakes hidden among the hills are saints, and the sea too is a saint who praises God without interruption in her majestic dance.
>
> The great, gashed, half-naked mountain is another of God's saints. There is no other like him. He is alone in his own character; nothing else in the world ever did or ever will imitate God in quite the same way. That is his sanctity.
>
> The goodness of the world, stricken or not, is incontestable and definitive. If it is stricken, it is also healed in Christ.

Are these not poems to the original blessing (and goodness) of things? It is interesting that these passages, taken from his *New Seeds of Contemplation*, follow on his ever deeper entry into the mind of Meister Eckhart.

Merton says that there is "one point on which I most profoundly disagree with the Barthians" and that is the following: "Our very creation itself is a beginning of revelation. Making us in His image, God reveals Himself to us, we are already His words to ourselves!" This too sounds very much like original blessing.

Merton on Original Sin

When it comes to the topic of original sin, Merton clearly wrestled with the topic. Contrary to what Ratzinger wrote about me, I do not deny original sin, but I deny its prominence. It must *never* take precedence over original blessing, and I decry the fact that it has never been defined as such. Thus it hangs in the wind and becomes a screen for projecting one's deepest fears and doubts. For women, their original sin is being women; for homosexuals, it is being homosexual; for people of color, it is being a person of color. It can take a lifetime to overcome this sociological bad messaging, which a floating "original sin" notion projects onto others.

In my book *Original Blessing*, I define original sin as dualism, which I see as the sin behind sins. Lately I have been taken by the language of the great psychologist Otto Rank, who talks about "original wound." (Being Jewish, he does not recognize original sin.) For him, our original wound is the separation we feel on leaving our mother's womb. All of life and its hardest moments ring the bell of this original separation — whether we are talking about death, sickness, divorce, betrayal, and so on — and so we all have to work at healing that wound. What is the medicine? For Rank, it is the *"unio mystica,"* the mystical union itself, and he says we undergo this union "in love and in art."

As early as 1959 in his journals, Merton was questioning the concept of original sin as it was popularly understood in the monastery:

> Yesterday in chapter a theological conference over the fate of unbaptized infants. It is a silly but symbolic question. With all our solemn theology of the mercy of God we still cannot devise a better system than one which involves the damnation of innocents....In questions like these I think Wisdom mocks the theologians — the men who so solemnly imagine they are supposed to know and settle everything.... The presuppositions are so childish and embarrassing....It is a very good subject on which to say nothing.

Merton deals with original sin in his dialogues with Suzuki and in a very late book, *Zen and the Birds of Appetite*, where he speaks of Eckhart's teaching that we possess with God "a basic unity *within ourselves* at the summit of our being where we are 'one with God.'" But we are distanced from this summit, so "the tragedy is that our consciousness is totally alienated from the inmost ground of our identity. And in Christian mystical tradition, this inner split and alienation is the real meaning of 'original sin.'" Our "true identity is the 'birth of Christ in us.'" This constitutes the cleansing of the original sin (dare I say: of separation from divinity?). As a path to this inner self, Merton invokes Eckhart's teaching about cracking open the outer shell to get to the inner. "As Eckhart says: 'The shell must be cracked apart if what is in it is to come out, for if you want the kernel you must break the shell. And therefore if you want to discover nature's nakedness you must destroy its symbols and the farther you get in the nearer you come to its essence. When you come to the One that gathers all things up into itself, there you must stay.'" Merton comments: "The real way to study Zen is to penetrate the outer shell and taste the inner kernel which cannot be defined. Then one realizes in oneself the reality which is being talked about."

Merton takes up his theme of original sin as alienation in responding to Suzuki's "mythical language in which the Fall of Man is described in the Bible and the Church Fathers, to distinct advantage psychologically and spiritually." He tells us that Suzuki interprets the Fall "in terms of man's alienation from himself." I should note that the Fall is not at all identical with original sin, as the Jews talk about the Fall but never about original sin. It seems that Merton did not understand this very important distinction, which I did not until around 1973, when a Jewish student of mine at Barat College raised the question. In any case, Merton adds that Paul Tillich, under the influence of psychology, was closer to Augustine than we think, that Jung says the Fall is "inscribed in our nature" as "symbolic archetypes," and that the Fathers of the Church (as well as the biblical writers, too, no doubt) were much more concerned with this archetypal significance than with the Fall as an "historical event." Merton also invokes Erich Fromm as one who "intuitively grasped the importance of this symbol."

Merton's treatment of original sin here clearly puts distance between it as an historic fact in contrast to its power as a "symbol" or "symbolic archetype" or "myth." Merton actually says that the Fathers of the Church as well as the biblical writers saw it in the latter fashion. By rendering it as a symbol or archetype, this certainly loosens the screws on the nailed-down doctrine of original sin. This does seem to come closer to the biblical and Jewish teaching of the Fall as a story of how humans err.

In a journal entry on November 8, 1959, Merton described how Claude Tresmontant, a Catholic philosopher, "says very convincingly that perhaps original sin is not sin which society inherited from one individual but sin which each individual contracts from society (Adam = man in the collective sense)." Merton called this a "very important idea that one must break with the exterior, 'tribal,' mechanical and collective society to which one is passively subject, and isolate oneself in order to be actively united in a *spiritual* community which transcends national, social and especially tribal limitations." In a 1966 article entitled "Camus and the Catholic Church," Merton again cited Tresmontant on original sin, writing that Tresmontant "restates in purely catholic terms exactly what Camus means by being a 'Rebel' against 'the absurd.' Tresmontant wrote: 'Tertullian said one is not born a Christian. One becomes a Christian.' The access to Christianity represents a new birth.... One can then legitimately distinguish between the state which precedes this new birth and the state which follows it. The state which precedes this new birth is the state which the Church calls 'original sin.'" Here Merton calls original sin a "state" we are born into rather than an individual blotch on one's newborn soul.

Merton offers an odd comment when he says Suzuki addressed original sin "in just the same simple natural way as the Fathers of the Church like St. Augustine or St. Gregory of Nyssa did." I don't think Augustine's teachings on original sin were the least bit simple or natural — in fact, Augustine identifies original sin with our concupiscence and with our sexuality, and it was Augustine who created a mammoth split between nature and spirit. Augustine's doctrine of original sin puts down the body, in contrast to a Jewish-based spirituality that respects the world and the body and represents an altogether different philosophy. Augustine not only invented the term "original sin" but he also defined spirit as "whatever is not matter." He and Plato thereby set up the ultimate dualism, from which we have inherited a suspect attitude toward sexuality and our bodies and the earth. This issue still haunts the Western consciousness, and certain papal teachings thrive on it, such as on issues of birth control, homosexuality, and others, which ignore what science has learned about sexuality. To me, Augustine's radical separation of matter from spirit is anything but "simple and natural" — it is very convoluted and decidedly anti-natural.

Nor does it reflect a consistency in Merton's thought regarding original sin. In Merton's second to last book, *Zen and the Birds of Appetite*, he wrote, "The story of the Fall tells us in mythical language that 'original sin 'is not simply a stigma arbitrarily making good pleasures seem guilty, but a basic inauthenticity, a kind of predisposition to bad faith in our understanding of ourselves and of the world." Again, Merton invokes the "mythical language" of the Fall while equating it with "original sin," and this is a stretch, as I discuss above. But here he defines original sin as an inauthentic "predisposition" toward self and world. He states that Buddhism and biblical Christianity agree that humans are somehow out of right relationship to the world and to things in it, "or rather, to be more exact, they see that man bears in himself a mysterious tendency to *falsify* that relation, and to spend a great deal of energy in justifying the false view he takes of his world and of his place in it." He cites the Buddhist concept of avidya, which is more than mere ignorance but is "the root of all evil and suffering because it places man in an equivocal, in fact impossible position." At the same time, Merton writes, "Christianity attributes this view of man and of reality to 'original sin.' " He invokes the Buddhist concept of dukkha, where in "every movement desire tends to bear ultimate fruit in pain rather than lasting joy, in hate rather than love, in destruction rather than creation." As examples of this delusion, Merton cites the H-bomb and the Nazi extermination camps.

In his very last talk delivered two hours before his death,

Merton again took up "the myth of original sin," comparing it to the Buddhist concept of avidya or fundamental ignorance. "Both Christianity and Buddhism agree that the root of man's problems is that his consciousness is all fouled up and he does not apprehend reality as it fully and really is.... Consequently, Christianity and Buddhism look primarily to a transformation of man's consciousness — a transformation, and a liberation of the truth imprisoned in man by ignorance and error."

Thus we see that Merton was forever searching for a meaning of original sin — right up to the end of his life. He was continually looking for a language to make some sense of it. At times he came up with psychological language (inauthenticity and alienation) and Buddhist language (avidya and dukkha) and societal language (Tresmontant). What is clear is that he was not content with the concept hanging loose by itself, and he quietly distanced himself (by silence) from the idea of original sin as our sexuality, which is so prominent in Augustine. Rather, he broadened it, seeing examples in our technology and creativity, our power to create H-bombs and extermination camps. Merton deserves credit for opening up a discussion on original sin, which is a discussion that has engaged my work as well.

In my book *Creativity: Where the Divine and the Human Meet*, I propose that maybe original sin is the guilt we feel for exercising our creativity, and I invoke the story of Prometheus who, like Adam, paid a severe price for stealing the gift of the gods. I was not aware at the time I wrote that book that in *Raids on the Unspeakable*, Merton devoted an entire chapter, called "Prometheus: A Meditation," to this myth. In it, Merton described Prometheus's despair, which derived from the

> terror of facing and fully realizing his divine sonship, in Christ, and in the Spirit of Fire Who is given us from

heaven. The fire Prometheus thought he had to steal from the gods is his own identity in God, the affirmation and vindication of his own being as a sanctified creature in the image of God....In the eyes of Prometheus, to be himself was to be guilty.

Christ differs from Prometheus because the fire arrives as a gift from God — one does not have to steal it or take on guilt because of it. For, Merton wrote, "in reality God cannot seek to keep anything good to Himself alone," and for this reason the God-gift of creative fire is a grace, a freebie. We are tempted by despair "because we think our life is important to ourselves alone, and do not know that our life is more important to the Living God than it is to our own selves...there is nothing we can steal from Him at all, because before we can think of stealing it, it has already been given."

In a journal entry, Merton developed another angle on Prometheus, whom he called an "archetypal representation of the suffering Christ. But we must go deeply into this. Prometheus startles us by being more fully Christ than the Lord of our own clichés — I mean, he is free from all the falsifications and limitations of our hackneyed vision which has slowly emptied itself of reality." In my reflection on Prometheus, I write: "Both the Prometheus story and the Adam and Eve story connect the 'stealing of the Divine creativity' with death. In this context, the resurrection story of Christianity becomes an affirmation of our creativity, an act of permission to carry on our Divine likeness without guilt and without fear. Not even the fear of death. We are now free to live, i.e. to create."

I believe Merton's "last word" on original sin is presented in a brilliant poem composed late in his life. Tellingly, he called it "First Lesson about Man."

Man begins in zoology
He is the saddest animal
He drives a big red car
Called anxiety....
Whenever he goes to the phone
To call joy
He gets the wrong number
Therefore he likes weapons
He knows all guns
By their right names
He drives a big black Cadillac
Called death
Now he is putting anxiety
Into space
He flies his worries
All around Venus
But it does him no good....
Man is the saddest animal
He begins in zoology
And gets lost
In his own bad news.

Notice how Merton sees humanity as "the saddest animal" and ever seeking bigger, brighter things, along with more weapons and war, to fill a void in our souls. We get lost in our "own bad news." Yes, an original sin ideology can do that to us. It is very bad news, and it feeds the needs of a consumer-driven economy. For I believe consumer capitalism is the secular version of original sin. It teaches us through its advertising preachers that we lack what it takes to be happy or strong, and we need outside redemption — the compulsive purchase of goods — to stand tall. If we began our teachings with original blessing, presumably the news would not be so bad, and what seems a self-fulfilling prophecy would not happen and we would be freer of the gods of consumerism, which, in fact, consume *us*.

Heresy #5: "Matthew Fox
Does Not Condemn Homosexuals"

Cardinal Ratzinger got that right, for sure. How can we condemn something that science has proven is found in at least 464 other species and is found in every human community? About 8 percent of the human population is gay or lesbian; that is just the way it is. If we apply St. Thomas's principle that "a mistake about creation results in a mistake about God," then the persistence of homophobia in the name of religion is worship of a false God. The God of creation is not homophobic, no matter what popes tell us. The God of creation is biased in favor of diversity. This is true in so much of nature, but it is surely true when it comes to human sexual attraction. So let it go at that. To worship a homophobic Deity is therefore idol worship. It is difficult to count the damage that religion and its righteous preachers have dumped on homosexuals over the centuries, filling them with shame and guilt and regret for their basic humanity and sexuality. It is religion that is sinful, not people who may be gay or lesbian (though as human beings, all are capable of sin). Recently, when returning from a trip, Pope Francis was asked by reporters about homosexual priests, and he said: "Who am I to judge?" Pope Francis got it right; the cocksure homophobes are wrong. Homosexuality has become the Galileo case of our day — once again religion is hiding its head in the sand and ignoring what science has learned, as it did with the discovery that the earth travels around the sun. Pope John Paul II removed the Catholic Church's condemnation of Galileo after four hundred years — so how many centuries will it take this time for organized religion to listen to science?

Merton on Sexuality

Thomas Merton's basic view on sexuality is laid out in his 1962 book, *New Seeds of Contemplation*, where he wrote: "Sex is by no means to be regarded as an evil. It is a natural good, willed by God, and entering into the mystery of God's love and God's mercy toward men [*sic*]." Merton did not speak out on homosexuality per se, which is not altogether surprising. We must remember that gay rights concerns only broke through our national consciousness after the Stonewall riots in Greenwich Village in New York City on June 28, 1969. This occurred a full seven months after Merton's death, and before that, the topic of homosexuality was not much on political or cultural agendas. Yet there is some evidence that Merton's father was bisexual and that Tom knew this as a child.

Regarding sexuality in general, however, Merton did express himself, and we see a decided transformation in his thought. As a young man, Merton was quite licentious, and he lived an essentially bawdy lifestyle for years. This continued until his religious conversion and his entrance, at age twenty-six, into a strict monastic community that required a celibate lifestyle. All this he wrestles with at some length in his autobiography, in which he pretty much abides by the dualistic and guilt-tainted theology of St. Augustine. Merton expresses guilt over his rowdy days at Cambridge, where he enrolled in 1933, which included fathering a child and abandoning the child's mother, as well as his excessive partying at Columbia University in New York City, where he enrolled in 1935. In his notebook, he commented on one such party while at Columbia, which occurred even after his conversion to Catholicism. He wrote: "Missie. Some girl, like [Ginny] said,...'The party Sunday night — scotch-type whiskey.' Swimming in the creek 3 AM. Everyone furiously drunk."

He then criticized and denounced himself as a sinner deserving of "terrible damnation," since he'd committed a worse act than Pilate's sin or those executioners who pounded the nails in Jesus's hands. He compared his conduct to that of Hitler and

Stalin, blaming himself and everyone else who was "violent and lustful and proud and greedy and ambitious." His conversion experience occurred on a trip to Cuba in April 1940. Afterward, he engaged in similar exaggerated beratings of himself, which found fertile theological ground in the writings of St. Augustine. After all, Augustine had his own rather tawdry youth, and he also fathered an illegitimate child (though he stayed with the child's mother for a number of years). Both wrote autobiographies containing exaggerations of guilt.

Years later, Merton was using very different language to evoke sexuality, such as in this quote from a May 1965 journal entry that described his move to the hermitage (and which I cite in chapter 4): "The silence of the forest is my bride and the sweet dark warmth of the whole world is my love and out of the heart of that dark warmth comes the secret that is heard only in silence, but it is the root of all the secrets that are whispered by all the lovers in their beds all over the world." This passage, I think, conveys the *context* in which he recognizes lovemaking — it is part of the warmth of the universe. It is cosmic. Such talk is not the rigid dualism of some monastic writers but rather an opened soul that recognizes the sexual energy and beauty that is embedded in all of our relationships, including and especially our relationship with nature. This is not a sexual attitude of judgment but of ecstasy. It is, if anything, pansexuality at work.

The same idea shines through in his poem "The Harmonies of Excess" written in 1968:

The hidden lovers in the soil
Become green plants and gardens tomorrow
When they are ordered to re-appear
In the wet sun's poem
Then they force the delighted
Power of buds to laugh louder

They scatter all the cries of light
Like shadow rain and make their bed
Over and over in the hollow flower
The violet bonfire.

This poem expresses marvelously the larger dimension of sexuality, the presence of the power of generation in all of nature; it carries our sense of sexuality beyond moralizing because it carries us beyond anthropomorphism. It carries us into the arena of sexual mysticism — and even the flowers do it! There is a "violet bonfire" to behold from lovers "in the soil" and those who "make their bed" over and over. He culminates this passage with an explicit recognition of the presence of the Cosmic Christ in sexual experience.

Slowly slowly
Comes Christ through the garden
Speaking to the sacred trees
Their branches bear his light
Without harm.

The trees, too, bear the "light of Christ" and are "sacred." After all, he did say, "I am the vine," didn't he? Clearly, Merton is hinting at the redemption of the Garden of Eden, blessed by the arrival of the Christ who takes his time to show up. Sexuality, too, is sacred and light-filled, Christ-filled.

One commentator on Merton's poetry says that "Merton was not opposed to sexuality but rather to the perversion of it that seemed to be part of America's heritage." Merton invokes the English Ranters, who in the seventeenth century opposed the Puritan establishment in England and stood for "the essential goodness and divinity of all life — including sexuality." They were persecuted and suppressed by the religious establishment of the day. In his poem "Impious Doctrine," written late in his life in 1968, Merton put the following words into the leading Ranter's mouth:

"Nay, I see that God is in all creatures,
Man and Beast, Fish and Fowle,
And every green thing from the highest cedar to the ivey
    on the wall;
And that God is the life and being of them all....
Sin is the dark side of God but God is not the author of sin."

Here Merton applies a Cosmic Christ and panentheistic theology ("God is in all creatures") to the question of sexuality in general.

In my book *The Coming of the Cosmic Christ*, I call for turning from Augustine's "regret" for our sexuality to a creation-based "praise" for sexuality, and I invoke the Bible's Song of Songs for championing such a perspective. I write, "The Cosmic Christ is radically present to all sexuality in all its dimensions and possibilities." The Cosmic Christ is present with the sexual *anawim* (which includes homosexuals in a homophobic culture). Otto Rank incisively recognized that beginning in the fourth century (Augustine's time), "as an expression of will, sexuality became evil, guilty, and a cause of death," carrying as it did the full weight of the culture's need for survival and immortality. This "ideology of fertilization" was responded to by an ideology of celibacy, which loses its power when perverted into a goal in itself. In the passages above, Merton is very much in sync with my writings on the Cosmic Christ and sexuality.

Consider for example this passage I called "The Cosmic Christ Speaks on Sexuality":

The Cosmic Christ might speak thus on the topic of sexuality: "Let religion and the churches abandon their efforts to be 'houses of sublimation.' Instead reenter the cosmic mystery that sexuality is and teach your people, young and old, to do the same, remembering justice, remembering responsibility as intrinsic to the mystical experience. All lovemaking (as distinct from 'having sex') is Christ meeting Christ. Love beds are altars. People are temples encountering temples, the holy of holies receiving the holy of holies. Wings of cherubim and seraphim beat to the groans and passions of human lovers, for the cosmic powers are there eager to enhance the celebration. The sacred moments of sexual ritual are not inferior to any other cosmic liturgy. Re-learn the art of lovemaking as a genuine art, as meditation experience. Know that in making love the very process is the way. I am there. I am the way. Go beyond 'being in love' to being the presence of cosmic love embodied and reflected in two human lovers. Deanthropocentrize being in love, yet localize it and ground it in personal commitment to another. Sexual love will help you to do this, reminding you even of your finiteness in the midst of infiniteness, of your mortality in the midst of beauty's everlastingness, of the future in the midst of the now."

In the late 1970s, I invited Sister Therese Lentfoehr, Thomas Merton's good friend, to be a visiting teacher at our Institute of Culture and Creation Spirituality (ICCS) program at Mundelein College in Chicago. While there, she regaled us with stories of the picnics she and Merton shared on the monastery grounds. I was impressed that she and Thomas had maintained their friendship, which began with a common interest in poetry well before his entrance into the Trappist community, and I was struck that she could be critical of his poetry to his face — and that he had the humility to take the criticism and learn from it. While with us, she shared what she called Merton's "Zen poetry." When she read his words "I am a bell," I practically fell out of my chair. This was a profoundly feminine image for a heterosexual man at that time, and it spurred me to research other mystics on the subject of gender stretching, or what we might call deconstructing and reconstructing one's sexual identity.

Sure enough, I found that the majority of Teresa of Avila's images for her soul were masculine, and Meister Eckhart and John of the Cross used mostly feminine images, like Merton. I discovered that the mystic and the celibate are not afraid to cross gender roles — in fact, he or she may be driven to it to survive psychically (reflecting Jung's thesis about the anima/animus dialectic). I think it speaks well of Merton's own sexual awareness that he questioned cultural rigidity around sexuality and sexual roles. For this reason, and for his deep commitment to justice, I think Merton would have responded very favorably to the awakening of gay consciousness that emerged after his death.

Furthermore, Merton spoke of the importance of being true to oneself, and this gets to the heart of today's homosexual awakening. On this point, Merton was unbending. He wrote that people are "at liberty to be real or unreal...be true or false, the choice is ours." He insisted that we not hide behind masks that cover up our true selves; he wrote that some people wear "one mask and now another and never if we so desire to appear with our own true face." The true self is to come first, for "we have a choice of two identities: the external mask which seems to be real and which lives by a shadowy autonomy for the brief moment of earthly existence," and the true or inner self. But to live with the hidden, inner person is to give oneself "eternally to the truth in whom [one] subsists." Living under a mask, playing a role, makes a person "itch with discomfort," till some must eventually pay "a psychiatrist to scratch him."

Merton, unlike Augustine, evolved on the subject of sexuality. He came to a place where he could melt the dualisms that much of Christianity had inherited from Plato and realize that human love need not be separate from God love — sexuality and spirituality, matter and spirit, could themselves marry. In his journal on August 30, 1959, Merton recalled meeting a sister of one of

his brother monks, calling her "charming, intelligent and honest."
He enjoyed spending time with her discussing her agnosticism,
among other things. He commented: "Anyone with two grains of
sense will probably detect behind all this a sort of sexual attraction. Certainly not explicit or overt, but spiritualized. Well. So
what? Does that invalidate anything I have said? We are human
and our humanity is part of the mystery of Christ, and there is
hardly any spontaneous human affection that does not have some
sex in it somewhere."

"I always obey my nurse": Merton's Love Affair

The evolution of Merton's attitude toward sexuality was partly
the influence of the nondualistic spirituality of Meister Eckhart
and of Zen. But it also reflected the deeply personal transformation that occurred when he fell in love with a woman named
Margie in early 1966. Merton was then fifty-one and recovering
from a back operation in the hospital. Margie was half his age, a
twenty-five-year-old Catholic nurse who massaged his back as he
recuperated, and before long they fell in love and had an affair.
This helped Merton heal a spiritual dualism and move even further
from Augustine's Fall/redemption philosophy to that of Creation
Spirituality. In April 1966, three months after meeting Margie, he
wrote: "All I know is that I love [Margie] so much I can hardly
think of anything but her. Also I know that in itself this love is a
thing of enormous value (never has anyone given herself to me
so completely, so openly, so frankly, and never have I responded so
completely)." He continued, "I see how badly I need her love to
complete me," and her "womanness blends with the man I am,
and we are one being....Again, I now realize I had found something, someone, that I had been looking for all my life."

In 1958, he had written: "My worst and inmost sickness is the
despair of ever being truly able to love, because I despair of ever

being worthy of love.... I do not really love my Order as it is. I am suspicious of its inmost aims and desires, I wonder if they have anything to do with Christ and with love. I seriously wonder, all the time the fault is probably mine."

During his recovery in the hospital, Merton wrote a love poem to Margie called "I Always Obey My Nurse."

> I always obey my nurse
> I always take care
> Of my bleeding sin
> My fractured religion.

Merton acknowledged his break with his vow of celibacy. But the experience also woke him up on several levels, including his belief system. Like many religious, he was rediscovering human love in the context of a certain "fractured religion." One should keep in mind that, after the Second Vatican Council, many priests and nuns were experimenting with their sexuality. A great exodus from religious orders was occurring. For example, in my Dominican province, two of the "student masters" (the priests overseeing the brothers in training) left to marry, as did the "novice master." Indeed, of the fourteen priests I was ordained with in 1967, only two remain in the priesthood and order today. Further, Brother Antoninus (Bill Everson), a Dominican poet whose work Merton respected, and who visited Merton at Gethsemani, left the Dominicans after sixteen very visible and fruitful years to marry a woman he had been involved with for some time. It was a time of experimentation, no doubt, and of the return of love.

In this context, Thomas Merton's affair was not unique. It was part of the post-Vatican II zeitgeist in the Catholic Church, which was not spared the "sexual revolution" of the sixties. Many priests and Catholic sisters left religious life to get married, and Merton was not immune from such happenings. He, of course, did not leave his monastic life, but he did leave behind, once and for all, a religious ideology that was built on dualisms of mind and body, spirit and matter, which has haunted religion in the West for centuries.

Ross Labrie offers this observation about Merton's love experience: "Although the experience undermined his feeling of integrity as a religious man, it had the unexpected effect of strengthening some of his deepest beliefs, as can be seen in the concluding refrain: 'And God did not make death!' " In other words, eros was returning to Merton's soul. Merton assisted in deconstructing both the imperative of celibacy and a dualistic doctrine that has often (not always) supported it. In opposition to the latter, he concluded that one can indeed love God and a human in the same love. Indeed, in his final talk, speaking to monks and nuns gathered in Bangkok, he offered an opinion that celibacy was not necessarily the future of monastic life. He told a friend that "conditions had changed, and that celibacy, even for a monk, was a thing of the past." No doubt this was one of the deep lessons he learned from his temporary detour from his vow of celibacy. This is not unlike Father Bede Griffiths's remarks to me shortly before he died that "the future of monasticism is not with monks but with laypeople."

On August 20, 1968, the anniversary of his third year of residence in his hermitage, Merton burned Margie's letters in the fireplace as a ritual marking the end of his relationship with her. Author Mark Shaw comments:

> Their sacred moments of togetherness included clandestine meetings in Dr. Wygal's office, where they first felt the warmth of each other's bodies and enjoyed passion beyond Merton's comprehension; the time spent at the Louisville airport on Derby day, where the two snuggled and shared inner feelings about love; the picnics at Gethsemani, where emotions erupted into a sexual togetherness; and a

multitude of sharing encountered at every turn. They knew the love affair was over, but the love they had known would last forever.

It took great courage for Merton to end such a relationship and opt anew for his celibate lifestyle. He respected Margie in the process, and she moved on as well, eventually getting married and becoming the mother of two boys. Margie never wrote an "exposé" or in any way exploited the experience she shared with Thomas Merton. It seems to me that both handled the experience with considerable maturity, mutual respect, and yes, love.

It is significant that Merton never regretted the affair; in fact, he called it a "miracle." He saw it as a God-given transformation that taught him, finally, what human love was all about. He had not experienced authentic love with a woman previous to entering the monastery — he had been too immature to have undergone such love. But after the experience with Margie, Merton knew he would never again be a man who, he said, "did not know or love in a deep mysterious way, because we gave ourselves to each other almost as if we were married." Biographer Michael Mott said Merton "loved greatly and was greatly loved. He was overwhelmed by the experience and it changed him forever.... Thomas Merton never again talked of his inability to love, or to be loved." In his journal on December 2, 1967, Merton wrote about receiving "some rather touching fan mail" from a man and a woman "both thanking me for my 'Notes on Love' (in *Frontier*) and saying how much they agreed. How right I was, what an unusual viewpoint, etc. Well, if these notes helped two people to love each other better and with more trust in love's truth, then all that happened between me and M. was worthwhile. I feel sad about M."

Yet Margie was still on his mind three weeks later.

A card from M. today: thought of her suddenly the other day, almost saw her it was so vivid. That was the day the card was mailed....Certainly I feel less real, somehow, without our constant communication, our sense of being in communion (so intense last year). The drab, futile silences of this artificial life, with all its tensions and its pretenses: but I know it would be worse somewhere else. And marriage, for me, would be terrible. Anyway, that's all over. In a month I'll be 53, and no one in his right mind would get married for the first time at such an age.

Yet this afternoon I wondered if I'd really missed the point of life after all. A dreadful thought!

On April 22, 1967, Merton wrote, "So in a way it is liberation day — and I have made up my mind to be what I am supposed to be (Finally!)." In mid-May he made the decision that his journals should not be published until twenty-five years following his death (his wishes were respected in this regard) — and that the Margie episode ought not be excised from them. "I have no intention of keeping the [Margie] business out of sight." He did not want to present a false self but to tell the full story of his journey. "The affair with [Margie] is an important part of it — and shows my limitations as well as a side of me that is — well, it needs to be known too, for it is part of me." On August 20, 1968, shortly before his trip to Asia, he performed the ritual of letting the relationship go. "Today, among other things, I burned M.'s letters. Incredible stupidity in 1966! I did not even glance at any one of them."

In the end, Merton experienced a gradual healing of Augustine's dualistic and antisexual and antiwomen attitude, and this reconciliation contributed to his love affair and was in fact occurring in the church at large. Merton did not regret the episode so much as learn from it, and he hoped others would learn from it. But it was not the last word. He returned to his vocation as a monk and as a hermit before he left for Asia, and he was seriously looking at other eremitical venues where he might live on his return, while still staying connected to his motherhouse, Gethsemani Abbey.

The bottom line is not about celibacy but about love. As John's epistle says, "Love is from God; everyone who loves is born of God and knows God. Whoever does not love does not know God, for God is love.... There is no fear in love, but perfect love casts out fear; for fear has to do with punishment, and whoever fears has not reached perfection in love" (1 John 4:7–8, 18). That Merton was able to navigate both a celibate life for twenty-some years and then a temporary discovery of human love to its fullest and then return to a celibate life is to his credit.

In many ways I see Merton's journey as a nail in the coffin of Augustinian, fear-of-women, fear-of-body, fear-of-sex spirituality. We should thank Merton for his willingness to carry that burden to its logical conclusion...and beyond. Several years ago, I was asked to speak to a large gathering of male and female Benedictines on the occasion of the anniversary of 1,500 years of the order's existence, and I chose to speak on Hildegard of Bingen and her connection to the Creation Spirituality tradition. Afterward, a Benedictine scholar and monk came up to me and said: "You are right. Our tradition fell away from our creation-centered roots beginning in the seventeenth century. Augustinian dualism has indeed leaked into Benedictine theology some three centuries ago." But Merton, trusting his intuition, had the courage to work beyond it. It is clear that he, unlike Augustine, learned ultimately to hold no regrets about his humanity and sexuality. He treated his partner with great respect, and mutually they agreed on their painful separation.

While Augustine, like Merton, led a somewhat profligate life as a young man, he never matured enough — even though he lived to be seventy-six years old — to recognize that his need for discipline as a youth was not something to build a theology on. In contrast, and to his credit, Merton, who died at just fifty-three years of age, was wise enough to make love the bottom line for building a theology of sexuality and spirituality. In doing so he lay the groundwork for deconstructing Augustinian guilt and regret around our bodiliness and our sexuality, and he gave us the direction in which to reconstruct such a theology. We are indebted to him for his honesty and his courage in moving beyond Augustine, Thomas à Kempis, and Tanquerey when it comes to our sexuality.

Heresy #6: "Matthew Fox Prefers the Four Paths He Talks about to the Traditional Three Paths of Purgation, Illumination, and Union"

The good cardinal is correct. I certainly do prefer the Four Paths of Creation Spirituality to the three paths of purgation, illumination, and union as naming our journey to the Divine (and the Divine to us). First, those three paths are not found anywhere in the Bible. They come from Neoplatonist philosophers Plotinus (204–270) and Proclus (412–485) by way of the sixth-century Syrian monk Denis the Areopagite. While emphasizing the One that permeates all reality and thus speaking to a unitive experience common to all mysticism, nevertheless, neither was a Christian and neither knew the Bible or the theme of the incarnation of the Divine. Being Platonists, their view of the role of matter in our lives was badly skewed and buttressed a class consciousness that takes one far from the message of Jesus, who supported the *anawim*, or those without a voice in society. So why has the "classical" spiritual journey been named by them, rather than using Jewish and biblical language? I have purposely and deliberately tossed out these terms as a valid naming of the spiritual journey inspired by the prophets of Israel and of Jesus.

I am not alone in this. For example, I mention in chapter 3 the

Jewish rabbi from Switzerland, who was a student with Gershom Scholem and who so enthusiastically endorsed the Four Paths as Jewish (while decrying the three paths as not Jewish). This man was 100 percent correct. The Four Paths are Jewish; therefore, they are biblical, while the three paths are not. Notice what is missing from the three paths: there is not a word about justice, not a word about creativity, not a word about joy. When people grow up spoiled, purgation or loss is often a kick-start to a spiritual awakening. But for most of humanity — which is not spoiled as such — the breakthrough is meant to happen via awe and wonder and praise, the Via Positiva. Life contains enough of its own suffering and pruning and lessons of loss and letting go. We don't have to add to the suffering through ascetic overload. The three paths leave out the basic teachings of Jesus and the prophets, including justice and compassion. Why would the Christian tradition hold on to them — unless perhaps it served political interests like empire building?

As chapters 4 through 7 show, Thomas Merton grew from the three paths to the Four Paths of the Creation Spirituality journey. To this, I would add a final point. In his 1967 letter to me, Merton said that we have to move beyond Adolphe Tanquerey: "The Tanquerey approach just won't do." He was correct. And at the heart of Tanquerey's anti-body and justiceless spiritual teaching is the three-fold path of purgation, illumination, and union. Enough said.

Heresy #7: "Matthew Fox Works Too Closely with Native Americans"

I find this to be the most bewildering of all the heresies attributed to me. What does it mean to "work too closely with Native Americans"? It is true that I try to work often and as closely as possible with Native Americans, and I have had the privilege of having a number of Native American teachers (and some students) in my life. They have taught me much that is important about the spiritual journey, about the sacredness of Mother Earth and her creatures and our bodies, and about ceremony in particular. I think of Franciscan Sister José Hobday, a Seneca woman chosen by her tribe at seven years old to be a storyteller — and she was a great one. I think of Buck Ghosthorse, a Lakota teacher who joined our faculty after having dreams for ten years that he should work with white people because they are in charge and aren't very smart. He showed up at our ICCS program at Holy Names College unannounced, having driven cross country with his wife and all their earthly belongings because he was called by his dreams. He taught courses with us on Native American spirituality, and he set up a sweat lodge on campus that served students, faculty, and staff alike. We learned so much.

After three years with us he moved to the state of Washington to start his own community, which included sundance and many other ceremonies. He offered these, as his dreams dictated to him, to Native Americans and non–Native Americans alike. I was privileged to undergo a vision quest with him in the foothills of the Seattle-area mountains as well as several sundances near Goldendale, Washington. Native ceremonies and the drumming and ancient songs that accompany them are food for my soul. I am forever indebted to Buck, who died a few years ago but left his sundance community under the leadership of his two sons, Paul and Chad, and his wife, Vicki.

I have been privileged to work with and learn from Aboriginals in Australia as well as Maori peoples in New Zealand and indigenous people in Scandinavia. Other teachers include Navajo painter David Paladin (whose wife invited me to comment on his work for an exhibition after he died) and Apela Colorado, who was on my faculty at the University of Creation Spirituality and who led me through some ceremonies in her adopted islands of Hawaii. And with Linda Neale and her husband, elder Ron McAfee, who live in the Portland, Oregon, area and who invited me to pen a preface to Linda's excellent book *The Power of Ceremony: Restoring the Sacred in Our Selves, Our Families, Our Communities*. A Canadian First Peoples person, who was a student in our program, was a Vietnam War veteran who taught me a deep lesson from his tribal training about growing from a soldier into a warrior.

Is all this "working too closely with Native Americans"? I see it as a simple admission that the West does not hold all the answers. Indigenous people have much to teach us and especially in this time of crisis with Mother Earth. How much racism is involved in saying I work too closely with Native Americans? I suspect that Mr. Ratzinger was unnerved to hear that there was a Native American sweat lodge on a Catholic campus in Oakland, California.

Lately I have been working with native peoples of California to combat the completely misguided attempts of the Vatican to canonize Franciscan friar Junipero Serra, who founded the mission system in the state. Scholarship now abounds to put a lie to the mythology that he loved and protected the Native Americans. In fact he was torturing them, beating them, destroying their families and culture and spiritual practices, and killing them in what were in effect death camps. Far from being a saint, Serra was a zealous colonizer-in-chief, a racist, and a white supremacist driven by a sick theology that cared almost nothing about life so long as his charges were baptized to go to heaven when they died. The first visitor to see the missions was a French sea captain who compared them to the slave plantations he had observed in the Caribbean. A very just comparison, indeed.

During a trip in 2015 to Bolivia, Pope Francis apologized for the "crimes" committed by missionaries. But to canonize one of their worst, which he did, is, I am sorry to say, a crime in itself. In the fifteenth century, popes used the "Discovery Doctrine" to give supposed legitimacy to the conquest of new territory in the name of the "Christian empire." I wonder what Jesus — who was himself murdered by an empire — would say.

Merton on American Indigenous History

Thomas Merton was very aware of Native American suffering, and he frequently took up the cause of indigenous peoples in the Americas. As Ross Labrie writes, Merton "deals particularly with the Mayan culture, which he regarded as one of the noblest and most peaceful in history." Merton cited from the *Book of Chilam Balam of Tizimin* (1951), which gives the Mayan version of the Spanish conquest of America. He criticized the missionaries, in Labrie's words, "who had failed to see the beauty of the Mayan rituals" even as he painted a picture of "the graceful, ritual dancing of the men and women" of the tribe in prayer. Labrie said that "pre-colonial Mayan culture was for Merton a symbol of the paradise that is possible for all." But this paradise of living interdependently with nature was ripped apart first by raids from the warlike Toltecs and then most grievously by the arrival of the Spaniards. In his major poem *The Geography of Lograire*, written in 1968, Merton wrote:

Redneck captains with whips
Fire in their fingers.

Nor did he spare the religious invaders:

Friars behind every rock every tree
Doing business
Bargaining for our souls
Book burners and hangmen.

Merton's book *Ishi Means Man*, which includes a foreword by Dorothy Day, celebrates the wisdom found in America's indigenous peoples. In it, he commented on a Sundance for Peace and the "mystical" practices of fasting and vision quests. He demonstrated an awareness and appreciation of the power of cosmic rituals. These, he felt, accomplished a full integration

> into a cosmic system which was at once perfectly sacred and perfectly worldly.... "Self-realization" in such a context implied not so much the ego-consciousness of the isolated subject in the face of a multitude of objects, but the awareness of a network of relationships in which one had a place in the mesh. One's identity was the intersection of cords where one "belonged." The intersection was to be sought in terms of a kind of musical or aesthetic and scientific synchronicity — one fell in step with the dance of the universe, the liturgy of the stars.

Merton got it — the marriage of psyche and cosmos that cosmic rituals renew, a sense of belonging in a network of relationships. He also addressed the long history of oppression of native peoples.

> In putting the Indian under tutelage to our own supposedly superior generosity and intelligence, we are in fact defining our own inhumanity, our own insensitivity, our own blindness to human values....His reservation existence — somewhat like the existence of an orphan in an asylum — is as close to non-existence as we can get him without annihilating him altogether....It means that as far as we are concerned the Indian (like the Negro, the Asian, etc.) is permitted to have a human identity only in so far as he conforms to ourselves and takes upon himself our identity.

He mocked the ideology behind colonialism when he wrote that the native peoples "seemed to be owners of the whole continent, until we arrived and informed them of the true situation. They were squatters on land which God had assigned to us.... We could see at a glance, we understood without the slightest hesitation, that they were only *aboriginal* owners. They never had any legal title to the real estate." Thus we placed them, "with the help of the military," on reservations.

His essay "Ishi: A Meditation" begins with the following stark words: "Genocide is a new word. Perhaps the word is new because technology has now got into the game of destroying whole races at once. The destruction of races is not new — just easier." Ishi was the last survivor of the Yahi people, who were hunted for a bounty on their heads in California for fifty years, and Merton was responding to a new study by Theodora Kroeber, *Ishi in Two Worlds: A Biography of the Last Wild Indian in North America* (published in 1964). Merton celebrated "the courage, the resourcefulness, and the sheer nobility of these few stone age men struggling to preserve their life, their autonomy and their identity as a people." He respected the "hidden life" of this tribe, which had been reduced to twenty people, who for twelve years learned to live "invisible and as unknown." Eventually, only Ishi remained with his sister and sick mother, and when they died, Ishi surrendered to the white race on August 29, 1911. Fortunately, an anthropologist at the University of California at Berkeley took him in and treated him well for the remaining four and a half years of his life.

Merton compared the Ishi story to the contemporary goings-on in the Vietnam War, and he compared the Vietnam War to the American Indian wars of a hundred years ago. "Viet Nam seems to have become an extension of our old western frontier, complete with enemies of another 'inferior' race.... What a pity that so many innocent people have to pay with their lives for our obsessive fantasies." Merton asked us to consider

the spectacle of our own country with its incomparable technological power, its unequaled material strength, and its psychic turmoil, its moral confusion and its profound heritage of guilt which neither the righteous declarations of Cardinals nor the moral indifference of "realists" can do anything to change! Every bomb we drop on a defenseless Asian village, every Asian child we disfigure or destroy with fire, only adds to the moral strength of those we wish to destroy for our own profit.

In his essay "The Sacred City" — which was no doubt a response to theologian Harvey Cox's book *The Secular City*, which was in vogue in Merton's day — Merton spoke of the recent archaeological findings in Mexico's Oaxaca Valley and concluded that "three things" stood out in comparison with our contemporary urban world. "The indifference to technological progress, the lack of history, and the almost total neglect of the arts of war." This provided an "entirely different conception of man and of life," which can be characterized as "a network of living interrelationships....In plain and colloquial terms it is a difference between a peaceful, timeless life lived in the stability of a continually renewed present, and a dynamic, aggressive life aimed at the future."

Thus, in *Ishi Means Man*, Merton did not romanticize indigenous history but drew valuable lessons from it for our own time and for the ongoing examination of our own conscience. Elsewhere, Merton composed a myth of indigenous history in which he wrote how "the spirits have held out toward us in their hands in silence, and in their hands their orchids and oranges.... They have sung to us, they have followed us, friendly.... They have enticed us; they have flown seductively about our heads; they have vanished into the sky. We have not understood their playful modes. We have fought Eros." This last sentence lays bare so much of what ails Western culture and religion — it has been fighting Eros. It is afraid of the Via Positiva. The Book of Wisdom in the

Bible defines wisdom this way: "This is wisdom, to love life." Since Eros is about love and passion for life, to be wise is to be erotic and vice versa. Since playfulness is part of creativity, there will be no creativity without Eros and play. Didn't Thomas Aquinas say that the nearest thing to contemplation is play? Patriarchy and capitalism indeed fight Eros (and in the process reduce it to pornography). All dualism makes a foe of Eros. But indigenous religion, which has been called "aboriginal Mother Love," does not despise play or Eros.

Given Merton's involvement with and admiration of indigenous wisdom, would he, too, have been accused of "working too closely with Native Americans"?

Creation Spirituality as an Ecological Spirituality: From Heresy to Orthodoxy

In chapters 8 and 9, I have invited Thomas Merton to sit in on my "heresy trial" with Cardinal Ratzinger. As I've shown, I think Merton is very much on my side vis-à-vis these seven very nebulous charges. To me, these charges reveal how deeply threatened the Vatican establishment was by the Creation Spirituality tradition and how out of touch it was with its oldest authentic spiritual tradition.

They say the heresy of today morphs into the orthodoxy of tomorrow, and that seems to be happening now. In June 2015, Pope Francis released an encyclical on ecology entitled "*Laudito Si*: On Care for Our Common Home." With this, the accusations hurled at me in a time of gross ignorance in the Vatican seem to be melting before the far greater issues of developing an eco-spirituality. This is of course what the Creation Spiritual tradition is all about, and always has been: the sacredness of nature — including our own. In July 2015, I wrote a response to the encyclical entitled "Pope Francis' Encyclical and the Coming of Age of Creation

Spirituality." One of the principal architects of the encyclical, Sean McDonagh, in fact studied with me in our master's program in Creation Spirituality. Sean is an Irish missionary priest working in the Philippines, and he has published several solid books on spirituality and ecology since graduating from our program.

Thomas Berry celebrates Merton's contribution to ecology and spirituality when he acknowledges Merton's "nature writings" as an "all-pervasive aspect of his writings." These take on an "added significance," Berry writes, "since, in the future, the understanding of nature, its infinitely diverse modes of expression, and the need to develop a mutually enhancing mode of human presence to the natural world will be a central concern in every phase of human activity." Berry continues: "An absence of a sense of the sacred is the basic flaw in many of our efforts at ecologically or environmentally adjusting our human presence to the natural world. It has been said, 'We will not save what we do not love.' It is also true that we will neither love nor save what we do not experience as sacred." Berry continues:

> There is a certain futility in the efforts being made — truly sincere, dedicated, and intelligent efforts — to remedy our environmental devastation simply by activating renewable sources of energy and by reducing the deleterious impact of the industrial world. The difficulty is that the natural world is seen primarily for human use, not as a mode of sacred presence primarily to be communed with in wonder and beauty and intimacy. In our present attitude, the natural world remains a commodity to be bought and sold, not a sacred reality to be venerated....Eventually only our sense of the sacred will save us. Merton's gift...is this sense of the sacred throughout the entire range of the natural world.

As Berry recognizes, Merton recovers that sacred sense for us all.

CHAPTER TEN

"The greatest orgy of idolatry the world has ever known"

Merton on Religion, Fundamentalism, and Empires

From now on, everybody stands on his own feet. . . . The time for re-lying on structures has disappeared.

— THOMAS MERTON

P art of Thomas Merton's prophetic work was his criticism of organized religion itself. In a correspondence with Henry Miller in 1962, Merton spoke bluntly about his ambivalent feelings about religion:

> In the whole question of religion today: all I can say, I wish I could really see what is there to see. Nobody can see the full dimension of the problem, which is more than a problem, it is one of those things you read about in the apocalypse. There are no problems in the apocalypse, just monsters. This one is a monster.
>
> The religion of religious people tends at times to poke out a monster head just when you are beginning to calm

down and get reassured. The religion of half-religious people doesn't tend: it bristles with heads...the dull eyes, the
ears that now listen to all the stars and decode their message
into something about business upswing.

This is the greatest orgy of idolatry the world has ever
known, and it is not generally thought by believers that
idolatry is the greatest and fundamental sin....Anyone who
sells out to even a small, inoffensive, bargain cheap idol has
alienated himself and put himself into the statue and has to
act like it, which is he has to be dead....The time is short,
and all the idols are moving....Strange that the individual is
the only power that is left.

These words seem particularly prescient given the rise of fun-
damentalisms in all the world's religions (Christianity included)
since Merton's day up to and including the apocalyptic-based
ideological extremism of ISIS that is inciting fear and angst in the
world. Clearly, Merton was not mesmerized by superficial religious
shibboleths of any kind. He was critical of religion and its often
dark history in general, and that included the history of his own
Christian tradition, whether talking of the friars who attended the
conquistadores in conquering the Native American populations,
or of the monasteries in Europe that went along with Hitler, or of
his experience within his own order with fellow monks, abbots,
lazy theologians, critical inquisitors, and censors who resisted his
attempts to speak up against the American empire.

I have no doubt that Merton, had he lived, would have had at
least as much angst and would have undergone at least as many
attacks from the church hierarchy as did I. Merton's frustration
was tempered somewhat by a clear theological distinction both he
and I hold to: that the kingdom/queendom of God is one thing,
and the church is quite another.

Christianity: A Cult of the Dead Body of Christ?

Merton was alert to the signs of the times — including the idols of sick religion. On Easter Sunday, 1967, he preached a homily at his monastery, in which he proclaimed:

> Our Christian religion too often becomes simply the cult of the dead body of Christ compounded with anguish and desperation over the problem of moving their immovable stone that keeps us from reaching him.
>
> This is no joke. This is what actually happens to the Christian religion when it ceases to be a really living faith and becomes a mere legalistic and ritualistic formality. Such Christianity is no longer life in the Risen Christ but a formal cult of the dead Christ considered not as the Light and Savior of the world but as a kind of divine thing, an extremely holy object, a theological relic. ... Christ becomes a shadow. At last He becomes a corpse-like figure of wax. Yet people go to extraordinary lengths to venerate this inert object, to embalm it with all kinds of perfumes, and to make up fantastic tales about what it can do to make you rich and happy by its powerful magic.

Calling Christianity a "cult of the dead body of Christ" is strong language indeed. Merton's prophetic critique does not spare the church. What is the medicine he offers? He urged a renewal of the individual, a rebirth from within, since "the individual is the only power that is left." Institutions — including religious ones — can no longer be trusted. Merton, like many living through the 1960s, developed a deep suspicion of institutions, so much so that in his very last talk given to Asian monks and nuns he cited Chögyam Trungpa Rinpoche, who said, "From now on, Brother, everybody stands on his own feet." Merton commented: "To my mind, that is an extremely important monastic statement. If you forget everything else that has been said, I would suggest you remember this for the future." He elaborated: "We can no longer rely on being supported by structures that may be destroyed at any moment by a political power or a political force.... The time for relying on structures has disappeared."

1968: A Tumultuous Year for Religion

Two religious bombs exploded in 1968, Merton's last year with us. The first was Pope Paul's encyclical *Humanae Vitae*, which appeared on July 25 and restated the church's opposition to birth control. The pope ignored the opinion of the very board he appointed to study the subject and instead reaffirmed the old teaching. At the time, this split the church wide open, and the rupture has continued to this day. The encyclical essentially stood by the teachings of Augustine and all those who followed him. According to Augustine, all sex has to be justified by having babies. To this day, the Roman Catholic Church is split over this one-sided teaching, which has created "neurotics for orthodoxy" (to quote a Latin American bishop) and has become the rallying cry for rightists fiercely promoting an "authentic Catholicism." A bishop from India shortly before Pope Francis's election talked about a "civil war in the church," with birth control being the litmus test of supposed orthodoxy. Supposedly, the number one issue is "Do you believe in birth control or not?" I am certain that the number one reason so many good Catholic priests abandoned ship in the fifteen years following that ill-fated encyclical was because they could no longer in good conscience preach fidelity to the principles of *Humanae Vitae*.

However, Pope Francis has opened the door somewhat on the subject. First, he has declined to emphasize it (and he has criticized those who put "all their theology in a condom"). Second, he has stated that Catholics are not to reproduce like rabbits. And most recently, in his encyclical on the environment, he has denounced dualisms of spirit versus matter.

A second momentous church event of 1968 was the Medellín Conference, which was held in Medellín, Colombia. This gathering of Latin American bishops, operating in the spirit and teachings of the Second Vatican Council, spoke in its final document released on September 6, 1968, about the "injustice [that cries] to the heavens" throughout Latin America. The solutions it offered included a "preferential option for the poor" and the establishment of "base communities" of ordinary lay Catholics who would be schooled in the teachings of justice to be found in the Bible. The goal was to liberate people from the "institutional violence" of poverty, and the work of Paulo Freire and "conscientization" of people was emphasized.

This conference gave a green light to the movement later known as Liberation Theology, which took hold rapidly not only in so-called third world countries but in industrialized countries as well. Yet this created a backlash, particularly in America under President Ronald Reagan. His National Security Council met just three months after he was inaugurated in January 1981 to address just one question: "How can we destroy Liberation Theology in Latin America?" They concluded that they could not destroy it, but they could split the church. They found a willing partner in Pope John Paul II, who came from Soviet-dominated Poland and was elected to the papacy in 1978. Pope John Paul II, along with his hatchet man, Cardinal Ratzinger, laid waste to this vital movement over several decades. Together, they expelled or silenced over 106 Catholic theologians. I was one of them, and I list the others in my book *The Pope's War*, which lays out this history. Eventually, all those cardinals sympathetic to Liberation Theology were replaced with conservative men who were often members of the fascist organization Opus Dei. This effectively killed what the Latin American church had given birth to in response to the spirit and teachings of Vatican II. The CIA rejoiced, and in exchange, they contributed thousands upon thousands of dollars to the Vatican coffers, some of which was earmarked for Poland's Solidarity movement.

One thing I find quite surprising is that there is no mention of either the Medellín Conference or *Humanae Vitae* in Merton's work. Both occurred before his October trip to Asia. Perhaps the monks found it wiser to edit both these controversial events from the papers they released from Merton's estate, or maybe Merton himself felt it wiser not to comment on the encyclical, as he had other priorities while preparing for his Asian journey. As we will see, he was very reluctant to speak on topics of sexual morality. And the real impact of the Medellín declaration, which appeared just a month before his departure for Asia, was not felt immediately and certainly not in North America.

Critiquing False Religion and Religious Fundamentalism

When it comes to institutional religion, Merton was conflicted. He reacted strongly to the fundamentalists supporting apartheid in South Africa:

> May 18, 1960. I was appalled to realize what terrible things are happening in Southern Africa. I had thought vaguely that *Apartheid* was something like race-prejudice in our own South, like our own segregation which is bad enough. But this is much more. A completely degraded, concentration camp existence, not in misery only but in squalor, degradation and suffering. Beating and killing — the bodies lying on the ground in Sharpeville.
>
> The Afrikaaners are Christian fundamentalists. Bible Christians. What an indictment of Christianity! Yet if they

read the Bible they would know what they were doing. And we too!!

Merton did not only criticize South Africa. He put the light on the United States as well.

> At least, some of us know that we don't see and that we are secondly, stupid, befogged, helpless. That our vague good will can do nothing. And we are snowed under by useless goods, objects, foods, furniture, clothes, things, that keep in movement our absurd society of advertising and commerce. We consume and waste and throw away and everyone else in the world starves, and starves miserably. The best that can be said is that we don't *want* it to happen that way. But it does.

Merton criticized the abuse of religion in politics and addressed the question of whether religion can indeed become the "opiate of the people," as Karl Marx proposed. Merton wrote, "When religion becomes a mere artificial façade to justify a social or economic system — when religion hands over its rites and language completely to the political propagandist, and when prayer becomes the vehicle for a purely secular ideological program, then religion does tend to become an opiate. It deadens the spirit." In such a situation, "religious zeal becomes political fanaticism. His faith in God, while preserving its traditional formulas, becomes in fact faith in his own nation, class or race. His ethic ceases to be the law of God and of love, and becomes the laws that might-makes-right: established privilege justifies everything, God is the *status quo*." Merton also criticized his own monastic system and its "monastic tradition" in Germany for going along with Hitler. He wrote in his journal in June 1963: "German monasteries which were very well up on patrology and monastic theology and which at the same time supported Hitler, and therefore, whether they knew it or not, were involved in Auschwitz, the Blitz, etc. etc."

Closer to home, in response to the Eichmann trial in 1963, Merton wrote: "What is religion, for the most part, in this country? A 'source of peace,' a refuge from conflict? So — an Eichmann factory, maybe! Certainly we preach the Cross, but not the cross of resistance; only the cross of submission. And never mind to what. Submission to power — any power that adjusts itself to the Church." Merton addressed a monk who said it was for the bishops to write about war, not Merton. His response? "How do you expect the bishops to say anything without the moral theologians? And the moral theologians? Sitting on their cans and preserving their reputations. This is one of the situations that keeps the Church half dead." So Merton saw himself operating amid a "half dead" church.

Back in 1959, before the Second Vatican Council was conceived, Merton ruminated about his problem with the church as institution and his complicity in it.

> What can I say about the great discovery of my need for the Church, that is for the Holy Spirit dwelling and acting in the Mystical Christ? It is something inexplicable, this greatest of all realities, this reality which is so well hidden by the false front and the externals and the unintended edifice. But I now realize that for a long time I have been slowly and severely tempted against the church and only with the first glimpse of a solution have I realized how deeply I was involved in the problem. And yet it is not really that much of a problem since the Spirit Himself (who helpeth our infirmity) both raises the question and answers it.

Critiquing His Monastery

Merton addressed the personal pain and suffering that came his way via the monastic system he was part of. He complained in a May 1963 journal entry about being asked to give too many conferences for visiting monks, and he questioned the mental stability of his abbot on more than one occasion. The monastery could be a very Via Negativa experience for him, clearly. "This I found very irritating and upsetting, for various subtle reasons, but I feel as if I had been partly flayed and salted because I am so aware of the implications and of the secret injustice that is done me by my abbot's neurosis."

In this journal entry, he was so upset that he could not sleep at night. He talked of being "worn down" and "easily discouraged":

> The depressions are deeper, more frequent. I am near fifty. People think I am happy.... I have stubbornly saved myself from becoming *absorbed* in the priesthood, and I don't know if this was cowardice or integrity. There seems to be no real way for me to tell.... I am not so sure about the others, the frustrating and seemingly pointless acts of mechanical obedience demanded purely and simply by the organizational pattern.

In July 1959, he complained mightily in his journal:

> I see no further reason for staying in the big overgrown, commercialized community with all its artificialities and stupidities. I honestly think that the situation here is almost helpless. The blind leading the blind — if not over a cliff, at least round in circles.... The systemic regularity that they would like to impose on everyone is empty and futile. A series of gestures and external acts without much inner meaning and hardly able to produce any spiritual fruit excepting the satisfied sense of duty that warms the heart of a conformist — when he has conformed.
>
> For the rest it seems only to produce warped and eccentric personalities.
>
> Not because of the Rule of St. B but because of the hopeless way in which it is interpreted here.

Merton called himself "a frustrated intellectual, pseudo-contemplative pseudo-hermit."

Merton also chafed under the issue of censorship of his writings — a lot of this censorship was not concerning faith and morals, but rather, as Ross Labrie puts it, "whether it was opportune for a particular book to be published. Anything at all, 'with or without reasons given,' he concluded, could cause a book to be stopped under this rubric." Merton chafed at being told by his abbot that he should not write about nuclear war.

> The argument that I am supposed to be a "contemplative" and therefore to remain silent is transparently artificial. True, this is a principle. But there is also a culpable silence. Silence is not an absolute, nor an end in itself....It would be to me a problem of conscience if I allowed myself simply to become the kind of monk they apparently want me to be — a conformist, not rocking the boat, not speaking out, passive, mute, indifferent.

These passages by Merton, in which he invokes the principle of "conscience," lead me to believe that he would have well understood my struggle with the American Dominicans and the Vatican and my willingness to speak out rather than to go silent. In my letters to Rome to defend my positions, I frequently invoked the law of conscience, especially the strong teachings from Thomas Aquinas on the primacy of conscience — teachings that have rarely been invoked in practice. For me, it was to little avail, obviously. The censorship problem for Merton reached a crescendo when his book *Peace in the Post-Christian Era*, which he finished in 1963, was denied permission to be published. One reason he wrote for small magazines such as *The Catholic Worker* was that the monastery less often censored his articles in modest magazines.

But Labrie believes that there was a bigger issue at stake that was triggered by the censors. It concerned Merton's vocational struggle. Labrie writes, "Merton's acutest problems with writing were the result of his own anxieties about his dual vocation as both contemplative and author. It was not just that writing took time away from contemplation but that it seemed at a certain point to subvert it." Contemplation and action, mysticism and prophecy, were in a battle within his soul. Merton wrote in his journal: "I am getting to dislike more and more the complacent emphasis of the term 'contemplative,' and its inherent capacity to encourage phariseeism." In 1959, wrestling with his vocation, he wrote:

> I really have no ideals. Perhaps what I really want is to get away from ideals and mental images of monasticism and simply live as best I can, just live.... The fact is, I do not want purely and simply to "be a hermit" or to lead a life purely and ideally contemplative. At the same time I want to break with all the fictions and pretense, all the façade and latent hypocrisy of the monastic community in which I live. Yet. I truly seek a very solitary, simple and primitive life with no special labels attached.

In many ways it seems to me that Merton was more at home with a contemplative/active spiritual vocation such as the Dominicans practiced (including Aquinas, Eckhart, and myself) than with an exclusively contemplative order such as the Trappists. On the other hand, with the Trappists, he undoubtedly found time and space to do the research, writing, inner work, and scholarship that he so desperately needed to do. He also clearly developed his mystical life, especially when he moved into the hermitage in the woods. With the Dominicans, he may have found too little time for research, which included the contemplative and inner research required for a deep spiritual journey, and maybe even more censorship. Eckhart's famous sermon on Martha and Mary, where he turns the tables on the traditional telling of the story, concludes that Martha is the mature one because she can do two things at once — contemplation *and* action — while Mary is immature and can only do one thing at a time, namely contemplation.

To resolve this, Merton might have profited from reading more of Eckhart, such as from his Via Transformativa sermons and treatises (which I offer in my book *Passion for Creation*). For according to Labrie, "the problem remained intellectually insoluble for him until his death." In art, the Via Positiva and the Via Creativa come together, along with the Via Negativa and the Via Transformativa. Indeed, for Merton solitude and silence (Via Negativa) were a prelude to art and creativity (Via Creativa). As Labrie put it, "it was this sensitivity to silence — to what lay behind the word — that motivated Merton's art as well as his life as a contemplative.... The artist and the contemplative in him were in agreement on this matter." Merton came to the conclusion that an art experience can become "analogous to the purity of religious contemplation," and experience lies beyond all art. He said, "A poem is for me the expression of an inner poetic experience and what matters is the experience, more than the poem itself." This is not unlike M. C. Richards saying that the greatest thing the potter produces is not the pot but the potter!

Merton also critiqued worship in the monastery. He found an "utter objectification" around the Sacred Presence in the Blessed Sacrament and complained that "we hide from ourselves by our very piety. Or our worship is often a way of deluding ourselves that we are paying our debts." In his journal, he fancied addressing his abbot this way (though he bit his tongue and did not do so): "I hate pontifical masses. I hate your idea of the liturgy — it seems to me to be a false, dead, repetition of words and gestures without spontaneity, without sincerity. You like to sing hymns because the melodies delight you. I can think of better ways in which to waste my time. The Africans with their drums have got it all over us. There is no routine with them. They are saying what they mean."

Merton also criticized the education and the educators in his monastery, as we saw in chapter 6.

Critiquing the Catholic Church

On February 8, 1959, Merton criticized a basic tenet of Catholicism, that of getting everyone to go to church, writing: "To get everybody back to 'going to Church' — that is not yet the answer. The idea is that men should live *first of all as men* — with all their human rights and dignities. Then as *Sons of God*, with their divine and spiritual prerogatives. If Sons of God — Then *Brothers in Christ*." Writing in 1962, Merton believed that the church was "full of a terrible spiritual sickness." In his letters, he wrote that he was "dispirited by the Christianity of 'individualism,' of 'formulas,' and of 'passive conformity,' and deeply disturbed by the silence of the Catholic Church and its clergy." He yearned that "the Catholic position on nuclear war was held as strict as the Catholic position on birth control." He observed that the "passivity…and worse still the active belligerency of some religious spokesmen, especially in this country, is rapidly becoming one of the most frightful scandals in the history of Christendom." He warned that the Bible is a "dangerous book" for those who really meditate on it, and he warned Catholic educators that religion can easily be bought. "Wealth and power know how important it is to have a 'kept' clergy and a 'kept' intellectual community — i.e. to have these two groups use their abilities and office to support in thought, word, deed, and spirit those allegiances that are in the interest of wealth and power."

Merton demonstrated an ambivalent attitude toward the Second Vatican Council at the start. He read Hans Küng's book *The Council, Reform and Reunion*, and praised it, but he confessed he was afraid of institutional backlash. Given the sad history of the Roman Catholic Church since the early seventies, his warnings sound eerily prescient.

> I am so afraid that the concept of "renewal" will turn out to be nothing more than a tightening of the screws on the poor rank and file religious, clergy, and layman who has been hog-tied for so long. This council is going to have to be a proof that we are not just a monolithic organization: because that is how such organizations renew themselves: by tightening their grip on the rank and file and re-asserting the perpetual rightness of the managers. If that happens this time, so help us it will be one of the most horrible scandals that ever took place. It will be a disaster. That, principally, is the object of my prayers: that it will be a real renewal, or a step toward it. But honestly, I am scared.

In this passage Merton accurately predicted what happened in the Catholic Church beginning with *Humanae Vitae* and culminating with the papacies of John Paul II and Benedict XVI. Reading this, I have little doubt that Merton would applaud my recent book on the dark side of the church, *The Pope's War*, which chronicled how these popes "tightened their grip" in order to preserve a "monolithic organization." The "horrible scandal" and "disaster" Merton feared has indeed taken place many times over. The church's hierarchy became dominated by radical right-wing groups like Opus Dei and Legion of Christ, and one result has been the pedophile priest scandals and their cover-up, all to protect the "monolithic organization" that he warned about.

These disasters and scandals are well-documented, and the conclusion I draw from them is quite clear: The Holy Spirit gave the world two debased popes in order to gut the Roman Catholic Church as we know it and therefore to begin a new Christ-path much closer to the teaching and person of Jesus than the church has become over the centuries.

In critiquing the church, Merton named — and predicted — something similar:

> We have to face the fact that we have traveled a long way from the real Christian center. Centuries of identification between Christian and civil life have done more to secularize Christianity than to sanctify civil life. This is not a popular idea. I wonder if anyone in our time has really faced it in a satisfactory way without either too much evasion, too total and too oversimplified a rejection of the secular and the temporal, or too complete a submission to it? The problem is enormous.

Responding to the Vatican Council

At the opening of the Second Vatican Council in 1962, Merton offered some guarded optimism and confessed that "I have been extremely heartened by the opening speech of John XXIII at the Vatican Council.... There are really deep and insistent notes of change and renewal. I am sure that if he gets any cooperation at all, the Council will certainly do good and even great things." The pope had called for "opening the windows" of the church and reaching out more to serve the world as it was and not as one would hope it would be. There was considerable backlash, of course, in the Curia, or administrative offices of the church, which were quite stale and closed minded. Merton brought up opposition from the Curia, but he believed Pope John would hold his own against them. Calling the opening of the council "tremendous," he repeated a joke that was going around about the nay-saying cardinals. "You know the Roman joke that is going around now? Question: Where are Cardinals Ottaviani and

Ruffini these days? Answer: Oh, haven't you heard? They are on their way to the Council of Trent." The Council of Trent was called in the sixteenth century in response to the Protestant Reformation. Suggesting the opponents of Vatican II were retreating four centuries was not so far off the mark — and many would say the same retreat was repeated under the papacies of John Paul II and Benedict XVI.

When it comes to strategies for church renewal, Merton did not countenance putting too much energy into projecting onto the hierarchy but rather sticking with the *sensus fidelium* (the conscience of practicing laypeople) at the ground level. He urged people to resist the "glorified infantilism" of always seeking answers from "above," that is, from ecclesial prelates.

> I am not in favor of the kind of pressure that strives to get Rome to approve this and condemn that. In the long run it tends to be glorified infantilism and it prolongs the infantile type of theological thought we are trying to get rid of.... The thing to realize is this: we are members of Christ, and we have a voice whether as priests or as laity. If we as members of Christ protest against total war, then it is already in some sense a work of the Church.

When the council ended, Merton wrote in his journal about how he was changed by it: "I am repeatedly thankful for this Council, for having lived at this time, for having learned so much from it. Certainly my own attitude to 'the world' will have to be modified. I have too easily and unthinkingly used the old *contemptus mundi* line as an evasion. However, this does not mean I do not remain a hermit. But it changes my attitude, anyway. Rightly so." On December 13, 1965, Merton wrote about how one necessary change was his anti-technology stance and his feelings that science all too easily sold its soul for purposes of war and, with pesticides, to chemical companies that destroy the earth.

A grace of the Council for me will have been the beginning of a change from a radically negative anti-science and anti-technology attitude to something more open and humane. For example when the big SAC B 52 flew low over the hermitage under the low ceiling of clouds it was possible for me to think of it as part of my own world, not just as "*their* damn plane.*"* Although that does not imply approval of the bomb, still, it is *my* world that builds the planes and flies them and there is something admirable about all that: it has at least good possibilities.

He foresaw tensions within the church as a result of the council. In an August 1964 diary entry, he wrote: "When one has lived through the pontificate of a John XXIII, one cannot go back to the old positions again. One has to see things forever in a new light. I know now that there are forces awakened in the church that will refuse to go back to sleep. I don't know what will come, but there may be momentous stresses and pressures."

His words have surely been accurate. Since the seventies, the church has been sinking under those "momentous stresses and pressures," and it has resorted to many of the "old positions" — including a preoccupation with sexual morality, centralization of decision making in Roman bureaucracies, and silencing theologians, even though the Second Vatican Council sought to empower local churches to make decisions and encouraged freedom of intellectual thought.

One of the defining issues of the council was the subject of the church as the people of God versus the church as hierarchy. The council spoke of the church as "the people of God," and this can itself be narrow thinking: Are non-Christians not also "people of God"? And what about non-humans? Are the four-legged and finned people and tree people not "people of God"? Nevertheless, it was a transformative language that moved people out of the "infantile" attitudes of father dependency and into a sense of their own responsibility for moral decision making. Merton applied this shift of thought to his novices, the youngest ones in the community whom he came to admire and love. He saw the church as the people and not so much as hierarchy, writing: "Especially love for and appreciation for the novices, realization of Christ's love for them: these are very important to me, sometimes makes all the difference. In them the Church is easily visible to me. More visible, I fear, than in Rome. I don't refer to the Council, for that too has had its charismatic visibility, at least in the beginning."

Conscience, Fidelity, and "Blind Obedience" in the Church

Merton recognized a built-in tension or "trial" around the issue of fidelity versus conscience in an organization like the church. He wrote:

> The great trial of fidelity in Christian life — a trial which springs from the fact that we too closely identify *fidelity to God* and *fidelity to external organization* in the Catholic Church. There are times when it seems that fidelity to God is *not* compatible with mere obedience to an external norm, where fidelity to God requires something else: certainly not revolt or disobedience, but a presentation of alternatives and deeper views.... The answer is in the church considered less as an organization than as a living body of interrelated freedoms. Fidelity belongs not so much to the realm of Law as to the realm of love. But it presupposes obedience and self-sacrifice.

Merton recognized how religion — and Catholicism in particular — can become an "obsession" or addiction, such as in this 1967 journal entry:

The whole thing is sickening. The mechanical, cause-and-effect, official machinery of Catholicism. Dreadfully dead, putrid. And yet people are committed to this insane validism, this unchristian obsession....It is the old hang-up on magic: following the instructions on the bottle to get the infallible effect. A monastery is a place where, though there are more detailed instructions on the bottle we follow them all meticulously, and the whole Church turns on with our magic tonic. Is LSD more honest? We do this because we think it makes us respectable: we are fully justified by Tierce, Sext, None, Vespers and Compline and blind obedience to the ascetic Dad, no matter how absurd.

The Church is a great treadmill, and when you turn it, it churns out an ineffable substance called grace, and he who gets his pail full is thereafter untouchable, impervious to everything, neither man nor God can tell him anything. He is justified. He is right.

After the Second Vatican Council ended, Merton criticized himself for going along with the game in the past:

I happened to glance through some old notes of mine — novitiate conferences on the vows — dating back ten years. Incredible and quite embarrassing. I was astonished to find them so legalistic, so rigid, so narrow. Yet in those days I thought myself quite broad and many regarded me as a dangerous radical. I was only doing what I thought I had to do — teaching what all the authorities held! That it now seems completely unrealistic and false is a sign that there has really been something of a revolution. Felt the same about the Bishops' Pastoral [titled "The Church in Our Day" and appearing in November 1967]....It seems to lack a real inner sense of the Church: they are still talking of a Church of *Law*, and they are in a bind they can't really get out of.

Merton addressed the preoccupation with papal gossip (I have coined the term "papalolatry"), and he suggested feeling sorry for Pope Paul: "why blame everything on the poor man who can't help being what he is — a curial official trained under Pius XII, with a few lively ideas on Catholic Action acquired in the '20's and '30's." He commented bluntly that "the whole institutional structure is questionable.... This is not for me. I can't be part of any of it, for or against. It all strikes me as a bit childish."

At one point, the publisher Sheed and Ward asked Merton to write a book on current sexual issues. Merton refused, thus distancing himself from the preoccupation with sexual morality that takes over many moralists in church thinking and was so much a part of the pre-Vatican II mentality. Rosemary Ruether wrote the following comment to Merton in April 1967: "I do not now nor at any time in the foreseeable future wish to write any books on marriage, divorce, birth control, women, celibacy, abortion, or sex." Referring to an article in *Look* magazine by Father James Kavanaugh, she believed Kavanaugh "has covered the field of Catholic sexology sufficiently — what a depressing article! It really made you feel that the church was so hopelessly neurotic and was screwing up so many people's lives that the world would really be better off if it disappeared from the face of the earth." Merton did not respond to this statement one way or the other, but no doubt it registered on him in some fashion. I suspect that he, like Rosemary, was years ahead of Pope Francis's complaint that some people let condoms guide their theology. Unfortunately, from the time of Merton's death in 1968 to Francis's papacy in 2013, that old "condom theology" prevailed through several papacies.

Merton on Church and State

Merton took up the thorny issue of church and state at least as far back as 1959 when he was writing his book on the Desert Fathers,

The Wisdom of the Desert. He had much to say about the radical break that is often needed between true and false religion, true and false patriotism. In the book, he described the fourth-century movement of young men who chose to go out to the desert to pray rather than submit to the norms of the empire — even and especially a newly "baptized" Christian empire.

> Society — which meant pagan society, limited by the horizons and prospects of life "in this world" — was regarded by them as a shipwreck from which each single individual man had to swim for his life.... These were men who believed that to let oneself drift along passively accepting the tenants and values of what they knew as society was purely and simply a disaster. The fact that the Emperor was now Christian and that the "world" was coming to know the Cross as a sign of temporal power only strengthened them in their resolve.

Merton did not see this protest as unrelated to the challenges of our own times — indeed, he drew some deep lessons from their actions. "These men seem to have thought... that there is really no such a thing as a 'Christian state.' They seem to have doubted that Christianity and politics could ever be mixed to such an extent as to produce a fully Christian society." This strikes me as miles away from St. Augustine's writing on the Christian empire, *The City of God*, which was penned in the fifth century in response to the fall of Rome to Alaric I, king of the Visigoths, in 410. One might say that Augustine offered up a sort of blueprint for the burgeoning "Christian empire." Merton put explicit distance between himself and Augustine's political views, which have permeated Western consciousness:

> Jaspers talks of the "Augustinian turnabout." At one moment Augustine is saying "let none of us say he has already found the truth. Let us look for it as though we did not yet

know it on either side" and then later he advocates using force against those who do not accept our faith. And apparently without feeling there is any problem. As the greatest of Catholic Doctors he has bequeathed this mentality to the entire Catholic Church — and to the Protestants as well, because he is as much their Father as ours! This is the mind of Western Christendom.

On numerous occasions, as we have seen, Merton criticized the consumer capitalism that underscores so much of American culture. He combined this critique with what has come to be known as the military-industrial-media complex in a single journal entry in 1962:

> Policy of TV industry-standardization — give what offends no one of the accepted groups — business, military.
>
> Aim — to keep everybody loyally and happily *consuming*.
>
> Consumership and the techniques of manipulating people and order them [to] consume as much as possible.
>
> The "American way of life" is the American religion.

In the same journal Merton wrote: "The idea of 'Christian civilization' is one of the most explosive myths we have.... I wonder if we have not after all had our chance and missed it. There have been 1600 years of 'Christian civilization' and not all of it has been very Christian."

In this chapter, we have seen how blunt Merton could be in his criticism of the idols of religion and culture, and he did not let monasticism itself off the hook. He was not reluctant to critique his own backyard — religion, the Catholic Church, and the Trappists, his own order. Nor did he spare himself, calling himself a "guilty bystander."

However, Merton also offered medicine for ailing religion, and this we will address in the next chapter.

CHAPTER ELEVEN

"Everything That Is, Is Holy"

Merton on the Cosmic Christ and Love in Action

We are other Christs.... In us, the image of God, which is complete and entire in each individual soul, is also, in all of us "the image of God."

— THOMAS MERTON

Thomas Merton was not content to just criticize religion or culture. He offered medicine as well, and he found it among the teachings and actions of the Desert Fathers and in the experience of the Cosmic Christ.

Wisdom from the Desert Fathers

The people we know today as the "Desert Fathers" were a movement of hermits in the fourth century who peopled the deserts of Egypt, Palestine, Arabia, and Persia. "They were the first Christian hermits" according to Merton, and they chose to abandon the cities of the pagan world to live in solitude. The Desert Fathers were far more radical than was Augustine — so, too, was Merton. They did not countenance cozying up to the emerging Christian empire. Rather, they fled to the mysticism of the desert.

In his 1960 book *The Wisdom of the Desert: Sayings from the Desert Fathers of the Fourth Century*, Merton stressed what the desert movement was *not*. In many ways he saw it as an important moment in the history of democracy — a rebellion against "a decadent state."

> The flight of these men to the desert was neither purely negative nor purely individualistic. They were not rebels against society. . . . They were men who did not believe in letting themselves be passively guided and ruled by a decadent state, and who believed that there was a way of getting along without slavish dependence on accepted, conventional values. . . . The Desert Fathers declined to be ruled by men, but had no desire to rule over others themselves. . . . They were eminently social.

What was their path to an authentic spirituality? It was not one of theological wordiness and esoteric doctrines — it was a path of experience, of spirituality more than academic debates. Merton wrote, "They sought a way to God that was uncharted and freely chosen, not inherited from others who had mapped it out beforehand. They sought a God whom they alone could find, not one who was 'given' in a set, stereotyped form by somebody else. . . . Their flight to the arid horizons of the desert meant also a refusal to be content with arguments, concepts and technical verbiage." They put experience front and center, and Merton urges us to do the same. Their wisdom is "at once primitive and timeless, and . . . enables us to reopen the sources that have been polluted or blocked up altogether by the accumulated mental and spiritual refuse of our technological barbarism. Our time is in desperate need

of this kind of simplicity.... The word to emphasize is *experience*."
Of course, experience is precisely what distinguishes spirituality
from either religion or theology as such. Religion is so often sociological structures, and theology is so often conceptual analysis,
but spirituality is primarily about experience. The Four Paths, for
example, are about the God-experience, the living of life in depth
that we are all busy doing.

What was at the heart of the teaching and the spiritual path
of the Desert Fathers that constituted their Via Transformativa?
Love. Throughout, Merton wrote, we "find a repeated insistence
on the primacy of love over everything else in the spiritual life:
over knowledge, gnosis, asceticism, contemplation, solitude,
prayer. Love in fact *is* the spiritual life, and without it all the other
exercises of the spirit, however lofty, are emptied of content and
become mere illusions. The more lofty they are, the more dangerous the illusion."

Merton understood such love to be a deep sense of compassion:

Love means an interior and spiritual identification with
one's brother, so that he is not regarded as an "object" to
"which" one "does good.".... Love takes one's neighbor as
one's other self, and loves him with all the immense humility and discretion and reserve and reverence without which
no one can presume to enter into the sanctuary of another's
subjectivity.... Love demands a complete inner transformation — for without this we cannot possibly come to identify
ourselves with our brother. We have to become, in some
sense, the person we love. And this involves a kind of death
of our own being, our own self. No matter how hard we try,
we resist this death.

Part of the path to compassion and the Via Transformativa
is a kind of dying (the Via Negativa). For the Desert Fathers, the

path also included the Via Positiva and a creation-based spirituality, as Merton recounted in this tale from the ancient texts: "A certain philosopher asked St. Anthony: Father, how can you be so happy when you are deprived of the consolation of books? Anthony replied: 'My book, O philosopher, is the nature of created things and any time I want to read the words of God, the book is before me.'" The desert, after all, is a very mystical place. Meister Eckhart commented on the holiness of the desert: "There is no place for two in the desert. There creation and Creator are one." This teaching of St. Anthony resonates with Eckhart, who said, "Every creature is a word of God and a book about God." It also resonates with Thomas Aquinas, who said, "Revelation comes in two volumes — Nature and the Bible."

Remember, the desert in the lands where the "Desert Fathers" flourished — Egypt, Palestine, Arabia, and Persia — was *the wilderness*. The wilderness is not just a refuge or sanctuary — it is also a place of revelation. No doubt the Desert Fathers had plenty of experience of that kind of union and communion, nature and human together, black, starry nights and light-filled days. They journeyed the paths of the Via Positiva, Via Negativa, Via Creativa, and Via Transformativa in nature and with the seasons amid animals and vegetation unique to the desert and its wilds. An intelligent student of mine from Arizona once wrote a convincing essay for me on "viriditas" (a word invented by Hildegard of Bingen, who lived in the green country of the Rhineland, which means "greening power") and "ariditas" that emphasized the powerful dynamic of living in the desert and its unique wilderness. Of course, Jesus, too, lived in a natural world that was more "ariditas" than "viriditas."

Another cure Merton offered for a compromised religion centered on a Cosmic Christ theology.

The Cosmic Christ in Merton

The Cosmic Christ theology was important to Thomas Merton. On several occasions he uses the term. "We are other Christs.... We ourselves are 'the Second Adam' because we ourselves are Christ. In us, the image of God, which is complete and entire in each individual soul, is also, in all of us 'the image of God.'...We ourselves are Christ and we are all dwelling in one another, by virtue of the unity of the divine image reformed by grace." In his journal Merton wrote: "Who am I? A Son of God.... My true self is the self that is spoken by God — 'Thou are My Son!' Our responsibility (ability and obligation to respond). Tremendous happiness and clarity (in darkness) is my response: 'Abba, Father!' "

Merton praises the "marvelous image" that Eckhart puts forth to name the "dynamic unity" of God and creatures, an image that "from the point of view of logic" does "not make sense, but as an expression of inexpressible insight into the very core of life, it is incomparable." Merton quotes Eckhart commenting on how the image of God in humans delights Divinity.

> In this likeness or identity God takes such delight that he pours his whole nature and being into it. His pleasure is as great, to take a simile, as that of a horse, let loose over a green heath, where the ground is level and smooth, to gallop as a horse will, as fast as he can over the greensward — for this is a horse's pleasure and nature. It is so with God. It is his pleasure and rapture to discover identity, because he can always put his whole nature into it — for he is this identity itself.

Merton sees in this passage Eckhart's "Christian doctrine of creation"; the distinction between Creator and creature does not have the last word. Merton said that what prevails is "a basic unity *within ourselves* at the summit of our being where we are 'one with God.'" That is the image of God in us, which is the spark of the soul in Eckhart's language, and the Cosmic Christ in my language.

When it comes to the Cosmic Christ in Merton, and his radical stance against Christianity as a religion, we should pay attention to what he tells us in *Zen and the Birds of Appetite* — a very late work of his published in 1968:

> In Christianity, too, as well as in Islam, we have various admittedly unusual people who see beyond the "religious" aspect of their faith. Karl Barth for instance — in the pure tradition of Protestantism — protested against calling Christianity "a religion" and vehemently denied that Christian faith could be understood as long as it was seen embedded in social and cultural structures. These structures, he believed, were completely alien to it, and a perversion of it. In Islam, too, the Sufis sought *Fana*, the extinction of that social and cultural self which was determined by the structural forms of religious customs. This extinction is a breakthrough into a realm of mystical liberty in which the "self" is lost and then reconstituted in *Baqa* — something like the "New Man" of Christianity, as understood by the Christian mystics (including the Apostles). "I live," said Paul, "now not I but Christ lives in me."

Merton pivoted to the Buddhist understanding of the Buddha nature in all things. "And in Zen enlightenment, the discovery of the 'original face before you were born' is the discovery not that one *sees* Buddha but that one *is* Buddha." In his book *Mystics & Zen Masters*, Merton compared the Zen teaching of a direct grasp of one's "Original face" to Paul's Christ-based mysticism: "Such is the attainment of the 'Buddha mind,' or 'Buddhahood.' (Compare the Christian expressions 'having the mind of Christ' [1 Cor 2:16], being 'of one Spirit with Christ,' 'He who is united to the Lord is one spirit' [1 Cor, 6:17].)" This is Cosmic Christ talk. Clearly, Merton is recognizing the Cosmic Christ — the Christ in all beings — as parallel to the Buddha nature experience in Buddhism.

Merton is echoing Meister Eckhart. In the very same sermon that Merton cited above in *Zen and the Birds of Appetite*, about the galloping horse, Eckhart also said: "Therefore I am cause of myself according to my being, which is eternal, but not according to my becoming, which is temporal. Therefore also I am unborn, and following the way of my unborn being I can never die. Following the way of my unborn being I have always been, I am now, and shall remain eternally.... In this breakthrough I discover that I and God are one." While Eckhart recognizes every creature as a Word of God and a book about God, he goes out of his way to speak about humans in particular as other Christs:

> In this Word the Father speaks my spirit, your spirit, and the spirit of every person who resembles the Word. And in this utterance you and I are true sons of God, as the Word himself is Son of the Father.... As I have said before the Father knows of no separation between you and him and no preference as to Father and Word, because the Father and you and everything that is and the Word are one in the same light.

Further, Eckhart wrote, "The nature assumed by God is common to all people without distinction of more or less. Therefore, it is given to every person to become the son of God, substantially indeed in Christ, but in himself or herself by adoption through grace.... Humanity and divinity are one personal being in the person of Christ."

Eckhart does not limit his theology to our *being other Christs* but to our *acting* like other Christs and imitating him and his compassion in our actions. Eckhart says that we are to be "doing his works" and "behaving exactly like Jesus.... Christ says here,

'Follow me.'...'Follow' is a command to act....Mold yourself in all your works on his pattern."

Merton invoked the Cosmic Christ of Meister Eckhart and indeed of the earliest Christian writer, Saint Paul. In his *New Seeds of Contemplation*, Merton wrote: "If we believe in the Incarnation of the Son of God, there is no one on earth in whom we are not prepared to see, in mystery, the presence of Christ." Again, he wrote: "We ourselves are the 'Second Adam' because we ourselves are Christ." In his journal on August 13, 1965, he wrote that each of us is an "epiphany" of God:

> The joy that I am *man*! This fact, that I am a man, is a theological truth and mystery. God became man in Christ. In the becoming what I am He united me to Himself and made me His epiphany, so that now I am meant to reveal Him, and my very existence as true man depends on this, that by my freedom I obey His light, thus enabling Him to reveal Himself in me. And the first to see this revelation is my own self. I am His mission to myself and through myself to all men. How can one see Him or receive Him if I despise or fear who I am — man? How can I love what I am — man — if I hate man in others?
>
> The mere fact of my manness should be an everlasting joy and delight....God did not become an angel. He became *man*.

Merton sees God in all things: "We do not see the Blinding One in black emptiness. He speaks to us gently in ten thousand things....He shines not on them but from within them." This, too, is Cosmic Christ teaching, that the Christ is present in all beings and is more than present — is radiating light and shining forth. Consider this poem entitled "O Sweet Irrational Worship":

> Wind and a bobwhite
> And the afternoon sun.

By ceasing to question the sun
I have become light,
Bird and wind.
My leaves sing.
I am earth, earth
All these lighted things
Grow from my heart....
Out of my nameless weeds
His foolish worship.

One commentator responded to this poem: "The earth song conveys Merton's consciousness of the ground of being." Indeed, it does — and it is Eckhart's consciousness also. Here lies a profound Cosmic Christ consciousness telling of the light in all things, ourselves included. We are all Cosmic Christs. All beings are: "Life is this simple: We live in a world that is absolutely transparent. The divine is shining through it all the time. This is not just a nice story or a fable — it is true." In chapter 4, I describe the stunning mystical breakthrough Merton experienced on the streets of Louisville, about which he exclaimed: "Thank God! Thank God! I am only another member of the human race like all the rest of them. I have the immense joy of being a man!" Later, commenting on his mystical experience, he observed: "There is no way of telling people that they are all walking around shining like the sun." This is Cosmic Christ talk, Cosmic Christ intuition at its fullest.

The Cosmic Christ is alive and well in Merton's theology, and he recognized both its personal and its social implications. He writes about the presence of "the pure glory of God" using rich Eckhartian imagery.

At the center of our being is a point of nothingness which
is untouched by sin and by illusion, a point of pure truth,
a point or spark which belongs entirely to God, which is

never at our disposal, from which God disposes of our lives, which is inaccessible to the fantasies of our own mind or the brutalities of our own will. This little point of nothingness and of absolute poverty is the pure glory of God in us. It is so to speak his name written in us, as our poverty, as our indigence, as our dependence, as our sonship. It is like a pure diamond, blazing with the invisible light of heaven. It is in everybody, and if we could see it we would see these billions of points of light coming together in the face and blaze of a sun that would make all the darkness and cruelty of life vanish completely.... I have no program for this seeing. It is only given. But the gate of heaven is everywhere.

Yes, the Cosmic Christ is all about the "glory of God" in everyone and everything. It is everywhere. The Cosmic Christ experience also affects society.

The Cosmic Christ as an Alternative to the Idolatry of Christian Empires

In liberation theologian Joerg Rieger's thoughtful book *Christ & Empire: From Paul to Postcolonial Times*, he traces the history of Christ talk and empire talk. Rieger begins with the early church's resistance to the Roman Empire, and he traces the evolving developments of God and empire through the eras of early colonialism, late colonialism, and neocolonialism. Ultimately, Rieger asks whether a Cosmic Christ theology can offer a more authentic view than the imperial versions of Christ served up in Christian history. To me, this speaks to the issue of the papal bulls of the fifteenth century, which are collectively known as the "Discovery Doctrine," in which popes actually spoke about the "Christian empire." These popes gave legal legitimacy to Portuguese and Spanish imperial ambitions to invade Africa and the Americas because the inhabitants there were not Christian and therefore the nations were not sovereign. Rieger warns us that "even a cursory glance at the history of empire reveals that empires have often been justified and supported by theological means."

How to cut this cord? Rieger proposes that maybe a Cosmic Christ theology might offer such a new start. There is much about a Cosmic Christ theology that can redeem us from narrow and dangerous worldviews based on racial and cultural superiority. Merton anticipated Rieger's Liberation Theology perspective, for he also proposed the Cosmic Christ consciousness as an alternative to a "barbarous" empire consciousness. Merton wrote:

> The greatest sin of the European-Russian-American complex which we call "the West"... [is] above all *its unmitigated arrogance towards the rest of the human race*. Western civilization is now in full decline into barbarism (a barbarism that springs *from within itself*) because it has been guilty of a twofold disloyalty: to God and to Man. To a Christian who believes in the mystery of the Incarnation, and who by that belief means something more than a pious theory without real humanistic implications, this is not two disloyalties but one. Since the Word was made Flesh, God is in man, God is in *all men*. All men are to be seen and treated as Christ. Failure to do this the Lord tells us, involves condemnation for disloyalty to the most fundamental of revealed truths. "I was thirsty and you gave me to drink. I was hungry and you gave me to eat..." (Matthew 25:42). This could be extended in every possible sense: and is meant to be so extended, all over the entire area of human needs, not only for bread, for work, for liberty, for health, but also for truth, for belief, for love, for acceptance, for fellowship and understanding.

Here Merton is appropriately referencing the historic Jesus in Matthew 25 speaking a Cosmic Christ theology: every person, and especially a needy one, is another Christ. He continues:

One of the great tragedies of the Christian West is the fact
that for all the good will of the missionaries and coloniz-
ers...they could not recognize that *the races they conquered
were essentially equal to themselves and in some ways supe-
rior*.... Where they failed was in their inability to *encounter
Christ* already potentially present in the Indians, the Hindus
and the Chinese.

Here Merton applies a Cosmic Christ theology to history and
politics and empires. A Via Transformativa, indeed.

The Cosmic Christ archetype also addresses anthropocentrism
of many kinds. It offers a substrate for a genuine eco-theology, for
it brings back the reality of the sacredness of creation. Just as
Teilhard de Chardin was chagrined that he could not find people, lay or theologian, who were interested in the Cosmic Christ,
Merton had the same problem, saying that the "cosmic mediation
of Christ" as found, for example, in Paul's letter to the Colossians
(1:15–17) left him "astounded that they receive so little attention
from Christians today."

In a recent study entitled *Kabbalah and Ecology: God's Image
in the More-Than-Human World*, Rabbi David Seidenberg builds
an entire eco-theology on the Jewish concept of *the image of God
in every creature*, which he proves is present in the entire Jewish
tradition, from the Bible and Midrash through the Kabbalah, rabbinic texts, and Maimonides. As I have written, this is the exact
meaning of the Cosmic Christ as well as the Buddha nature archetype. We now have three great religious traditions celebrating the same reality and providing together a theological basis
for ecology, providing powerful medicine for any temptations to
anthropocentrism or fundamentalism. Recognizing the Christ (or
Buddha nature or Image of God) in every creature is the first step
in resacralizing our understanding of the earth and her creatures
and therefore the first step in a truly more-than-narcissistic attitude toward the rest of creation.

Merton's Cure for Fundamentalism
and Contemporary Idol Worship

What about fundamentalism? Fundamentalism is a process of projection and of objectifying God, and Merton reminds us "when God becomes object, he sooner or later 'dies,' because God as object is ultimately unthinkable. God as object is not only a mere abstract concept, but one which contains so many internal contradictions that it becomes entirely nonnegotiable except when it is hardened into an idol that is maintained in existence by a sheer act of will." God as object therefore *invites atheism*, and I find myself atheist in that very sense: I, too, reject a God who is object. Merton recognized that for the Cartesian consciousness "the 'other,' too, is object.... Is a genuine I-Thou relationship possible *at all* to a purely Cartesian subject?" Merton warned:

> It would be pointless here to go into the ancient Biblical polemic against "idols of woods and stone." There are much more dangerous and much more potent idols in the world today: signs of cosmic and technological power, political and scientific idols, idols of the nation, the party, the race. These are evident enough, but the fact that they are evident in themselves does not mean that people do not submit more and more blindly, more and more despairingly to their complete power. The idol of national military strength was never more powerful than today, even though men claim to desire peace.

In contrast to God as object, Merton saw another option.

> Another, metaphysical, consciousness is still available to modern man. It starts not from the thinking and self-aware subject [that is, not from anthropocentrism] but from Being, ontologically seen to be beyond and prior to the subject-object division. Underlying the subjective experience of the individual self there is an immediate experience of

Being. This is totally different from an experience of self-consciousness. It is completely nonobjective. It has in it none of the split and alienation that occurs when the subject becomes aware of itself as a quasi-object. The consciousness of being (whether considered positively or negatively and apophatically as in Buddhism) is an immediate experience that goes beyond reflexive awareness. It is not "consciousness *of*" but *pure consciousness*, in which the subject as such "disappears."

Merton speaks out on the importance of the "act of Being," which he sees as more primal than mere "becoming" or "process." He wrote this passage in 1968, not long before he died: "Afflicted as I am with an incurable case of metaphysics, I cannot see where the idea of Godhead as process is more dynamic than that of godhead as *pure act*. To one who has been exposed to scholastic ontology and has not recovered, it remains evident that the activity of *becoming* is considerably less alive and dynamic than the *act of Being*."

Metaphysics has been so disclaimed by modern philosophy that most people have forgotten the term altogether. But Merton claims to possess an "incurable" case of it. What is metaphysics? It is a study of being. Eastern Orthodox scholar David Bentley Hart has written convincingly of this same theme in his fine book *The Experience of God: Being, Consciousness, Bliss*, where he calls upon both Western and Eastern Wisdom traditions to recover the experience of being. He criticizes much of contemporary religion for forgetting a God of being and settling for superficial projections, both in theism and atheism.

Eckhart surely underwent what Merton calls the "immediate experience of Being" that is behind all being. He spoke of how "is-ness is God" and God is the "ground of all being," and he taught that we make contact with Divinity so that "our ground and his ground are the same." Thomas Aquinas also spoke of God as the "Source without a source" and as Being itself, and he beckoned us toward this realm of the being behind being where all holiness and energy and being resides. The results of such a God aware- ness spill over into our action, as Merton noted: "This form of consciousness assumes a totally different kind of self-awareness from that of the Cartesian thinking-self which is its own justifi- cation and its own center. Here the individual is aware of himself as a self-to-be-dissolved in self-giving, in love, in 'letting-go,' in ecstasy, in God — there are many ways of phrasing it."

Merton's and my work very much coincide here. Merton talks of "ecstasy" as being an experience of the self dissolving, and I take up this experience in my early book *Whee! We, Wee All the Way Home: A Guide to Sensual Prophetic Spirituality*. In that book, I considered ecstasy the breakthrough moment in our spiritual journey, while later I came to call this the Via Positiva and Via Negativa. Indeed, I open the book with a passage from Merton: "The first step in the interior life, nowadays, is not, as some might imagine, learning *not* to see and taste and hear and feel things. On the contrary, what we must do is begin by unlearning our wrong ways of seeing, tasting, feeling, and so forth, and acquire a few of the right ones."

I distinguish what I call "natural ecstasies" — including friendship and experiences in nature, art, music, lovemaking, study of truth, work, and so on — as invitations to ecstasy and the experience of God in ecstasy. But also we have, thanks to our spiritual traditions, what I call "tactical ecstasies," and what some in the past might have called "ascetic exercises," such as fasting, vegetarianism, celibacy, chant, yoga, mantras, meditation, and so on — which accomplish the same thing natural ecstasies do and which can supplement and refire our natural ecstasies. These, too, lead us to a God-experience. By definition, ecstasy "takes us

out of ourselves" and accomplishes a breakthrough out of ego-
consciousness into something bigger (thus the "Whee!" of ecstasy
leads to "We"). Our ecstatic moments can constitute our satori
or breakthrough experiences, which Eckhart talks about when
he says "in breakthrough I learn that God and I are one." The
"wee" in the title refers to our work of fighting injustice — one
feels very small at times when facing powers, principalities, and
institutions.

Merton praises the indigenous peoples of Africa, telling us
that the Africans' "reverence for life and for the sacred, creative
dynamism of life, expressed in his art and in his symbolism, could
be extremely deep and pure," for example, in depicting animals.
He points out how for this reason the killing of animals was eventually prohibited in India, where "one encounters an even deeper
level of communion: the level of *being itself*. Man and the animal
are finally seen as sharing in the ontological mystery of being,
they are somehow one 'in God the Creator.' Or as Hinduism
would say the *Atman* is one in them both."

For Merton our encounter with Being includes a "metaphysical intuition of Being...an intuition of a *ground of openness*, indeed of a kind of ontological openness and an infinite generosity
which communicates itself to everything that is. 'The good is dif-
fusive of itself,' or 'God is love.' Openness is not something to
be acquired, but a radical gift." In other words, a grace. Here,
Merton names the grace that is the Via Creativa, and he sounds
strikingly like Meister Eckhart, who says:

> Human beings should be communicative and emanative
> with all the gifts they have received from God. Saint Paul
> says, "What is there that we have not received from him?"
> (Cf 1 Co: 4:7). If human beings have something that they
> do not bestow on others, they are not good. People who do
> not bestow on others spiritual things and whatever bliss is

in them have never been spiritual. People are not to receive and keep them for themselves alone, but they should share themselves and pour forth everything they possess in their bodies and souls as far as possible, and whatever others desire of them.

Eckhart tells us that we must "of a necessity be and remain in being and in the foundation. There is where God has to touch you with his onefold being without the mediation of any image." Remain one with Being and all grace flows.

Merton posed the following question in his next to last book: "Supposing that the only authentic Christian experience is that of the first Christians, can this be recovered and reconstructed in any way whatever? And if so, is it to be 'mystical' or 'prophetic'? And in any case, *what is it?*" He answers his question the way I do — with the marriage of mysticism and prophecy. He wrote: "The important thing is not to *oppose* this gracious and prophetic concept to the metaphysical and mystical idea of union with God, but to show where the two ideas really seek to express the same kind of consciousness or at least to approach it, in varying ways." This is the both/and approach that I describe in my work and that I find laced throughout the Creation Spirituality tradition — Merton included. Here lies the very meaning of compassion. As Eckhart says, "Compassion is where peace and justice kiss," and "compassion means justice." I find in the term "compassion" that the marriage of mysticism and justice (mysticism and passion) gives birth to the warrior energy (prophecy and justice-making), which awakens to preserve what we love or cherish. "The prophet is the mystic in action," as William Hocking declared early in the twentieth century. This names well, I think, the mature journey that Merton came to name so beautifully and to live out so fully.

Merton's photograph of a battered circle, a wagon wheel. Did Merton travel a full and "perfect circle"?

A Way to God and the "Perfect Circle" of Merton's Spiritual Journey

Better to study the germinating waters of my wood
And know this fever: or die in a distant country
Having become a pure cone
Or turn to my eastern abstinence
With that old inscrutable love cry
And describe a perfect circle.

— THOMAS MERTON

Several of Merton's friends say that he told them he felt he would not live a long life. Otto Rank defines the artist as "one who wants to leave behind a gift." Perhaps this is why Merton worked so diligently and generously in birthing the many and varied gifts he left us in a relatively short lifetime — he was eager to leave many gifts behind. Matthew Kelty, a fellow monk who sometimes worked with Merton as a private secretary, observed that Merton "had a great reverence for time, had a sacramental view of it." Kelty also said that in 1968 when Merton left for the

East, he had arranged all his papers in such good order that some were led to believe "that he had some certainty that his end was at hand. Everything seemed just a little too tidy." The gifts Merton left behind were immense. Kelty writes, "When you consider the vast amount of writing the man did in his lifetime, the total output staggers you" — especially when you weigh in his other responsibilities besides writing, such as being novice master for ten years and the regular monastic choir requirements, his correspondence, his study, and more. Kelty concludes: "When you recall that his health was hardly the best and that he never had the services of a regular secretary until just prior to his death, it turns out that he was a veritable work horse, which is to say that he made very good use of his time." Yes, we are recipients of lavish giving on Merton's part.

Merton's Premonitions of His Death

Merton alluded to a possible early death on several occasions. On his forty-fifth birthday, he wrote in his journal: "I never thought to have had such a thing as a forty-fifth birthday. Yet here it is. Why was I always half convinced I would die young? ... Life is a gift I am glad of, and I do not curse the day when I was born. On the contrary, if I had never been born I would never had had friends to love and be loved by, never have made mistakes to learn from, never have seen new countries." On December 24, 1962, Merton wrote in his journal that he would die "probably within a few years, say five or ten — if not much sooner." In fact, it would be six years hence. In *Conjectures of a Guilty Bystander*, written a few years before his death, he wrote: "I think sometimes that I may soon die, though I am not yet old (forty-seven)...." On December 20, 1966, Merton wrote the abbot that he was looking forward to finding "a real quiet, isolated place where no one knows I am (I want to disappear)." Strange! His final public words were identical — when he ended his conference at the gathering in Bangkok on December 10, 1968, his last words were "Now I am going to disappear." Two hours later he was dead.

He described a dream he had about "walking toward the center, without quite knowing where I was going. Suddenly I came to a dead end, but on a height, looking at a great bay, an arm of the harbor." John Howard Griffin tells us that Merton photographed such a place overlooking the Bangkok River shortly before he died, and that very picture, which Griffin reproduces, was in his camera at the time of his death.

In a particularly uncanny premonition of his death, Merton wrote about electrocution: "To the abyss: the eyes of fire, the lamps with bony wings, the escape around the Equator....It is time for the nerve which electrocutes. The mass flash of feeling. Everything is recorded on a memorandum pad. Hell summons the neuter verb. The bird rests finally atop a thunderbolt." Several lines later, in a poem called "The Secret," he calls himself a bird: "I am a bird which God made." Merton died at the hands of technology, electrocuted, but whether by accident or by intention is not yet determined.

Another precognitive intuition about his death arises in *Cables to the Ace*, composed in the last year of his life.

> Better to study the germinating waters of my wood
> And know this fever: or die in a distant country
> Having become a pure cone
> Or turn to my eastern abstinence
> With that old inscrutable love cry
> And describe a perfect circle.

Merton did die in a distant country, and he did turn toward the East. Did he also live and die "a perfect circle"? The fact that he died twenty-six years to the day after he entered the monastery almost sounds like a perfect circle to me. In chapter 5, I quoted a poem that includes the line "in my ending is my meaning." Is this the truth in this instance? Is the union of ending and beginning, as in a circle, where meaning is to be found?

A "Way to God"

In his 1967 letter to me, which I reproduce in chapter 2, Merton wrote about how our shared vocation is to provide "the way to God," since that is what people are looking for. Those people included, of course, himself and myself. I think the two of us were on a parallel pathway and that both of us were somewhat surprised at how much work needed to be done, historically and theologically, to undo certain entrenched ecclesial habits and regulations as well as frozen theological dogmas to render a viable path for today. I think we both underestimated the amount of resistance we would encounter along the way, including in ecclesial circles and in our orders. But nevertheless I think we both found a viable way to God for our times, and I call it (with indebtedness to our common mentor, Pere Chenu) *the Creation Spirituality path*. It includes a Cosmic Christ awareness and an original blessing consciousness and the Four Paths of the Via Positiva, Via Negativa, Via Creativa, and Via Transformativa.

Merton did not discover this path overnight. His journey was a gradual one. The church, too, has been evolving. In many respects I recognize Thomas Merton as doing what many artists do — he carried the burdens of our culture and even our species on his shoulders and wrestled with them his whole life long. Of course, a special dimension to that burden was the religious inheritance of our culture. His religious conversion, like that of St. Augustine in the fourth century, followed a rather promiscuous lifestyle as a ribald young man. Both fathered illegitimate children and more or less abandoned them. Both were immature and pretty much driven by their lusts, and with Merton alcohol and intense partying played a significant role as well.

The conversion experience for both was a black-and-white experience, and Merton chose a very severe and highly disciplined order in which to start his life over at the age of twenty-six. There he found, some might say, the "missing mother" of his childhood in Mother Church and the "missing father" in his father abbot. Unlike Augustine, Merton became an orphan as a child. He tells us all this in his autobiography, *The Seven Storey Mountain*. In great part Merton picked up on Augustine's theology of dualism and regret and introspection that marks Fall/redemption religion.

But there were holes in that view of the world and of faith that Merton gradually, in what he himself called a "circle," moved far beyond. In doing so he was in some fashion carrying the church and even society with him. He rejected dualism; he rejected antiwomen bias; he rejected anti-body and anti-nature ideology; he questioned original sin and its Augustinian connection to our sexuality. He rejected original sin insofar as it implied anthropocentrism as well as patriarchal pessimism. And he strongly rejected the "Christian empire" ideology that reflected Augustine's worldview and writings and with it much of Christian history right up to today.

Merton wrote, "At present the Church is outgrowing what one might call the Carolingian suggestion. This is a world view which was rooted in the official acceptance of the Church into the world of imperial Rome, the world of Constantine and of Augustine, of Charlemagne in the west and of Byzantium in the east." He described the religion that buttressed that imperial consciousness as preaching a "world radically evil and doomed to hell [and] ransomed from the devil by the Cross of Christ and is now simply marking time...until the judgment." This religious viewpoint sounds very familiar to the preaching we still hear today from fundamentalists of all stripes. Merton recognized what Chenu taught: that there is another tradition "we find in the thought of Aquinas, Scotus, Bonaventure, Dante, a basically world-affirming and optimist view of man, of his world and his work, in the perspective of the Christian redemption." He recognized that in the "flourishing years of the twelfth and thirteenth centuries we see a harmonious synthesis of nature and grace, in which the created world itself is an epiphany of divine wisdom and love, and, redeemed in and by Christ, will return to God with all its beauty restored by the transforming power of grace, which reaches down to material creation through man and his work. Already in St. Thomas we find the ground work for an optimistic Christian affirmation of natural and world values in the perspective of an eschatological love." In contrasting these two religious worldviews Merton is explicitly speaking of the distinction between the Fall/redemption and pessimistic tradition of Augustine (and others) in contrast to the "original blessing" worldview of Creation Spirituality.

Merton evolved from teaching about Eckhart as a dangerous heretic in the midfifties to adopting him as a spiritual master through the intercession of Dr. Suzuki after 1959. He rejected the exclusivity of salvation through the Catholic Church alone, instead reaching out to other faith traditions, both East and West.

Though Merton lived a much shorter life than Augustine, he grew far more, and in his maturity, he corrected the dualisms of his monastic youth and learned what human love is. Augustine never did. Merton celebrated that love was at the heart of the Desert Father's resistance to the empire. Merton also had the courage to leave the story of his love experience unedited for future generations to ponder. He found many allies to assist him, and Meister Eckhart was ally number one — along with Eastern philosophers and practitioners, poets, scientists, artists, novelists, photographers, and more.

Merton's journey, therefore, was from Fall/redemption Catholicism to Creation Spirituality, which regrounds religious consciousness not primarily in sin but in blessing and praise and gratitude for existence itself, for life, for being (the Via Positiva). Merton saw the cosmos as sacramental and wrote that "the created world itself is an epiphany of divine wisdom and love." One Merton scholar commented on this passage by saying that "in his rejection of a negative view toward the material world, Merton certainly could be considered an advocate of what has come to be called 'creation spirituality.'"

Merton honored the Via Negativa mostly around the experiences of deep solitude and silence and the richness of the nothingness experience and of just doing nothing. In this way he was confronting the American spirit of "can-do" and excessive activism and learned to live, in Eckhart's words, "without a Why." In doing this he was also learning to calm the reptilian brain, since that brain is calmed by lying in the sun — doing nothing — just being. Here, too, he was speaking to a profound need of our time, to develop the mindfulness that can combat the excessive reptilian brain power trips that so dominate a patriarchal and imperial culture in its last days.

Merton wrestled constantly with the Via Creativa as his vocation, and no place more than in his tornness between solitude and community. Of course, he lived the Via Creativa generously through his prodigious birthing of books and articles and conferences as well as in his photography, his cultivation of friendships, his immense volume of correspondence, his calligraphy, his music, his teaching, and more.

And of course he rediscovered the Via Transformativa — indeed, he offered us a definition of compassion in his final talk that we can all live with and start practicing anew. His sensitivity to injustice — whether racial or ecological or economic or gender or political — was fine-tuned, and it came from a place of passion, not a place of cerebral consciousness or academic privilege and rational intellectualisms. He came to a full awareness and indeed *experience* of the Cosmic Christ, not the empire's Christ. For instance, he wrote: "The world was created without man, but the new creation which is the true Kingdom of God is to be the work of God in and through man. It is to be the great, mysterious, theandric work of the Mystical Christ, the New Adam, in whom all men as 'one Person' or one 'Son of God' will transfigure the cosmos and offer it resplendent to the Father."

Thus he moved far beyond the Christology of the Nicene Creed, fashioned as it was by Emperor Constantine himself, who called and abetted the Council of Nicaea upon being converted to Christianity in the fourth century. That creed has almost nothing of the teachings of Jesus in it — it is all about elevating Jesus to the exclusive status of the Christ. It ignores Jesus's teaching — that Eckhart knew so well and that Merton repeated on numerous occasions — that we are all "other Christs."

As for sexuality, so burning a topic for the dominant culture, here Merton underwent a great circle of a journey. From misusing women as a young man, to practicing celibacy via considerable ascetic tactics as a young monk, to rediscovering the intrinsic sexual (and blessing-filled) nature of all of reality, to breaking his vows while learning of human love for the first time as a responsible adult, to then returning to his monastic vows of celibacy — Merton traveled a path that many people undergo in some fashion. Here, too, he separated from St. Augustine who, after all, is the father of the anti–birth control hysteria in modern Catholicism (since he taught that all lovemaking is sinful and must be justified by having children).

Merton also overcame his patriarchal consciousness, turning late in his life (though he was only fifty-one years old) to a young, thirty-one-year-old feminist theologian, Rosemary Ruether, for advice and counsel. He also drew on many other women for their wisdom to nourish his intellectual and spiritual life, from Rachel Carson to Julian of Norwich, from Denise Levertov to Flannery O'Connor, from Sister Therese Lentfoehr to Mechtild of Magdeburg, from Dorothy Day to Valerie Delacorte, from Marguerite Porete to Teresa of Avila, and more. (Though, like most clerics of his generation, he rarely if ever had a woman teacher in his life.) The women's movement was just emerging in his day, and he did not ignore it nor belittle it but reached out to it to learn from it while it was just getting off the ground.

Merton's "Full Circle" Journey

In all these ways, Merton did indeed travel a "full circle." Most of all, he circled away from Augustine and his Platonic dualisms. This speaks to the integrity and the courage and the awareness of Merton. Augustine contributed to the building of empire and the Christianizing of it; Merton was critiquing the reigning empire right up to the end — and his critique may have cost him his life.

The circle Merton journeyed took him back to his artistic and nature-based roots, which were grounded in his early days with his artist parents in the foothills of the Pyrenees mountains, but the connections go much further back than that. They go back to the original Benedictine ideal of prayer and work and the blessing of the earth, of living close to the land; back to the Desert Fathers, who found God and love in the wilderness, not in society and its ecclesial institutions and ambitions; and back to his Celtic roots and ancestors in Wales. Merton wrote: "It is the Welsh in me that counts: that is what does the strange things, and writes the books, and drives me into the woods. Thank God for the Welsh in me, and for all those Birds, those Celts." (Bird was the family name of Merton's Welsh grandmother.) They go back to the Jesus of the Gospels, who was a peasant prophet nurtured on the Wisdom tradition of Israel (which itself is land-based, not city- and Temple-based), and back to the prophets and wisdom teachings of the Hebrew Bible. Jesus was initiated into his wisdom in the desert wilderness by John the Baptist, who taught him practices that would make him a prophet but which would also arouse the deep antipathy of an empire.

Merton also underwent antipathy from an empire. We now know that Merton was spied upon and his mail was illegally intercepted by the FBI and CIA. Did they also end his life prematurely? It is very likely. In that regard, too, Merton followed the path of his model, Jesus.

Merton spoke of life as a circle also in this passage from *Conjectures of a Guilty Bystander*:

> This is the whole meaning and heart of all existence, and in this all the affairs of life, all the needs of the world and of men, take on their right significance: all point to this one great return to the Source.... The "return" is the end beyond all ends, and the beginning of beginnings.
>
> To "return to the Father" is not to "go back" in time, to roll up the scroll of history or to reverse anything. It is a going forward, a going beyond, for merely to retrace one's steps would be a vanity on top of vanity, a renewal of the same absurdity in reverse.
>
> Our destiny is to go on beyond everything, to leave everything, to press forward to the End and find in the End our Beginning, the ever-new beginning that has no end.

Merton also traveled a circle insofar as he took up what I call prayer as a "radical response to life," wherein prayer is understood to be *both* our mystical "root response to life (our Yes)" *and* our prophetic "root response to life (our No)." The former is about love. The latter is about fighting injustice and the warrior energy that takes. The mystic is a lover; the prophet is a warrior. We are all called to be both. Merton was both. Merton answered the question in a similar way to mine when he criticized those who merely want "to transform others" but flee from their own inner transformation. For instance, he ends his book *Mystics & Zen Masters* with this passage:

> Is there not an optical illusion in an eschatological spirit which, however much it may appeal to *agape*, seeks only to transform person and social structures *from the outside?* Here we arrive at a basic principle, one might almost say an ontology of nonviolence which requires further investigation.

I hear Merton saying that the great battleground even for social transformation has to take place within ourselves, on the inside, in the realm of spirituality therefore. Otherwise we may be busy projecting our unfinished issues onto others or onto ideologies of many stripes. If one creates a Trinity of Yes and No in response to Life (Spirit), one has another circle. Living life deeply becomes a circle.

In defining prayer as "a radical response to *life*," I am echoing Merton's call to "seek a deeper dimension of consciousness than that of a horizontal movement across the surface of life." We are in agreement about the essence of spirituality. A "radical" response is a nonhorizontal and a non-surface-like approach to life. I appreciate the fact that "life" is at the center of his call for a deep response — as it is to my understanding of prayer. Merton wrote: "If we reflect and think, we sense that the whole meaning of our life consists in this yes to God. Something in us wants to say this yes....All life flows out of this deep yes to God."

Merton also discourses on the word "response," saying,

"Maturity is the capacity for free and authentic *response*. Once again, this demands something more than psychological adjustment. It calls for divine grace." He recognizes that "the new man lives in a world that is always being created and renewed. He lives in this realm of renewal and of creation. He lives in life.... Newness is there all the time." "Life" is a frequent synonym for God among mystics such as Hildegard, Aquinas, Eckhart, and more.

Merton's mentor and mine, Meister Eckhart, also describes life as a circle: "being is a circle for God," and the soul is a "circle of the world," and humans are meant to be a "circle...filled with the spirit of the Lord." For Eckhart, life is a "flowing out" and a "flowing back." We flow out of the Godhead when we come into history and being and the realm of the Creator God, and we flow back to the Godhead when we return to our Source. Thus, a circle. The Four Paths of Creation Spirituality, which Merton traveled in depth, also constitute a circle insofar as they name the ever-expanding spiral from the Via Positiva to the Via Transformativa and back to the Via Positiva again.

Another example of Merton's cyclical journey can be found in a reflection of an ex-Dominican monk whom he respected and who visited him at Gethsemani, William Everson (former Brother Antoninus). Everson speaks this way about the archetypal "hero's journey": "The mono-myth is the cyclical path of the hero, built of three parts: a separation from the known world, an initiation and penetration into another world, and the return back to this world." Meister Eckhart says a similar thing when he reports that "a person works in a stable; that person has breakthrough. What does he do? He returns to the stable." I think it can be said that Merton's journey does parallel the cyclical path that Everson, the hero's myth, and Eckhart name: Surely Merton separated himself from the world on entering the monastery, he immersed himself thoroughly into that world, and he also in many respects emerged in a return that included critiquing and traveling with new eyes into the world he once left.

Merton spoke of life as a pilgrimage similar to *anga*, or pilgrimage in the Zen tradition: "The purpose of *anga* is to convince the monk of the fact that his whole life is a search, in exile, for his true home." In many ways that was Merton's life: a search, a pilgrimage, a never-ending journey for truth and light. A return to the Source. And the sharing of what he found. The circle is complete, but it is not a closed circle as long as we are alive. It is open, like a spiral.

When Merton tells us that "in my ending is my meaning," he names a kind of circular journey. If meaning is present at our birth, and we gradually find it in our journey and in a unique way in our ending, then we have traversed a sort of circle. What are some lessons of meaning from Merton's particular and quite special ending? Among them we might name the following:

1. He left the security of the monastery, exhibiting a willingness to risk.
2. He discussed rather loudly before his journey about seeking a more fully eremitical existence outside the monastic community (but not cutting ties with it).
3. During his journey East, he found individuals and experiences that affected him deeply; in other words, he continued expanding his ecumenical and interfaith consciousness, East and West together.
4. He exhibited an ever-expanding prophetic awareness, one that led to action in his reflections on Karl Marx.
5. He continued his deep exploration of contemplation, since he was talking to monastics in his final talk two hours before he died.
6. He displayed the primacy of the role of compassion, which was a key component of his final talk.

7. Surprise.

8. He experienced possible martyrdom for his commitment to peace and dialogue over war and the jingoism that feeds it.

Thus, Merton experienced a full circle that carried him beyond Western culture and religion and ideology. As part of his meaning, he became an example of a world consciousness, as distinct from a nationalistic one. In this context, we might reflect again on a passage that appeared in chapter 5.

> As soon as a man is fully disposed to be alone with God, he is alone with God no matter where he may be — in the country, the monastery, the woods or the city. The lightning flashes from east to west, illuminating the whole horizon and striking where it pleases and at the same instant the infinite liberty of God flashes in the depths of that man's soul and he is illumined. At that moment he sees that though he seems to be in the middle of his journey, he has already arrived at the end. For the life of grace on earth is the beginning of the life of glory. Although he is a traveler in time, he has opened his eyes, for a moment, in eternity.

It is for this reason, I think, that I was so taken when I saw one of Merton's photographs at the Thomas Merton Center and asked to reproduce it in this book. It is of an old wagon wheel, very beaten up and with many chipped and broken pieces on it, demonstrating how it has survived through years of a rugged existence. I think this photograph by Merton speaks loudly about his own journey: every circle is perfect, but our life journeys are rugged — as his certainly was — with many broken pieces and wounds acquired along the way. Meister Eckhart says when we are born we flow out of the Godhead into the world of creation and history and many challenges, but that when we die we return to the Godhead. Thus, life, death, and return constitute another circle. But we return with plenty of scars and rugged edges, just as Merton's photograph reminds us.

Thus we are all invited not only to celebrate Thomas Merton's accomplishments and his courage at living out his vocation fully but to call on him to inspire our own vocations as we journey our own pilgrimages, traveling our own circles and spiraling our own paths amid the profound challenges facing not just our culture but our species at this critical time in history. In his letter to me, Merton wrote that people are looking for a "way to God." He was, too. He found a way, and he wrote about it and he traveled it and he tested it. He walked his talk. May we journey with the same candor, courage, and imagination as Merton mustered for his — with the same Spirit at our backs and in our hearts. May we, like he, journey back and forward to our true Source along a way called Creation Spirituality.

Acknowledgments

I wish to thank the Thomas Merton Center at Bellarmine University in Louisville for their invitation to speak on the occasion of the Merton Centennial on the topic of "Vocation, Merton and Myself." Also I thank Mark Steiner of Creative Connections for cosponsoring that event and the daylong workshop that followed. Both events inspired this book. I also want to thank Owsley Brown III, chair of the 2015 Festival of Faiths held in Louisville, Kentucky, under the auspices of the Center for Interfaith Relations, and especially for the moving evening program of jazz music dedicated to Merton's memory that brought alive a significant dimension of his soul and its loves. That night, jazz musician Dick Sisto shared his music and his stories of interacting with Merton as a young man in the last years of Merton's life and how they shared a love of jazz, Zen meditation, and Christian mysticism. Gratitude for that magical evening of Thomas Merton remembrance!

I want to thank several generations of monks at the Abbey of Our Lady of Gethsemani for being a loyal brother to Thomas Merton, both during and after his death, and for keeping his works alive and in circulation, including his posthumously published journals. I wish to acknowledge with gratitude Gray Henry and Jonathan Montaldo for their fine volume of essays by over a hundred different authors, *We Are Already One: Thomas Merton's Message of Hope*, published in celebration of the centenary of Merton's birth and acknowledging his role in their spiritual journeys (and for the opportunity to offer my own modest essay among the others).

I want to thank New World Library and Jason Gardner, this book's chief editor, for welcoming and subsequently publishing this book; Jeff Campbell for his astute and detailed editing of my manuscript; and Mel Bricker for his work on permissions. I extend a hearty appreciation to Dr. Paul Pearson, director and chief archivist of the Thomas Merton Center at Bellarmine University for his rapid and knowing responses to queries I sent his way. Also to Anne McCormick, trustee of the Merton Legacy Trust, for granting permission for me to publish Thomas Merton's letter to me.

Finally, to all those scholars, some of whom are acknowledged in this book by way of endnotes and the bibliography, a big shout-out for entering into the deep and varied world of Thomas Merton and for sharing some of the gifts you have returned with. And to those millions of persons worldwide who, like myself, have been graced by the presence of Thomas Merton in our lives and who are committed to keeping his work alive so others, including future generations, may be so blessed.

Permission Acknowledgments

Pages ix and 16: "Letter to Matthew Fox." Used with permission of the Merton Legacy Trust.

Pages xviii, 14, and 80: Photographs of Thomas Merton. Used with permission of the Merton Legacy Trust and the Thomas Merton Center at Bellarmine University.

Page 147: "Backpacking in the Hereafter" poem by M. C. Richard. Reprinted with permission of Black Mountain College Museum and Art Center, Asheville, North Carolina. Gratitude to Julia Connor, editor.

Page 242: Photograph by Thomas Merton. Used with permission of the Merton Legacy Trust and the Thomas Merton Center at Bellarmine University.

All of Thomas Merton's poetry quoted in *A Way to God* is reprinted from the following works: *Cables to the Ace or Familiar Liturgies of Misunderstanding* by Thomas Merton, *The Collected Poems of Thomas Merton* by Thomas Merton, *Selected Poems of Thomas Merton* by Thomas Merton, and *Words and Silence: On the Poetry of Thomas Merton* by Sister Thérèse Lentfoehr. All poems are reprinted by permission of New Directions Publishing Corp.

Endnotes

Dedication

Page vii, *"seek a deeper dimension"*: Thomas Merton, *Zen and the Birds of Appetite* (New York: New Directions, 1968), 25.

Introduction

Page xvii, *"Shall this be the substance of your message?"*: Thomas Merton, *Raids on the Unspeakable* (New York: New Directions, 1966), 6.

Chapter One. "The sign of Paris is on me, indelibly!": My Intersection with Thomas Merton

Page 1, *"It is important to have seen the jagged"*: Thomas Merton, *Conjectures of a Guilty Bystander* (New York: Doubleday Image, 1968), 186–87.

Page 4, *"The big wound bleeds"*: Thomas Merton, *A Search for Solitude: Pursuing the Monk's True Life: The Journals of Thomas Merton, Volume Three, 1952–1960*, ed. Lawrence S. Cunningham (San Francisco: HarperSanFrancisco, 1996), 370–71.

Page 4, *Later, in 1967, Merton spoke at some length about Winandy's*: Thomas Merton, *The Springs of Contemplation* (New York: Farrar, Straus & Giroux, 1992), 59–60.

Page 5, *"Since language has become a medium"*: Thomas Merton, *Cables to the Ace or Familiar Liturgies of Misunderstanding* (New York: New Directions, 1967), 3.

Page 5, *Perhaps the most impactful piece for me was Chenu's article*: M. D. Chenu, "The End of the Constantinian Era," *Listening* (Autumn 1967), 170–71.

Page 6, *"How much we have done to lead"*: Thomas Merton, *Turning Toward the World: The Pivotal Years: The Journals of Thomas Merton, Volume Four, 1960–1963*, ed. Victor A. Kramer (San Francisco: HarperSanFrancisco, 1996), 272–73.

Page 6, *Luce called America the nation "most chosen"*: Matthew Fox, *Religion USA: An Inquiry into Religion and Culture by Way of "Time" Magazine* (Dubuque, IA: Listening Press, 1971), 53.

Page 6, *"Otto of Friesing was so convinced"*: Merton, *Turning Toward the World*, 273–74.

Page 7, *"The true responsibility — to receive"*: Ibid., 274.

Page 7, *"one of the men who spearheaded American"*: Matthew Fox, editorial, *Listening* (Autumn 1966), 170.

Page 10, *"M. D. Chenu's article on Theology"*: Merton, *Turning Toward the World*, 272.

Page 10, *"It is important to have seen the jagged"*: Merton, *Conjectures of a Guilty Bystander*, 186–87.

Page 10, *"The sign of Paris is on me"*: Ibid., 181.

Page 11, *"If you are lucky enough to have"*: Ernest Hemingway, *A Moveable Feast* (New York: Charles Scribner's Sons, 1964), iii.

Page 12, *"Ash Wednesday, February 16, 1994"*: Matthew Fox, *Confessions: The Making of a Post-Denominational Priest* (San Francisco: HarperSanFrancisco, 1996), 245–46.

Chapter Two. "The first place that comes to my mind": Merton's 1967 Correspondence with Me

Page 15, *I reproduce here the original correspondence*: Personal correspondence from Father Thomas Merton, January 23, 1967.

Page 17, *"the future of spirituality is creation spirituality"*: Personal correspondence from Father Bede Griffiths. My dialogue with Father Bede at Holy Names College, "Spirituality for a New Era," is available on tape from the Matthew Fox Legacy Project at 33dennis@sbcglobal.net.

Page 18, *"Don't worry about the Vatican"*: Matthew Fox, *The Pope's War: Why Ratzinger's Secret Crusade Has Imperiled the Church and How It Can Be Saved* (New York: Sterling Ethos, 2011), xiii.

Page 19, *"Asceticism was not the ideal"*: Abraham J. Heschel, *The Prophets* (New York: Harper & Row, 1962), 258.

Page 20, *To his credit, in his 2015 encyclical on the environment*: Pope Francis, *Laudato Si': On Care for Our Common Home* (Vatican City,

Rome: Libreria Editrice Vaticana / Our Sunday Visitor, 2015), section 98, http://w2.vatican.va/content/francesco/en/encyclicals/documents/papa-francesco_20150524_enciclica-laudato-si.html.

Page 20, *"a frustrated intellectual, pseudo-contemplative"*: Thomas Merton, *The Other Side of the Mountain: The Journals of Thomas Merton: Volume Seven, 1967–1968*, ed. Patrick Hart (San Francisco: HarperSanFrancisco, 1998), 302.

Page 21, *"I am not enough of a theologian"*: Cited in Mary Tardiff, ed., *At Home in the World: The Letters of Thomas Merton & Rosemary Radford Ruether* (Maryknoll, NY: Orbis Books, 1995), 22.

Page 23, *"It is hard to describe his face"*: Thich Nhat Hanh, "Introduction to Thomas Merton's 'Contemplative Prayer,'" in *Sacred Journeys and the Legacy of Thomas Merton* (Louisville, KY: Center for Interfaith Relations, 2015), 57.

Page 23, *Merton devoted the final pages of his book*: Thomas Merton, *Mystics & Zen Masters* (New York: Farrar, Straus & Giroux, 1967), 285–88.

Page 23, *"In our monasticism, we have been content"*: Thomas Merton, *Woods, Shore, Desert: A Notebook, May 1968* (Santa Fe: Museum of New Mexico Press, 1982), 48.

Chapter Three. "Eckhart is my lifeboat": Merton Encounters Meister Eckhart

Page 25, *"Eckhart trusted men to recognize"*: Merton, *Conjectures of a Guilty Bystander*, 53–54.

Page 25, *"Meister Eckhart may have limitations"*: Ibid.

Page 26, *"Sister Katryn to be an obscure descendent"*: Merton, *Woods, Shore, Desert*, 42.

Page 27, *"Eckhart's thoughts come most closely"*: D. T. Suzuki, *Mysticism: Christian and Buddhist* (London: The Buddhist Society, 2002), xix.

Page 27, *"He was a great man who was pulled"*: Merton, *Conjectures of a Guilty Bystander*, 53–54.

Page 28, *Cognet devoted two chapters to Eckhart*: Louis Cognet, *Introduction aux Mystiques Rhéno-Flamands* (Paris: Desclee et Cie, 1968), 11–105.

Page 29, *I was bowled over to learn from Sister Therese Lentfoehr*: Sister Therese Lentfoehr, *Words and Silence: On the Poetry of Thomas Merton* (New York: New Directions, 1979), 55.

Page 30, *"A catholic monk and…this volume is dedicated"*: Matthew Fox, ed., *Western Spirituality: Historical Roots, Ecumenical Routes* (Santa Fe, NM: Bear & Company, 1981), 6–7. The book was originally published by Fides/Claretian Press in 1979.

Page 32, *"A modest purpose behind this"*: Ibid., 11.

Page 32, *In* Western Spirituality, *I also published*: Ibid., 215–48.

Page 32, *"The path of which I speak is"*: Cited in Matthew Fox, *Passion for Creation: The Earth-Honoring Spirituality of Meister Eckhart* (Rochester, VT: Inner Traditions, 1991), 165. Originally titled *Breakthrough: Meister Eckhart's Creation Spirituality in New Translation.*

Page 32, *In* Western Spirituality, *I took to task the*: Fox, *Western Spirituality*, 260.

Page 33, *"Opened a new translation…loyal to this principle"*: Merton, *Search for Solitude*, 298.

Page 34, *In his essay "Buddhism and the Modern World"*: Merton, *Mystics & Zen Masters*, 16, 28, 283.

Page 35, *"In a sermon of Eckhart"*: Merton, *Turning Toward the World*, 341.

Page 35, *"No man can see God…a wilderness (Eckhart)"*: Merton, *Cables to the Ace*, 28, 59.

Page 35, *"Reading Basho again. Deeply"*: Merton, *Other Side of the Mountain*, 27. Unless otherwise noted, here and elsewhere italics are reproduced as in the original.

Page 36, *"The perfect act is empty…you have begun"*: Merton, *Cables to the Ace*, 27.

Page 36, *"Desert and void. The Uncreated"*: Ibid., 58.

Page 37, *I have described Eckhart's indebtedness to Porete*: Matthew Fox, *Meister Eckhart: Mystic-Warrior for Our Times* (Novato, CA: New World Library, 2014), 88–92.

Page 37, *"Had two good long talks with Suzuki"*: Thomas Merton, *Dancing in the Water of Life: The Journals of Thomas Merton, Volume Five, 1963–1965*, ed. Robert E. Daggy (San Francisco: HarperSanFrancisco, 1997), 113–14.

Page 37, *"I saw Dr. Suzuki only in two brief"*: Merton, *Zen and the Birds*, 62, 65.

Page 38, *"In the following pages I attempt"*: Suzuki, *Mysticism*, 1.

Page 39, *"the Christian mystic closest…in Eckhart"*: Merton, *Zen and the Birds*, 9, 13, 136.

Page 39, *"Although Dr. Suzuki accepted the current"*: Ibid., 63.

Page 40, *"he is someone to whom I am"*: Merton, *Turning Toward the World*, 306.

Page 40, *"Eckhart says in perfectly orthodox"*: Merton, *Zen and the Birds*, 75–76.

Page 40, *"His taste for paradox…Countries in his time"*: Ibid., 12–13.

Page 41, *"If it is the case that man"*: Ibid., 9.

Page 42, *"Blessed are the pure in heart"*: Thomas Merton, *Learning to Love: The Journals of Thomas Merton, Volume Six, 1966–1967*, ed. Christine M. Bochen (San Francisco: HarperSanFrancisco, 1998), 92.

Page 43, *"was written in a kind of isolation"*: Thomas Merton, *New Seeds of Contemplation* (New York: New Directions, 1962), ix–xi.

Page 43, *"extract an almost complete philosophy"*: Cited in Fox, *Passion for Creation*, 402.

Page 44, *"If the deepest ground of my being"*: Thomas Merton, *Contemplation in a World of Action* (New York: Doubleday Image, 1973), 171.

Page 44, *Eckhart preached this Christology time and*: See Fox, *Passion for Creation*, 325–37.

Chapter Four. "Contemplation…is spiritual wonder": Merton and the Via Positiva

Page 47, *"Contemplation is the highest expression"*: Merton, *New Seeds of Contemplation*, 1.

Page 48, *"Our real journey in life is interior"*: Thomas Merton, *The Asian Journal of Thomas Merton*, eds. Naomi Burton, Brother Patrick Hart, and James Laughlin (New York: New Directions, 1973), xxix.

Page 49, *"The frustration of the American"*: Thomas Merton, *Search for Solitude*, 169.

Page 50, *He moved from a "Climbing Jacob's ladder"*: I describe this contrast in "Sexuality and Compassion: From Climbing Jacob's Ladder to Dancing Sara's Circle," in Matthew Fox, *A Spirituality Named Compassion: Uniting Mystical Awareness with Social Justice* (Rochester, VT: Inner Traditions, 1999), 36–67. The book was originally published in 1979.

Page 50, *Eckhart teaches the Via Positiva when*: Fox, *Western Spirituality*, 220–22.

Page 51, *"I stepped out of the north wing"*: Merton, *Conjectures of a Guilty Bystander*, 304.

Page 51, *Eckhart, too, offers a rich meditation on horses*: Fox, *Western Spirituality*, 222.

Page 51, *"Contemplation is the highest expression"*: Merton, *New Seeds of Contemplation*, 1.

Page 52, *"We will recover our sense…moon into its orbit"*: Thomas Berry, *The Great Work: Our Way into the Future* (New York: Bell Tower, 1999), 49, 166, 170, 174.

Page 53, *"The strictly scientific view of the universe"*: Merton, *Conjectures of a Guilty Bystander*, 296.

Page 53, *"Heisenberg's Physics and Philosophy is"*: Ibid., 297.

Page 54, *"Warm sun. Perhaps these yellow"*: Thomas Merton, *The Collected Poems of Thomas Merton* (New York: New Directions, 1977), 400.

Page 54, *"The worshipful cold spring light"*: Merton; *Woods, Shore, Desert*, 46.

Page 54, *"'All blue is precious,' said"*: Ibid., 28.

Page 55, *"It is a city I love. Flying"*: Merton, *Asian Journal*, 171.

Page 55, *"The clouds of the morning parted"*: Ibid., 155–56.

Page 56, *"I met a woman and child walking"*: Ibid., 92.

Page 56, *"The boy was charming and"*: Ibid., 97–98.

Page 56, *"No blade of grass is not blessed"*: Merton, *Collected Poems*, 331.

Page 56, *"Every plant that stands in the light"*: Merton, *Raids on the Unspeakable*, 106.

Page 57, *"The rain has stopped"*: Ibid., 23.

Page 57, *"Here in this wilderness I have"*: Ibid., 10.

Page 57, *"Dance in this sun, you tepid idiot"*: Ibid., 107.

Page 57, *"Most impressive mountains I've seen"*: Cited in Kathleen Deignan, ed., *When the Trees Say Nothing: Writings on Nature: Thomas Merton* (Notre Dame, IN: Sorin Books, 2003), 155.

Page 58, *"Beauty of the sunlight falling"*: Ibid., 146.

Page 58, *"Late afternoon — a good rainstorm"*: Ibid., 138–39.

Page 59, *One Merton scholar has counted over eighteen*: Monica Weis, *The Environmental Vision of Thomas Merton* (Lexington, KY: University Press of Kentucky, 2011), 71.

Page 59, *"the Psalms then are the purest"*: Ibid., 68.

Page 59, *It has been said that Merton "celebrated gratefully"*: Deignan, *When the Trees Say Nothing*, 32–33.

Page 60, *"His engagement with nature…experience of God"*: Ibid., 22, 32.

Page 60, *"I live in the woods out of necessity"*: Ibid., 22–23.

Page 60, *"In time…his unique subjectivity"*: Ibid., 23.

Page 60, *"obviously symbolize the Celtic culture"*: Ross Labrie, *The Art of Thomas Merton* (Fort Worth, TX: Texas Christian University Press, 1979), 150.

Page 61, *"Yesterday, in Louisville, at the corner"*: Cited in Gray Henry and Jonathan Montaldo, eds., *We Are Already One: Thomas Merton's Message of Hope* (Louisville, KY: Fons Vitae, 2014), 100.

Page 62, *"And the deepest level of communication"*: Merton, *Asian Journal*, 308.

Page 62, *"We all share what Merton calls"*: Henry and Montaldo, *We Are Already One*, 118–19.

Page 63, *"As Thomas Berry put it"*: Deignan, *When the Trees Say Nothing*, 18.

Chapter Five. "I shall certainly have solitude…beyond all 'where'": Merton and the Via Negativa

Page 65, *"What it all comes down to is"*: Merton, *Search for Solitude*, frontispiece.

Page 65, *"Nothing in all creation…stillness and a silence"*: Fox, *Western Spirituality*, 233.

Page 66, *"The Word lies hidden in the soul"*: Fox, *Meister Eckhart*, 40.

Page 66, *"the doorway of God's house...and from all forms"*: Ibid., 40–41.

Page 66, *"How then should one love"*: Ibid., 41.

Page 67, *"Be still"*: Cited in Lentfoehr, *Words and Silence*, 55–56.

Page 68, *"The whole"*: Ibid., 58.

Page 68, *"Contemplation is essentially a listening"*: Thomas Merton, *Contemplative Prayer* (Garden City, NY: Doubleday Image, 1971), 90.

Page 68, *"the most powerful prayer"*: Fox, *Meister Eckhart*, 42–43.

Page 69, *"love winter when the plant"*: Merton, *Collected Poems*, 353.

Page 69, *"I still have the feeling that the lack"*: Merton, *Asian Journal*, 149.

Page 70, *"If you seek a heavenly light"*: Merton, *Collected Poems*, 340–41.

Page 70, *"The deepest level of communication"*: Merton, *Asian Journal*, 308.

Page 70, *"In the interior life there should"*: Merton, *Contemplation in a World*, 358.

Page 71, *"There will always be a place...of slaves and robots"*: Merton, *Raids on the Unspeakable*, 22.

Page 71, *"In reality, prayer is useless"*: Matthew Fox, *Prayer: A Radical Response to Life* (New York: Jeremy P. Tarcher/Putnam, 2001), 26.

Page 71, *"the sickness that lies in wait"*: Merton, *Raids on the Unspeakable*, 21.

Page 71, *"against the community of living men"*: Otto Rank, *Art and Artist* (New York, Agathon Press, 1975), 406.

Page 72, *"true spiritual living includes the"*: Matthew Fox, *Wrestling with the Prophets: Essays on Creation Spirituality and Everyday Life*, (New York: Jeremy P. Tarcher/Putnam, 2003), 209.

Page 72, *"God is superessential...your gums about God"*: Fox, *Meister Eckhart*, 37, 38–39.

Page 73, *"My love is darkness!"*: Cited in Lentfoehr, *Words and Silence*, 73.

Page 73, *"Closer and clearer"*: Ibid., 56.

Page 73, *"Let there always be quiet"*: Cited in Henry, *We Are Already One*, 95.

Page 74, *"A flat impersonal song...Circles the empty ceiling"*: Cited in Lentfoehr, *Words and Silence*, 68–69.

Page 75, *"God glows and burns...God and nothing else"*: Fox, *Passion for Creation*, 279–80, 289.

Page 75, *"Fire, turn inward"*: Merton, *Collected Poems*, 353.

Page 76, *which Eckhart, by the way, attributed to*: See Fox, *Meister Eckhart*, chapter 10.

Page 76, *"Merton takes the Zen...in the midst of being' "*: Lentfoehr, *Words and Silence*, 57–58.

Page 76, *"The color of the wall depends"*: Fox, *Western Spirituality*, 225–26.

Page 76, *"as they were when they were"*: Fox, *Passion for Creation*, 216–17.

Page 77, *"The way that is most yours"*: Cited in Lentfoehr, *Words and Silence*, 107.

Page 77, *"But to each of us there is"*: Ibid.

Page 77, *"The more you seek God"*: Matthew Fox, *Meditations with Meister Eckhart* (Santa Fe, NM: Bear & Co., 1982), 52.

Page 77, *"To enter there is to become"*: Lentfoehr, *Words and Silence*, 107.

Page 77, *"This is a good retreat"*: Merton, *Asian Journal*, 158.

Page 78, *"We must learn an inner solitude"*: Fox, *Western Spirituality*, 238.

Page 78, *"I am the utter poverty of God"*: Merton; *Woods, Shore, Desert*, 24.

Page 78, *"When one has learned to let"*: Fox, *Meditations with Meister Eckhart*, 63.

Page 78, *"As soon as a man is fully disposed"*: Thomas Merton, *Thoughts in Solitude* (New York: Farrar, Straus & Giroux, 1956), 93.

Chapter Six. "Something in my nature": Merton and the Via Creativa

Page 80, *"the camera became"*: John Howard Griffin, *A Hidden Wholeness: The Visual World of Thomas Merton* (Boston: Houghton Mifflin, 1979), 50.

Page 81, *"There is something in my nature"*: Labrie, *Art of Thomas Merton*, 3.

Page 82, *"The theology of creativity will"*: Thomas Merton, "The Theology of Creativity," in Brother Patrick Hart, ed., *The Literary Essays of Thomas Merton* (New York: New Directions, 1981), 360.

Page 82, *"becoming fruitful as a result ... begets his eternal Word"*: Fox, *Passion for Creation*, 282–84.

Page 83, *"All that has been said"*: Merton, *Contemplative Prayer*, 84.

Page 83, *"The function of image, symbol"*: Ibid., 90.

Page 84, *"Yesterday Fr. Chrysogamus played"*: Merton, *Search for Solitude*, 283.

Page 84, *In a Cosmic Mass, multiple generations of worshippers*: Go to www .thecosmicmass.com to learn more about the Cosmic Mass; there is online instruction and advice for inaugurating one in your community.

Page 85, *"I think the whole thing needs"*: Thomas Merton, *The Springs of Contemplation* (New York: Farrar, Straus & Giroux, 1992), 175–76.

Page 85, *"Then the angel said ... in all his works"*: Fox, *Passion for Creation*, 336, 409.

Page 86, *"the Son comes into ... must emerge from within"*: Ibid., 371, 405, 407.

Page 86, *"Let us be proud of the words"*: Cited in Lentfoehr, *Words and Silence*, 142.

Page 86, *"without realizing, completely toward it"*: Merton, *Conjectures of a Guilty Bystander*, 187.

Page 87, *"the camera became in ... in his emulsions"*: Thomas Merton and John Howard Griffin, *A Hidden Wholeness: The Visual World of Thomas Merton* (Boston: Houghton Mifflin, 1979), 50.

Page 87, *"In Christian terms [suchness] is"*: D. T. Suzuki, *Zen and Japanese Culture* (New York: Panentheon Books, 1959), 228.

Page 87, *"The best photography ... thought you saw"*: Merton, *Asian Journal*, 153.

Page 87, *"was not a 'photographer.' For"*: Merton, *Woods, Shore, Desert*, xi.

Page 87, *"I sent contact prints to John"*: Merton, *Asian Journal*, 248.

Page 88, *"On my last visit with him before"*: Merton and Griffin, *Hidden Wholeness*, 91–92.

Page 88, *"I am also inspired by Merton's practice"*: Henry, *We Are Already One*, 94.

Page 89, *"Merton's photographs inspire me"*: Ibid.

Page 89, *"there ceases to be any distinction"*: Cited in Labrie, *Art of Thomas Merton*, 16–17.

Page 89, *"Your work is your yoga and it can"*: Merton, *Springs of Contemplation*, 204–5.

Page 89, *"Thomas Merton referred to his...leave the viewer free"*: Merton and Griffin, *Hidden Wholeness*, 51–52.

Page 90, *"The Dylan songs blasted the still"*: Merton and Griffin, *Hidden Wholeness*, 103.

Page 91, *"When psalms surprise me"*: Cited in Lentfoehr, *Words and Silence*, 54.

Page 91, *"Poetry is not ordinary...his fourfold vision"*: Merton, *Asian Journal*, 204.

Page 92, *"Aestheticism which fails to integrate"*: Ibid., 288.

Page 92, *"No art form stirs or moves me"*: Merton, *Conjectures of a Guilty Bystander*, 307.

Page 93, *"a warm, saintly old man...great experience"*: Merton, *Asian Journal*, 32–33.

Page 93, *"I am able to approach...one aesthetic illumination"*: Ibid., 233, 235.

Page 94, *"My Asian pilgrimage has come clear"*: Ibid., 236.

Page 94, *"named himself not only...neo-surrealist technique"*: Lentfoehr, *Words and Silence*, 2.

Page 94, *"recognized as an important figure"*: Labrie, *Art of Thomas Merton*, 167.

Page 95, *"There is something in my nature"*: Ibid., 3.

Page 95, *"The natural basis for this theology"*: Cited in Lentfoehr, *Words and Silence*, 143.

Page 96, *"an apostolate of friendship"*: Henry, *We Are Already One*, 83.

Page 96, *"to the ever-widening circle of"*: Thomas Merton, *Cold War Letters*, ed. Christine M. Bochen and William H. Shannon (Maryknoll, NY: Orbis Books, 2006), xxv.

Page 96, *"Thomas Merton found no inconsistency"*: Merton and Griffin, *Hidden Wholeness*, 101.

Page 96, *"a good friend of mine"*: Merton, *Asian Journal*, 337–38.

Page 97, *"Beautiful little chapter on the"*: Merton, *Turning Toward the World*, 262.

Page 97, *"I want as many of the novices"*: Merton, *Conjectures of a Guilty Bystander*, 26–28.

Page 98, *"has a degree but has learned nothing"*: Merton, *Dancing in the Water*, 129.

Page 98, *"Christopher Dawson has remarked on"*: Merton, *Mystics & Zen Masters*, 80.

Page 98, *Merton talked in his* Asian Journal: Merton, *Asian Journal*, 248.

Page 99, *On the one hand, he called Heisenberg's*: Merton, *Conjectures of a Guilty Bystander*, 296–97.

Page 99, *"God does this: he begets"*: Fox, *Passion for Creation*, 303–4.

Page 99, *"God and this humble…begotten in you"*: Fox, *Western Spirituality*, 235, 236.

Page 100, *"a public Catholic intellectual…and discerning disciple"*: Henry, *We Are Already One*, 105.

Page 101, *"was a person in motion, always"*: Ibid., 93.

Page 101, *One point Rank makes that truly speaks*: Fox, *Wrestling with the Prophets*, 208.

Page 102, *"Instead of blending into the monastic"*: Mark Shaw, *Beneath the Mask of Holiness: Thomas Merton and the Forbidden Love Affair That Set Him Free* (New York: Palgrave Macmillan, 2009), 123.

Page 102, *called him a "harebrained neurotic"*: Ibid., 124.

Page 102, *"calling is not a means of livelihood"*: Otto Rank, *Art and Artist* (New York: Agathon Press, 1975), 371. My article "Otto Rank on the Artistic Journey as a Spiritual Journey, the Spiritual Journey as an Artistic Journey" speaks volumes to Merton's journey (in Fox, *Wrestling with the Prophets*, 199–213).

Page 102, *"to accept the artist in himself"*: Labrie, *Art of Thomas Merton*, 171.

Page 103, *"is a very good one for me now"*: Merton, *Collected Poems*, 288.

Page 103, *The story is told that when French philosopher*: Labrie, *Art of Thomas Merton*, 13.

Page 103, *"are to be sought less in the tracts"*: Merton, *Raids on the Unspeakable*, 21.

Page 104, *"No one seems to suspect that there might be"*: Merton, *Search for Solitude*, 250.

Page 104, *One of the conclusions of my doctoral*: Fox, *Religion USA*, 430–32.

Chapter Seven. "The prophetic struggle with the world": Merton and the Via Transformativa

Page 107, *"In the conflict between law"*: Merton, *Contemplation in a World*, 343–44.

Page 108, *"Every totalitarian regime is frightened"*: Walter Brueggemann, *The Prophetic Imagination* (Minneapolis: Fortress Press, 1978), 45.

Page 108, *"Merton saw the prophetic…of these problems"*: Labrie, *Art of Thomas Merton*, 12.

Page 109, *"the struggles and the general…hope, in imagination"*: Ibid., 13.

Page 109, *"The poets, the painters, the musicians…to such a work"*: Fox, *Prayer*, 140–41.

Page 110, *"one must look to Russian literature"*: Cited in James Kenney, "Fullness in Emptiness: The Development of a Russian Spiritual Vision," in Fox, *Western Spirituality*, 368.

Page 110, *"Let us obey life, and the Spirit"*: Merton, *Raids on the Unspeakable*, 160.

Page 110, *"Let us be proud of the words"*: Ibid.

Page 111, *"To prophesy is not to predict"*: Ibid., 159.

Page 111, *"sensed in the early years...revealed in death?"*: Fox, *Prayer*, 144, 145.

Page 112, *I laid this out many years ago in an article*: See Fox, *Wrestling with the Prophets*, 215–44.

Page 112, *"Art enables us to find ourselves"*: Matthew Fox, *Original Blessing: A Primer in Creation Spirituality* (New York: Jeremy P. Tarcher/Putnam, 2000), 199–200.

Page 112, *"is not to be learned...happened to you"*: Fox, *Western Spirituality*, 238, 241.

Page 112, *"God will be born in this just"*: Fox, *Passion for Creation*, 464.

Page 113, *Indeed, compassion is the "best name"*: Ibid., in sermons 30 and 31.

Page 113, *"Bread is given to us not"*: Fox, *Western Spirituality*, 242.

Page 113, *"What do the poor people do"*: Ibid., 243.

Page 114, *"In contemplation you serve...vision of God"*: Ibid.

Page 114, *"In the conflict between law and"*: Merton, *Contemplation in a World*, 343–44.

Page 114, *"Began reading Heschel's new book"*: Merton, *Turning Toward the World*, 286.

Page 115, *"Supposing that the only authentic"*: Merton, *Zen and the Birds*, 22.

Page 115, *"The true vocation of the monks"*: Cited in Suzanne Zuercher, *Merton: An Enneagram Profile* (Notre Dame, IN: Ave Maria Press, 1996), 190.

Page 115, *"the prophetic struggle...partly responsible"*: Henry, *We Are Already One*, 60.

Page 116, *"From Gerald Twomey's tellingly"*: Ibid.

Page 116, *"His critique of the Vietnam"*: Ibid., 106.

Page 116, *"Utah? It's dry. Far down"*: Merton, *Woods, Shore, Desert*, 54.

Page 117, *"What a miserable bundle...by criminal waste"*: Deignan, *Writings on Nature*, 47, 48, 51, 52.

Page 117, *"How absolutely true, and how"*: Merton, *Turning Toward the World*, 312.

Page 118, *"I have been shocked at a notice"*: Weis, *Environmental Vision*, 12.

Page 118, *"Carson's writing and...dreadful hatred of life"*: Ibid., 11, 16.

Page 119, *"A lot of water has gone"*: Merton, *Search for Solitude*, 303.

Page 119, *"January 12 marked a turning point"*: Weis, *Environmental Vision*, 9–10.

Page 120, *The reference to the "divine spark"*: See Fox, *Meister Eckhart*, 189–90.

Page 120, *"Having focused his social justice"*: Weis, *Environmental Vision*, 18.

Page 120, *"It is written: Our God"*: Thomas Merton, *The Wisdom of the Desert: Sayings from the Desert Fathers of the Fourth Century* (New York: New Directions, 1960), 55.

Page 120, *"The problem of getting technology"*: Tardiff, *At Home in the World*, 44–45.

Page 121, *"The machines bothered Merton"*: Labrie, *Art of Thomas Merton*, 2.

Page 121, *"Met a brother leading a young"*: Merton, *Search for Solitude*, 284.

Page 121, *"What is wrong with their"*: Merton, *Collected Poems*, 389.

Page 121, *"What can we gain by sailing"*: Cited in Labrie, *Art of Thomas Merton*, 132.

Page 122, *"Grand machines, all flame"*: Merton, *Collected Poems*, 241–42.

Page 122, *"I hear they are working on a bomb"*: Ibid., 391.

Page 123, *"That is why we must…what you have done"*: Ibid., 349, 373–74.

Page 123, *"Guns at the camp (I hear them suddenly)"*: Ibid., 228.

Page 124, *"instrument of war. Words of the clocks"*: Ibid., 252.

Page 124, *"refusal to accept mass-mind"*: Merton, *Turning Toward the World*, 343.

Page 124, *"at once primitive and timeless"*: Merton, *Wisdom of the Desert*, 11.

Page 125, *"the technical community of men"*: Labrie, *Art of Thomas Merton*, 134.

Page 125, *"is not evil, but it is"*: Tardiff, *At Home in the World*, 44.

Page 125, *"the mere rejection of modern technology"*: Thomas Merton, "Symbolism — Communication or Communion?" (for "The Mountain Path," India, 1965), 28. Paper sent by Merton to author with no further publication details.

Page 125, *"When the acceleration becomes"*: Thomas Merton, "Technology," 1. Paper sent by Merton to author with no further publication details.

Page 126, *"to restore to technological man"*: Ibid., 3.

Page 126, *"I can find no evidence that man"*: Ibid., 4, 5.

Page 126, *"The true renewal of the world"*: Ibid., 6.

Page 127, *"Race pride is revealed today"*: Merton, *Turning Toward the World*, 144.

Page 127, *"Martin Luther King, who is"*: Merton, *Conjectures of a Guilty Bystander*, 308.

Page 128, *"so subjective and so ineffectual … 'pushing' the police"*: Merton, *Turning Toward the World*, 317, 325–26.

Page 128, *"It all comes under the heading"*: Merton, *Raids on the Unspeakable*, 46.

Page 129, *"It is the sane ones…for 'sanity' at all"*: Ibid., 46–47.

Page 129, *"A Spirituality that preaches"*: Fox, *Original Blessing*, 293.

Page 129, *In the same vein, Merton critiqued the social*: Merton, *Springs of Contemplation*, 148.

Page 130, *"A Christian must be seriously concerned"*: Thomas Merton, "Vicit agnus noster, eum sequamur," 2. Paper sent by Merton to author with no further publication details.

Page 130, *"My interest in Buddhism has disturbed"*: Merton, *Asian Journal*, 160, 233.

Page 131, *"In speaking for monks"*: Ibid., 305.

Page 131, *"must not be construed as an escape"*: Merton, *Cold War Letters*, 17–18.

Page 131, *Laypeople know about this, too*: Fox, *Original Blessing*, 132–77.

Page 132, *"I find myself representing…witness to life"*: Merton, *Asian Journal*, 306.

Page 132, *He acknowledged that part of his vocation*: Cited in Tardiff, *At Home in the World*, 44.

Page 132, *"The whole idea of compassion"*: Merton, *Asian Journal*, 341–42.

Page 133, *"Marcuse's theory is that… 'We are monks also' "*: Ibid., 329, 334–35.

Page 133, *"the monk is essentially someone"*: Ibid., 329.

Page 134, *a "conversion" that I discuss in my*: Fox, *Pope's War*, 13–32.

Page 134, *"Eckhart has described and analyzed"*: Erich Fromm, *To Have or To Be?* (New York: Harper & Row, 1976), 59.

Page 134, *"To a healthy number of Marxists"*: Reiner Schurmann, *Meister Eckhart: Mystic and Philosopher* (Bloomington, IN: Indiana University Press, 1978), xii.

Page 134, *Marxist philosopher Ernst Bloch wrote*: Cited in Fox, *Wrestling with the Prophets*, 167.

Page 135, *"Nazareth, Beguines, mystics…prevents real change"*: Merton, *Woods, Shore, Desert*, 5, 6.

Page 135, *"I am coming to see clearly"*: Merton, *Dancing in the Water of Life*, 87.

Page 136, *"a theoretical dogma of what man"*: Fox, *Wrestling with the Prophets*, 168, 169.

Page 136, *"Truth needs no huckstering"*: Ibid., 171.

Page 137, *"Whether they are body…but from within"*: Ibid., 174, 175.

Page 137, *"Let me say this before rain"*: Merton, *Raids on the Unspeakable*, 9.

Page 137, *"Everyone is an Aristocrat…and of His desert?"*: Fox, *Wrestling with the Prophets*, 179.

Page 138, *In the original, Eckhart uses word*: Fox, *Passion for Creation*, 523.

Page 138, *"One thing is certain: Eckhart's"*: Fox, *Wrestling with the Prophets*, 181.

Page 138, *"All creatures are interdependent"*: Fox, *Passion for Creation*, 446.

Page 139, *"Somewhere, when I was in some plane"*: Merton, *Woods, Shore, Desert*, 41–42.

Page 140, *"the FBI did indeed have a file"*: Henry, *We Are Already One*, 103.

Page 142, *"It is said that the war"*: Merton, *Dancing in the Water*, 298.

Page 142, *"Same is the Ziggurat of everywhere"*: Merton, *Collected Poems*, 579.

Chapter Eight. "A *readable* theologian is dangerous":
Merton on the "Heresies" of Feminism

Page 143, *"I sometimes wonder why Rahner"*: Merton, *Turning Toward the World*, 342.

Page 144, *"I am reading Karl Rahner's essays"*: Ibid.

Page 145, *"the Goddess in all her manifestations"*: Marija Gimbutas, *The Language of the Goddess* (San Francisco: HarperSanFrancisco, 1989), 321.

Page 146, *It is no small thing that Buddhism*: I have treated the role compassion plays in the spiritual traditions of the world in Matthew Fox, *One River, Many Wells: Wisdom Springing from Global Faiths* (New York: Jeremy P. Tarcher/Putnam, 2000), 377–403.

Page 146, *"To feed the hungry means"*: Dorothee Soelle, *Theology for Skeptics: Reflections on God* (Minneapolis: Fortress Press, 1995), 92.

Page 147, *"Four children are singing"*: Julia Connor, ed., *Backpacking in the Hereafter: Poems by M. C. Richards* (Asheville, NC: Black Mountain College Museum, 2014), 31–32.

Page 149, *"When I read Flannery I"*: Merton, *Raids on the Unspeakable*, 42.

Page 149, *"women take an awful beating"*: Merton, *Springs of Contemplation*, 161–62.

Page 149, *"strange, ponderous fantasy…Earth hears him"*: Merton, *Raids on the Unspeakable*, 80–81, 82.

Page 150, *"What comes across in these"*: Tardiff, *At Home in the World*, xv.

Page 151, *"whether it was in fact…and lumber companies"*: Ibid., xvi, 41–42, 47.

Page 152, *"One of the things in monasticism"*: Ibid., 34–35.

Page 153, *"Asceticism is of no great"*: Fox, *Meditations with Meister Eckhart*, 58.

Page 153, *"On the other hand, the real"*: Tardiff, *At Home in the World*, 35–36.

Page 154, *"The language of religion"*: Soelle, *Theology for Skeptics*, 43–44, 50.

Page 154, *"ruling over everything else"*: Ibid., 49–50.

Page 154, *"Julian is without any doubt"*: Merton, *Cold War Letters*,104–5.

Page 155, *"She is a true theologian with greater"*: Merton, *Conjectures of a Guilty Bystander*, 211.

Page 155, *Merton also tells us that he read*: Ibid., 189.

Page 156, *Merton was so in league*: Ibid., 195.

Page 156, *"I think the evil in us all"*: Ibid., 154.

Page 156, *"Woman has been 'used' shamelessly"*: Ibid., 138–39.

Page 157, *Thomas Merton also cites Julian's*: Merton, *Mystics & Zen Masters*, 140, 143.

Page 158, *"God," he wrote, "is at once Father"*: Merton, *Collected Poems*, 367.

Page 158, *"Perhaps in a certain very primitive"*: Ibid.

Page 159, *"God is not only fatherly"*: Soelle, *Theology for Skeptics*, 93.

Page 159, *As I have indicated elsewhere, both Hildegard*: See Fox, *Hildegard of Bingen*, 111–31, and Fox, *Meister Eckhart*, 57–96.

Page 159, *"The suppression of women...receptive power"*: Bede Griffiths, *The Marriage of East and West* (Tucson, AZ: Medio Media, 2003), 151–52, 199.

Page 160, *In his important book* Chaos, Gaia, Eros: Ralph Abraham, *Chaos, Gaia, Eros* (San Francisco: HarperSanFrancisco, 1994).

Page 161, *"Hagia Sophia (Holy Wisdom) is...of the Father"*: Cited in Lentfoehr, *Words and Silence*, 47–48.

Page 162, *There is a rather untold story about his conversion*: My thanks to Mertonphile Dr. Gregory Chaney of Louisville, Kentucky, for his exciting research on this connection of Merton to the black Madonna in Cuba.

Page 162, *"Because the heavenly stars"*: Thomas Merton, *Selected Poems of Thomas Merton* (New York: New Directions, 1959), 4–5.

Page 162, *"The shadows fall. The stars appear"*: Merton, *Collected Poems*, 371.

Page 163, *"Now the Blessed Virgin...one Sister"*: Cited in Lentfoehr, *Words and Silence*, 48–49.

Page 163, *"Sophia had awakened in their"*: Merton, *Collected Poems*, 367.

Page 163, *"the theological substrata of the"*: Cited in Lentfoehr, *Words and Silence*, 47.

Chapter Nine. "Every non two-legged animal is a saint": Merton on Original Blessing and Other So-Called Heresies

Page 165, *"The saint knows that the world"*: Merton, *New Seeds of Contemplation*, 24.

Page 165, *And consider Meister Eckhart, who is*: Fox, *Passion for Creation*, 110–13.

Page 166, *"Every action of God is new"*: Ibid., 112.

Page 166, *"The soul is as young as"*: Ibid., 113.

Page 167, *"Merton's attitude had changed"*: Lentfoehr, *Words and Silence*, 41.

Page 167, *Merton speaks of the childlikeness of the*: Ibid., 48, 50.

Page 167, *"What a drawing, what a house"*: Merton, *Cold War Letters*, 174–75.

Page 169, *"There is in all visible things"*: Deignan, *Writings on Nature*, 179.

Page 169, *"Yet despite the innate tendency toward"*: William H. Shannon, Christine M. Bochen, and Patrick F. O'Connell, eds., *The Thomas Merton Encyclopedia* (Maryknoll, NY: Orbis Books, 2002), 332.

Page 170, *"Everything That Is...interested in themselves"*: Merton, *New Seeds of Contemplation*, 21, 24.

Page 170, *"The forms and individual characters"*: Ibid., 30–31.

Page 171, *"one point on which I most profoundly"*: Merton, *Dancing in the Water*, 279.

Page 172, *"Yesterday in chapter a theological"*: Merton, *Search for Solitude*, 264.

Page 172, *"a basic unity...being talked about"*: Merton, *Zen and the Birds*, 11–12, 13–14.

Page 173, *"mythical language in...of this symbol"*: Ibid., 64.

Page 173, *"says very convincingly that perhaps"*: Merton, *Search for Solitude*, 341.

Page 174, *"restates in purely catholic terms exactly"*: Thomas Merton, "Camus and the Catholic Church" (August 1966), 11. Paper sent by Merton to author with no further publication details.

Page 174, *I don't think Augustine's teachings*: Fox, *Western Spirituality*, 12.

Page 175, *"The story of the Fall...rather than creation"*: Merton, *Zen and the Birds*, 82–83.

Page 176, *"Both Christianity and Buddhism agree"*: Merton, *Asian Journal*, 332–33.

Page 176, *"terror of facing and fully realizing"*: Merton, *Raids on the Unspeakable*, 84.

Page 177, *"in reality God cannot seek to keep"*: Ibid., 88.

Page 177, *"archetypal representation of the suffering"*: Merton, *Search for Solitude*, 370.

Page 177, *"Both the Prometheus story and the"*: Matthew Fox, *Creativity: Where the Divine and the Human Meet* (New York: Jeremy P. Tarcher/Putnam, 2002), 125.

Page 178, *"Man begins in zoology"*: Merton, *Collected Poems*, 624–26.

Page 179, *"Sex is by no means to be regarded"*: Merton, *New Seeds of Contemplation*, 88.

Page 180, *"Missie. Some girl, like [Ginny] said"*: Shaw, *Beneath the Mask*, 56.

Page 181, *"violent and lustful and proud and greedy"*: Ibid.

Page 181, *"The silence of the forest is my bride"*: Merton, *Dancing in the Water*, 240. Deignan, *Writings on Nature*, 22–23.

Page 181, *"The hidden lovers in the soil"*: Merton, *Collected Poems*, 447–48.

Page 182, *"Slowly slowly"*: Ibid., 449.

Page 183, *"'Nay, I see that God is in all creatures'"*: Ibid., 522–23.

Page 183, *"The Cosmic Christ is radically present to all"*: Matthew Fox, *The Coming of the Cosmic Christ: The Healing of Mother Earth and the Birth of a Global Renaissance* (San Francisco: Harper & Row Publishers, 1988), 164, 171.

Page 183, *"The Cosmic Christ might speak thus"*: Ibid., 177–78.

Page 185, *Sure enough, I found that the majority*: Matthew Fox, "Searching for the Authentically Human: Images of Soul in Meister Eckhart and Teresa of Avila," in *Dimensions of Contemporary Spirituality*, ed. Francis A. Eigo (Villanova, PA: Villanova University Press, 1982).

Page 185, *"at liberty to be real…to scratch him"*: Shaw, *Beneath the Mask*, 203, 204.

Page 186, *"Anyone with two grains of sense"*: Merton, *Search for Solitude*, 323.

Page 186, *"All I know is that I love"*: Shaw, *Beneath the Mask*, 209.

Page 186, *"My worst and inmost sickness"*: Merton, *Search for Solitude*, 187.

Page 187, *"I always obey my nurse"*: Cited in Labrie, *Art of Thomas Merton*, 134–35.

Page 188, *"Although the experience undermined"*: Ibid., 135.

Page 188, *"conditions had changed, and that"*: Edward Rice, *The Man in the Sycamore Tree: The Good Times and Hard Life of Thomas Merton* (Garden City, NY: Image Books, 1972), 182.

Page 188, *"Their sacred moments of togetherness"*: Shaw, *Beneath the Mask*, 184.

Page 189, *"did not know or love"*: Ibid., 206.

Page 189, *"loved greatly and was greatly loved"*: Ibid., 206.

Page 189, *"some rather touching fan mail"*: Merton, *Other Side of the Mountain*, 19.

Page 189, *"A card from M. today: thought"*: Ibid., 29.

Page 190, *"So in a way it is…it is part of me"*: Shaw, *Beneath the Mask*, 180.

Page 190, *"Today, among other things, I"*: Merton, *Other Side of the Mountain*, 157.

Page 194, *We learned so much*: For a fuller picture of my work with indigenous people, see my autobiography, *Confessions*.

Page 195, *Scholarship now abounds to put a lie to the mythology*: See Elias Castillo, *A Cross of Thorns: The Enslavement of California's Indians by the Spanish Missions* (Fresno, CA: Craven Street Books, 2015). See also my review, Matthew Fox, "The Emerging Truth about Junipero Serra and the California Missions," *Tikkun*, July 10, 2015, www.tikkun.org /tikkundaily/2015/07/10/the-emerging-truth-about-junipero-serra -and-the-california-missions.

Page 196, *"deals particularly with…is possible for all"*: Labrie, *Art of Thomas Merton*, 152–53.

Page 196, *"Redneck captains with whips"*: Merton, *Collected Poems*, 493.

Page 197, *In it, he commented on a Sundance*: Thomas Merton, *Ishi Means Man* (Greensboro, NC: Unicorn Press, 1968), 8, 17.

Page 197, *"into a cosmic system which was"*: Ibid., 38–39.

Page 197, *"In putting the Indian under"*: Ibid., 9–10.

Page 197, *"seemed to be owners of the whole"*: Ibid., 6.

Page 198, *"Genocide is a new…identity as a people"*: Ibid., 25, 26, 28.

Page 198, *"Viet Nam seems to have become"*: Ibid., 32.

Page 198, *"the spectacle of our own country"*: Ibid., 30.

Page 199, *"The indifference to technological"*: Ibid., 63.

Page 199, *"the spirits have held out toward us"*: Merton, *Raids on the Unspeakable*, 137.

Page 200, *In July 2015, I wrote a response*: Matthew Fox, "Pope Francis's Encyclical and the Coming of Age of Creation Spirituality," *Tikkun*, July 6, 2015, www.tikkun.org/tikkundaily/2015/07/06/pope-franciss -encyclical-and-the-coming-of-age-of-creation-spirituality.

Page 201, *"since, in the future, the understanding"*: Deignan, *Writings in Nature*, 16.

Page 201, *"There is a certain futility in"*: Ibid., 18–19.

Chapter Ten. "The greatest orgy of idolatry the world has ever known": Merton on Religion, Fundamentalism, and Empires

Page 203, *"From now on, everybody stands"*: Merton, *Asian Journal*, 338.

Page 203, *"In the whole question of religion"*: Merton, *Cold War Letters*, 168–69, 170.

Page 205, *"Our Christian religion too often becomes"*: Thomas Merton, "Easter Homily" (September 1967), 4. Paper sent by Merton to author with no further publication details.

Page 205, *"To my mind, that is an extremely"*: Merton, *Asian Journal*, 338.

Page 207, *"Together they expelled"*: See Fox, *The Pope's War*, 106–144, 238–248.

Page 208, *"May 18, 1960. I was appalled…But it does"*: Merton, *Search for Solitude*, 391.

Page 209, *"When religion becomes…the* status quo*"*: Merton, *Contemplative Prayer*, 113.

Page 209, *"German monasteries which were very"*: Merton, *Dancing in the Water*, 330.

Page 210, *"What is religion…Church half dead"*: Ibid., 316.

Page 210, *"What can I say about the great"*: Merton, *Search for Solitude*, 263–64.

Page 211, *"This I found very irritating…the organizational pattern"*: Merton, *Turning Toward the World*, 324.

Page 211, *"I see no further reason for…pseudo-hermit"*: Merton, *Search for Solitude*, 302.

Page 212, *"whether it was opportune for a particular"*: Labrie, *Art of Thomas Merton*, 5.

Page 212, *"The argument that I am supposed"*: Merton, *Turning Toward the World*, 318.

Page 213, *"Merton's acutest problems with writing"*: Labrie, *Art of Thomas Merton*, 7.

Page 213, *"I am getting to dislike more"*: Merton, *Search for Solitude*, 250.

Page 213, *"I really have no ideals"*: Ibid., 285, 293.

Page 213, *Eckhart's famous sermon on Martha and Mary*: See Fox, *Passion for Creation*, 478–94.

Page 214, *"the problem remained intellectually…the poem itself"*: Labrie, *Art of Thomas Merton*, 9, 11, 22.

Page 214, *"we hide from ourselves…what they mean"*: Merton, *Search for Solitude*, 258, 259.

Page 215, *"To get everybody back to"*: Ibid., 258.

Page 215, *"dispirited by the Christianity…dangerous book"*: Merton, *Cold War Letters*, xxxii–xxxiii, 100.

Page 215, *"Wealth and power know how important"*: Thomas Merton, "Vicit agnus noster, eum sequamur," 1. Paper sent by Merton to author with no further publication details.

Page 216, *"I am so afraid that the concept"*: Merton, *Cold War Letters*, 120.

Page 217, *"We have to face the fact that"*: Ibid., 49–50.

Page 217, *"I have been extremely…Council of Trent"*: Ibid., 189, 190.

Page 218, *"I am not in favor of the kind"*: Ibid., 183.

Page 218, *"I am repeatedly thankful for"*: Merton, *Dancing in the Water*, 323.

Page 219, *"A grace of the Council for"*: Ibid., 324.

Page 219, *"When one has lived through"*: Ibid., 137.

Page 220, *"Especially love for and appreciation"*: Merton, *Turning Toward the World*, 265.

Page 220, *"The great trial of fidelity in"*: Ibid., 289–90.

Page 221, *"The whole thing is sickening"*: Merton, *Other Side of the Mountain*, 30.

Page 221, *"I happened to glance through"*: Ibid., 40.

Page 222, *"why blame everything on…a bit childish"*: Ibid., 8.

Page 222, *"I do not now nor…of the earth"*: Tardiff, *At Home in the World*, 54.

Page 223, *"Society — which meant pagan society"*: Merton, *Wisdom of the Desert*, 3.

Page 223, *"These men seem to have thought"*: Ibid., 4.

Page 223, *"Jaspers talks of the 'Augustinian'"*: Merton, *Dancing in the Water*, 61.

Page 224, *"Policy of TV industry-standardization"*: Merton, *Turning Toward the World*, 259.

Page 224, *"The idea of 'Christian civilization'"*: Ibid., 296–97.

Chapter Eleven. "Everything That Is, Is Holy":
Merton on the Cosmic Christ and Love in Action

Page 225, *"We are other Christs"*: Thomas Merton, *The New Man* (New York: Farrar, Straus & Giroux, 1961), 160.

Page 226, *"The flight of these men to"*: Merton, *Wisdom of the Desert*, 4–5.

Page 226, *"They sought a way…is* experience*"*: Ibid., 6, 11.

Page 227, *"find a repeated insistence on the"*: Ibid., 17.

Page 227, *"Love means an interior and spiritual"*: Ibid., 18.

Page 228, *"A certain philosopher asked"*: Ibid., 62.

Page 229, *"We are other Christs"*: Merton, *New Man*, 160–61.

Page 229, *"Who am I? A Son"*: Merton, *Search for Solitude*, 394.

Page 229, *"In this likeness or identity"*: Merton, *Zen and the Birds*, 11.

Page 229, *"a basic unity* within ourselves*"*: Ibid., 11–12.

Page 230, *"In Christianity, too, as well as"*: Ibid., 5.

Page 230, *"And in Zen enlightenment, the"*: Ibid.

Page 230, *"Such is the attainment of the"*: Merton, *Mystics & Zen Masters*, 17.

Page 231, *"Therefore I am cause of myself"*: Fox, *Passion for Creation*, 217–18.

Page 231, *"In this Word the Father"*: Ibid., 340–41.

Page 231, *"The nature assumed by God"*: Ibid., 347.

Page 231, *"behaving exactly like Jesus"*: Ibid.

Page 232, *"If we believe in the Incarnation"*: Merton, *New Seeds of Contemplation*, 296.

Page 232, *"We ourselves are the 'Second Adam'"*: Merton, *New Man*, 160.

Page 232, *"The joy that I am* man!*"*: Merton, *Dancing in the Water*, 280.

Page 232, *"We do not see the Blinding"*: Deignan, *Writings on Nature*, 28.

Page 232, *"Wind and a bobwhite"*: Merton, *Collected Poems*, 344.

Page 233, *"The earth song conveys Merton's"*: Labrie, *Art of Thomas Merton*, 133.

Page 233, *"Life is this simple: We live"*: This quote is from Thomas Merton's final talk as novice master on August 20, 1965, which was transcribed in *Cistercian Studies Quarterly* 5 (1970), 222.

Page 233, *"Thank God! Thank God! I am"*: Merton, *Search for Solitude*, 181–82.

Page 233, *"There is no way of telling"*: Merton, *Conjectures of a Guilty Bystander*, 157.

Page 233, *"At the center of our being"*: Ibid., 158.

Page 235, *"even a cursory glance at the history"*: Joerg Rieger, *Christ & Empire: From Paul to Postcolonial Times* (Minneapolis: Fortress Press, 2007), 5.

Page 235, *"The greatest sin of the European-Russian…and the Chinese"*: Merton, *Collected Poems*, 380–81.

Page 236, *"astounded that they receive so"*: Merton, *New Man*, 136–37.

Page 236, *As I have written, this is the exact*: Matthew Fox, "Toward an Eco-Theology of God's Image," *Tikkun*, July 1, 2015, www.tikkun.org /nextgen/toward-an-eco-theology-by-way-of-tselem.

Page 237, *"when God becomes...purely Cartesian subject?"*: Merton, *Zen and the Birds*, 23.

Page 237, *"It would be pointless here to go"*: Thomas Merton, "Symbolism — Communication or Communion?" (for "The Mountain Path," India, 1965), 25–26. Paper sent by Merton to author with no further publication details.

Page 237, *"Another, metaphysical, consciousness"*: Merton, *Zen and the Birds*, 23–24.

Page 238, *"Afflicted as I am with an incurable"*: Cited in Labrie, *Art of Thomas Merton*, 137.

Page 238, *Eastern Orthodox scholar David Bentley Hart*: David Bentley Hart, *The Experience of God: Being, Consciousness, Bliss* (New Haven: Yale University Press, 2013), 87–151.

Page 239, *"This form of consciousness assumes"*: Merton, *Zen and the Birds*, 24.

Page 239, *"The first step in the interior life"*: Matthew Fox, *Whee! We, Wee All the Way Home: A Guide to Sensual, Prophetic Spirituality* (Santa Fe, NM: Bear & Co., 1981), 3. The citation is from Thomas Merton, *No Man Is an Island* (Garden City, NY: Doubleday Image, 1967), 40.

Page 240, *"reverence for life...in them both"*: Merton, "Symbolism — Communication or Communion?," 20.

Page 240, *"metaphysical intuition of Being"*: Merton, *Zen and the Birds*, 24–25.

Page 240, *"Human beings should be communicative"*: Fox, *Passion for Creation*, 367.

Page 241, *"of a necessity be and remain"*: Ibid., 297.

Page 241, *"Supposing that the only...in varying ways"*: Merton, *Zen and the Birds*, 25.

Conclusion: A Way to God and the "Perfect Circle" of Merton's Spiritual Journey

Page 243, *"Better to study the germinating"*: Merton, *Cables to the Ace*, 51.

Page 243, *"had a great reverence...use of his time"*: Matthew Kelty, " 'The Man': A Monastic Tribute," in *Sacred Journeys and the Legacy of Thomas Merton* (Louisville, KY: Center for Interfaith Relations, 2015), 26–28.

Page 244, *"I never thought to have had"*: Merton, *Search for Solitude*, 372–73.

Page 244, *"probably within a few years"*: Merton, *Turning Toward the World*, 279.

Page 244, *"I think sometimes that I may"*: Merton, *Conjectures of a Guilty Bystander*, 170.

Page 244, *"a real quiet, isolated place"*: Merton, *Other Side of the Mountain*, 142.

284 A WAY TO GOD

Page 245, *"walking toward the center, without"*: Cited in Griffin, *Hidden Wholeness*, 146.

Page 245, *"To the abyss: the eyes…which God made"*: Merton, *Collected Poems*, 824, 829.

Page 245, *"Better to study the germinating"*: Merton, *Cables to the Ace*, 51.

Page 247, *"At present the Church…an eschatological love"*: Thomas Merton, *Contemplation in a World of Action* (Notre Dame, IN: University of Notre Dame Press, 1998), 161–62, 163.

Page 249, *"in his rejection of a negative"*: Shannon, Bochen, and O'Connell, *Thomas Merton Encyclopedia*, 543.

Page 250, *"The world was created without"*: Merton, *Zen and the Birds*, 132.

Page 251, *"It is the Welsh in me"*: Merton, *Conjectures of a Guilty Bystander*, 200–201.

Page 252, *"This is the whole meaning and"*: Ibid., 171–72.

Page 253, *"Is there not an optical illusion"*: Merton, *Mystics & Zen Masters*, 287–88.

Page 253, *"seek a deeper dimension of consciousness"*: Merton, *Zen and the Birds*, 25.

Page 253, *"If we reflect and think, we"*: Merton, *Springs of Contemplation*, 262.

Page 254, *"Maturity is the capacity for free"*: Merton, *Mystics & Zen Masters*, 280.

Page 254, *"the new man lives in a world that"*: Merton, *Collected Poems*, 269.

Page 254, *"being is a circle…of the Lord"*: Fox, *Meister Eckhart*, 215.

Page 254, *For Eckhart, life is a "flowing"*: Fox, *Passion for Creation*, 77.

Page 254, *"The mono-myth is the cyclical path of the hero"*: Steven Herrmann, *William Everson: The Shaman's Call, Expanded Edition* (Strategic Book Publishing, 2016), 299.

Page 255, *"The purpose of anga is to"*: Merton, *Mystics & Zen Masters*, 226.

Page 256, *"As soon as a man is fully disposed to be"*: Merton, *Thoughts in Solitude*, 96.

Select Bibliography

Primary Sources: Books by Thomas Merton

Merton, Thomas. *The Asian Journal of Thomas Merton.* Edited by Naomi Burton, Brother Patrick Hart, and James Laughlin. New York: New Directions, 1973.

————. *Cables to the Ace or Familiar Liturgies of Misunderstanding.* New York: New Directions, 1967.

————. *Cold War Letters.* Edited by Christine M. Bochen and William H. Shannon. Maryknoll, New York: Orbis Books, 2006.

————. *The Collected Poems of Thomas Merton.* New York: New Directions, 1977.

————. *Conjectures of a Guilty Bystander.* New York: Doubleday Image, 1968.

————. *Contemplation in a World of Action.* New York: Doubleday Image, 1973.

————. *Contemplative Prayer.* Garden City, NY: Doubleday Image, 1971.

————. *Dancing in the Water of Life: The Journals of Thomas Merton, Volume Five, 1963–1965.* Edited by Robert E. Daggy. San Francisco: HarperSanFrancisco, 1997.

————. *Ishi Means Man.* Greensboro, NC: Unicorn Press, 1968.

————. *Learning to Love: The Journals of Thomas Merton, Volume Six, 1966–1967.* Edited by Christine M. Bochen. San Francisco: HarperSanFrancisco, 1998.

————. *Mystics & Zen Masters.* New York: Farrar, Straus & Giroux, 1961.

————. *The New Man.* New York: Farrar, Straus & Giroux, 1961.

————. *New Seeds of Contemplation*. New York: New Directions, 1962.

————. *The Other Side of the Mountain: The Journals of Thomas Merton: Volume Seven, 1967–1968*. Edited by Patrick Hart. San Francisco: HarperSanFrancisco, 1998.

————. *Raids on the Unspeakable*. New York: New Directions, 1966.

————. *A Search for Solitude: Pursuing the Monk's True Life: The Journals of Thomas Merton, Volume Three, 1952–1960*. Edited by Lawrence S. Cunningham. San Francisco: HarperSanFrancisco, 1996.

————. *Selected Poems of Thomas Merton*. New York: New Directions, 1959.

————. *The Springs of Contemplation*. New York: Farrar, Straus & Giroux, 1992.

————. *Thoughts in Solitude*. New York: Farrar, Straus & Giroux, 1956.

————. *Turning Toward the World: The Pivotal Years: The Journals of Thomas Merton, Volume Four, 1960–1963*. Edited by Victor A. Kramer. San Francisco: HarperSanFrancisco, 1996.

————. *The Wisdom of the Desert: Sayings from the Desert Fathers of the Fourth Century*. New York: New Directions, 1960.

————. *Woods, Shore, Desert: A Notebook, May 1968*. Santa Fe: Museum of New Mexico Press, 1982.

————. *Zen and the Birds of Appetite*. New York: New Directions, 1968.

Merton's 1967 Correspondence: Articles & Teachings

In 1967, Thomas Merton sent me a package of writings, teaching notes, and documents. This section lists these writings, some of which I quote from in this book.

Articles by Thomas Merton

All of the following were sent as mimeographed copies, except for an excerpt from Erich Fromm's book. For Merton's own writings, he did not provide publication information, except for incomplete references in a few cases. I include as much information as he provided.

"Camus and the Catholic Church," August 1966, 17 pp.

"Comment on War Within Man," in Erich Fromm, *War Within Man* (American Friends Service Committee, 1963), 44–50.

"Easter Homily," September 1967, 5 pp.
"A Foreword to 'Marcel and Buddha,' " January 1967, 7 pp.
"Love and Solitude," March–April 1966, 10 pp.
"Preface to Vietnamese Translation of 'No Man Is an Island,' " 7 pp.
"Social Science and the Theology of War: Gordon Zahn," 2 pp.; attached to
    the article are a few handwritten notes by Merton.
"Symbolism — Communication or Communion?" written for "The Moun-
    tain Path," India, 1965, 29 pp.
"Technology," 7 pp.
"Vicit agnus noster, eum sequamur," 10 pp.; this article is about mass media
    and education.
"Wilderness and Paradise," written for "Cistercian Studies," November 1966,
    9 pp.

Merton's Teaching Notes

Merton also sent to me the following collations of notes that he
used to teach the history of monastic spirituality to the novices
and others. Subsequent to his death, many if not all of these have
been published.

"The Cistercian Fathers and Their Monastic Theology," Abbey of Gethse-
    mani Novitiate, 1963, 175 pp.
"Gallo Roman Monasticism/Cassian/The Regula Magistri/The Background
    to the Rule of St. Benedict," 96 pp.
"An Introduction to Christian Mysticism (From the Apostolic Fathers to the
    Council of Trent): Lectures Given at the Abbey of Gethsemani, 1961,"
    178 pp.
"Monastic Fathers: Selections from the Institutes of John Cassian, Abbot of
    Marseilles," 177 pp.
"Pre-Benedictine Monachism: Syria, Persia and Palestine," 87 pp.
"Pre-Benedictine Monasticism Series I & II." Abbey of Gethsemani Novi-
    tiate, 1963–64.

Secondary Sources for Merton

Deignan, Kathleen, ed. *Writings on Nature: Thomas Merton, When the Trees
    Say Nothing*. Notre Dame, IN: Sorin Books, 2003.
Henry, Gray, and Jonathan Montaldo, eds. *We Are Already One: Thomas
    Merton's Message of Hope*. Louisville, KY: Fons Vitae, 2014.

Labrie, Ross. *The Art of Thomas Merton*. Fort Worth, TX: Texas Christian University Press, 1979.

Lentfoehr, Sister Therese. *Words and Silence: On the Poetry of Thomas Merton*. New York: New Directions, 1979.

Merton, Thomas, and John Howard Griffin. *A Hidden Wholeness: The Visual World of Thomas Merton*. Boston: Houghton Mifflin, 1979.

Shaw, Mark. *Beneath the Mask of Holiness: Thomas Merton and the Forbidden Love Affair That Set Him Free*. New York: Palgrave Macmillan, 2009.

Suzuki, D. T. *Mysticism: Christian and Buddhist*. London: The Buddhist Society, 2002.

Tardiff, Mary, ed. *At Home in the World: The Letters of Thomas Merton & Rosemary Radford Ruether*. Maryknoll, NY: Orbis Books, 1995.

Weis, Monica. *The Environmental Vision of Thomas Merton*. Lexington, KY: University Press of Kentucky, 2011.

Zuercher, Suzanne. *Merton: An Enneagram Profile*. Notre Dame, IN: Ave Maria Press, 1996.

Primary Sources for Meister Eckhart

Fox, Matthew. *Meister Eckhart: A Mystic-Warrior for Our Times*. Novato, CA: New World Library, 2014.

Fox, Matthew. *Passion for Creation: The Earth-Honoring Spirituality of Meister Eckhart* (formerly, *Breakthrough*). Rochester, VT: Inner Traditions, 2000.

Index

Page references given in *italic type* indicate illustrations or material contained in their captions.

About the Author

M atthew Fox is an internationally acclaimed theologian and spiritual maverick who has spent the past forty years revolutionizing Christian theology, taking on patriarchal religion, and advocating for a creation-centered spirituality of compassion, justice, and resacralizing of the earth. He has written more than thirty books, which have sold over 1.5 million copies in sixty languages.

Originally a Catholic priest, Fox was silenced for a year and then expelled from the Dominican Order, to which he had belonged for thirty-four years, by Cardinal Ratzinger for teaching liberation theology and Creation Spirituality. Fox currently serves as an Episcopal priest, having received what he calls "religious asylum" from the Episcopal Church. With exciting results, he has worked with young people to create the Cosmic Mass (www.thecosmicmass .com) to revitalize worship by bringing elements of rave and other postmodern art forms to the Western liturgical tradition.

For thirty-four years, through his YELLAWE program, Fox has worked extensively and consciously to reinvent forms of education in master's and doctor of ministry programs with adults as well as inner-city high school students. A key to that reinvention, he believes, is putting creativity first.

In 1976 Matthew Fox founded the Institute in Culture and Creation Spirituality (ICCS) at Mundelein College in Chicago. The master's program was designed as an alternative to the overly heady academic pedagogy that dominated European-based models of education, in order to educate all the chakras including the heart. The program's faculty included many artists along with scientists and teachers from numerous faith traditions. After seven years Fox moved ICCS to Holy Names College in Oakland, California, where it thrived for twelve years. The program was eventually terminated in the wake of Fox's expulsion from the Dominican Order.

Rather than disband his superb ecumenical faculty, in 1996 Fox started the University of Creation Spirituality, where he was president, professor, chief fund-raiser, and recruiter for nine years. Its doctor of ministry degree was unique in the world, since it honored the inherently priestly work of *all* workers who are midwives of grace (Fox's definition of the priesthood archetype) in their work. It drew excellent students from a variety of professions, all of whom felt called to deepen their spirituality and to reinvigorate their work as agents of social transformation. Fox is currently working to resurrect the program with the Institute of Interfaith and Ecological Spirituality.

Fox and his writings have received numerous awards, including the Gandhi, King, Ikeda Peace Award from Morehouse College; the International Association of Sufism Annual Inspiration Award; the Tikkun Ethics Award; and the International Courage of Conscience Award from the Peace Abbey of Sherborn, Massachusetts, whose other recipients include the Dalai Lama, Mother Teresa, Ernesto Cardenal, and Rosa Parks. Fox is currently a visiting scholar at the Academy for the Love of Learning in Santa Fe, New Mexico, and lives in Oakland, California. For more information, see his website, www.matthewfox.org.